Network Administration with FreeBSD 7

Building, securing, and maintaining networks with the FreeBSD operating system

Babak Farrokhi

PUBLISHING

BIRMINGHAM - MUMBAI

Network Administration with FreeBSD 7

First published: April 2008

Production Reference: 1070408

Published by Packt Publishing Ltd.
32 Lincoln Road
Olton
Birmingham, B27 6PA, UK.

ISBN 978-1-847192-64-6

www.packtpub.com

Cover Image by Nilesh Mohite (nilpreet2000@yahoo.co.in)

Credits

Author

Babak Farrokhi

Reviewer

Roman Bogorodskiy

Acquisition Editor

Rashmi Phadnis

Technical Editor

Della Pradeep

Editorial Team Leader

Mithil Kulkarni

Project Manager

Abhijeet Deobhakta

Project Coordinator

Abhijeet Deobhakta

Indexer

Hemangini Bari

Proofreader

Nina Hasso

Production Coordinator

Aparna Bhagat

Cover Work

Aparna Bhagat

About the Author

Babak Farrokhi is an experienced UNIX system administrator and Network Engineer who worked for 12 years in the IT industry in carrier-level network service providers. He discovered FreeBSD around 1997 and since then he has been using it on a daily basis. He is also an experienced Solaris administrator and has extensive experience in TCP/IP networks.

In his spare time, he contributes to the open source community and develops his skills to keep himself in the cutting edge.

You may contact Babak at babak@farrokhi.net and his personal website at http://farrokhi.net/

I would like to thank my wife, Hana, for being the source of inspiration in my life. Without her support and patience I could not finish this project.

Next I'd like to thank the Technical Reviewer of the book, Roman Bogorodskiy (novel@FreeBSD.org) for his thorough review, great suggestions, and excellent notes that helped me to come up with the chapters even better.

I also want to thank PACKT and everyone I worked with, Priyanka Baruah, Abhijeet Deobhakta, Rashmi Phadnis, Patricia Weir, Della Pradeep and others for their patience and cooperation. Without their help I could not turn my scattered notes into a professional looking book.

About the Reviewer

Roman Bogorodskiy lives in Russia, Saratov. He is a student of the Mechanics and Mathematics faculty at the Saratov State University. At the time of writing, he was working on a diploma project. He is working as a Software Engineer in the one of the biggest ISPs of his hometown. He takes part in various open source projects and got his FreeBSD commit bit back in 2005.

Table of Contents

Preface   **1**

Chapter 1: System Configuration—Disks   **7**

Partition Layout and Sizes   **7**

Swap   **9**

   Adding More Swap Space   10

   Swap Encryption   12

Softupdates   **12**

Snapshots   **13**

Quotas   **15**

   Assigning Quotas   16

File System Backup   **18**

   Dump and Restore   18

   The tar, cpio, and pax Utilities   22

   Snapshots   23

RAID-GEOM Framework   **24**

   RAID0—Striping   24

   RAID1—Mirroring   26

   Disk Concatenation   27

Summary   **28**

Chapter 2: System Configuration—Keeping it Updated   **29**

CVSup—Synchronizing the Source Code   **30**

   Tracking –STABLE   31

   Tracking –CURRENT   33

Ports Collection   **34**

   Tracking Ports   34

   Portsnap   35

Security Advisories   **36**

   VuXML—Vulnerability Database   37

CVS Branch Tag	37
Customizing and Rebuilding Kernel	**38**
Rebuilding World	**40**
Binary Update	**42**
Recovering from a Dead Kernel	**43**
Summary	**45**
Chapter 3: System Configuration—Software Package Management	**47**
Ports and Packages	**48**
The Legacy Method	48
Software Directories	49
Packages	49
Ports	51
Package Management Tools	**55**
Portupgrade	56
portinstall	**56**
pkg_deinstall	**57**
portversion	**58**
pkg_which	**59**
portsclean	**59**
Portmaster	60
Summary	**60**
Chapter 4: System Configuration—System Management	**63**
Process Management and Control	**63**
Processes and Daemons	64
Getting Information about Running Processes—ps, top, and pgrep	65
Sending Signals to Running Processes—kill, killall, and pkill	67
Prioritizing Running Processes—nice and renice	68
Resource Management and Control	69
System Resource Monitoring Tools—vmstat, iostat, pstat, and systat	69
Process Accounting	72
Summary	**73**
Chapter 5: System Configuration—Jails	**75**
Concept	**75**
Introduction	**76**
Setting Up a Jail	**77**
Configuring the Host System	**78**
Starting the Jail	**80**
Automatic Startup	**81**
Shutting Down Jails	**82**
Managing Jails	**82**

Jail Security	**84**
Jail Limitations	**85**
Summary	**85**
Chapter 6: System Configuration—Tuning Performance	**87**
Tweaking Kernel Variables using SYSCTL	**88**
Kernel	**89**
SMP	91
Disk	**92**
File limits	92
I/O Performance	92
RAID	93
Network	**94**
TCP Delayed ACK	94
RFC 1323 Extensions	95
TCP Listen Queue Size	95
TCP Buffer Space	95
Network Interface Polling	96
The /etc/make.conf file	**97**
CPUTYPE	97
CFLAGS and COPTFLAGS	98
The /boot/loader.conf file	**98**
Summary	**99**
Chapter 7: Network Configuration—Basics	**101**
Ifconfig Utility	**101**
Configuring IP Address	106
Configuring Layer2 Address	107
Configuring IPX	107
Configuring AppleTalk	108
Configuring Secondary (alias) IP Addresses	109
Configuring Media Options	110
Configuring VLANs	112
Advanced ifconfig Options	113
Hardware Offloading	114
Promiscuous Mode	115
MTU	116
ARP	116
Static ARP	117
Monitor Mode	118
Configuring Fast EtherChannel	118
Default Routing	**119**
Name Resolution	**120**

Network Testing Tools	**121**
Ping	121
Traceroute	122
Sockstat	123
netstat	124
ARP	125
Tcpdump	126
Summary	**131**
Chapter 8: Network Configuration—Tunneling	**133**
Generic Routing Encapsulation (GRE) protocol	**134**
IPSEC	**136**
Operating Modes	137
Tunnel Mode	138
Summary	**144**
Chapter 9: Network Configuration—PPP	**145**
Setting up PPP Client	**146**
Setting up PPP Server	**149**
Setting up PPPoE Client	**152**
Setting up PPPoE Server	**153**
Summary	**155**
Chapter 10: Network Configuration—Routing and Bridging	**157**
Basic Routing—IP Forwarding	**158**
Static Routing	**160**
routed and route6d	**162**
Running OSPF—OpenOSPFD	**163**
Running BGP—OpenBGPD	**166**
Bridging	**169**
Filtering Bridges	171
Proxy ARP	**172**
Summary	**173**
Chapter 11: Network Configuration—IPv6	**175**
IPv6 Facts	**176**
Fact One—Addressing	176
Fact Two—Address Types	176
Fact Three—ARP	176
Fact Four—Interface Configuration	177
Using IPv6	**177**
Configuring Interfaces	177
Routing IPv6	**179**
RIP6	**180**

Multicast Routing	**181**
Tunneling	**181**
GIF Tunneling	181
Summary	**182**
Chapter 12: Network Configuration—Firewalls	**183**
Packet Filtering with IPFW	**184**
Basic Configuration	185
Ruleset Templates	187
Customized Rulesets	188
Logging	190
Network Address Translation (NAT)	191
Traffic Shaping	192
Packet Filtering with PF	**193**
PF Configuration Syntax	194
Controlling PF	197
Network Address Translation using PF and IPFW	**199**
Summary	**201**
Chapter 13: Network Services—Internet Servers	**203**
inetd Daemon	**204**
tcpd	206
SSH	**207**
Running a Command Remotely	208
SSH Keys	208
SSH Authentication Agent	210
SSH Tunneling or Port Forwarding	212
NTP	**213**
Syncing	213
NTP Server	214
DNS	**215**
BIND software	215
Operating Modes	215
Forwarding/Caching DNS Server	216
Authoritative	217
Monitoring	219
Optimizations	219
FTP	**221**
Anonymous FTP Server	221
Mail	**223**
Sendmail	224
Postfix	226

Web   **227**
    Apache   228
      Virtual Hosts   229
    Alternative HTTP Servers   230
Proxy   **230**
Summary   **233**

Chapter 14: Network Services—Local Network Services   **235**
    Dynamic Host Configuration Protocol (DHCP)   **236**
    dhclient   236
    ISC DHCPD   236
      DHCPD Configuration   237
    Trivial File Transfer Protocol (TFTP)   **239**
    Network File System (NFS)   **240**
    Server   240
    Client   241
    NFS Locking   243
    Server Message Block (SMB) or CIFS   **243**
    SMB Client   243
    SMB Server   244
      Authentication   246
      Samba Web Administration Tool (SWAT)   246
    Simple Network Management Protocol (SNMP)   **248**
    bsnmpd   248
    NET-SNMP   249
      Client Tools   250
    Printing   **251**
    lpd—Print Spooler Daemon   252
    Common UNIX Printing System (CUPS)   253
    Network Information System (NIS)   **254**
    NIS Server   255
      Initializing NIS Server   255
    Summary   **258**
    Index   **259**

Preface

This book is supposed to help Network Administrators to understand how FreeBSD can help them simplify the task of network administration and troubleshooting as well as running various services on top of FreeBSD 7 Operation System. FreeBSD is a proven Operating System for networked environments and FreeBSD 7 offers superior performance to run network services, as well as great flexibility to integrate into any network running IPv4, IPv6 or any other popular network protocol.

This book is divided into three segments—system configuration, network configuration, and network services.

The first segment of the book covers system configuration topics and talks about different aspects of system configuration and management, including disks management, patching and keeping the system up to date, managing software packages, system management and monitoring, jails and virtualization, and general improvements to system performance.

Second segment of the book actually enters the networking world by introducing basic network configuration in FreeBSD, network interface configuration for different layer 3 protocols, Tunnelling protocols, PPP over serial and Ethernet and IPv6. This segment also looks into bridging and routing in FreeBSD using various third party softwares. At the end, there is an introduction to various firewall packages in FreeBSD and details on how to configure them.

Third segment of the book deals with different daemons and network services that can be run on top of FreeBSD, including Local network services such as DHCP, TFTP, NFS, SMB as well as Internet services such as DNS, Web, Mail, FTP and NTP.

What This Book Covers

Chapter 1 looks into FreeBSD file system and disk I/O from a performance point of view. Several methods to optimize the I/O performance on a FreeBSD host are discussed in this chapter.

Chapter 2 discusses several methods and tools to keep a FreeBSD system up-to-date, including CVSUP to update source and ports tree and also customizing and updating system kernel and rebuilding the whole system from source.

Chapter 3 introduces FreeBSD ports collection, packages, and different methods to install, remove, or upgrade software packages on FreeBSD.

Chapter 4 covers basic information about daemons, processes, and how to manage them. You will also get familiar with various system tools to monitor and control process behavior and manage system resources efficiently.

Chapter 5 discusses virtualization in FreeBSD and introduces Jails from ground up. This chapter covers creating and maintaining Jails and scenarios in which you can benefit from these built-in virtualization facilities in FreeBSD.

Chapter 6 discusses performance tuning from different perspectives, including Disk I/O and Network, and how to get the most out of the modern hardware and multi-processor systems. It discusses various tweaks that can make your FreeBSD system perform much faster and more smoothly.

Chapter 7 deals with network configuration in FreeBSD in general, focusing mostly on network interface configuration for different network protocols such as IPv4, IPv6, IPX and AppleTalk. It also deals with basic network configuration and related configuration files and finally introduces some network management and testing tools.

Chapter 8 discusses tunneling in general and introduces various tunneling protocols, and mostly concentrates on GRE and IPSec tunneling.

Chapter 9 covers PPP configuration in FreeBSD including PPP over Ethernet protocol as both client and server.

Chapter 10 has a closer look at routing and bridging in FreeBSD using built-in bridging features and also different routing protocols including OSPF and BGP using third-party software.

Chapter 11 concentrates on IPv6 implementation in FreeBSD and gives more detail on interface configuration, routing IPv6 using RIP6, Multicast routing, and Tunneling protocols.

Chapter 12 introduces IPFW and PF tools for packet filtering and network address translation as well as traffic management on FreeBSD.

Chapter 13 has a quick look at various important protocols such as SSH, NTP, DNS, FTP, Mail, Web, and Proxying. It also introduces different pieces of software that you can use to set up these services on a FreeBSD host.

Chapter 14 looks into some network protocols that are mostly used inside an autonomous system or inside a datacenter or a local network, such as DHCP, TFTP, NFS, SMB, SNMP, NIS and Printing and introduces various pieces of software and setting them up on a FreeBSD host.

What You Need for This Book

Basically you need a host running FreeBSD 7 connected to your network. Your host can be any hardware platform that FreeBSD supports, including i386, sparc64, amd64, ia64, powerpc or pc98. You should download relevant FreeBSD installation CD images from FreeBSD project's FTP server at ftp://ftp.freebsd.org/pub/

There you will find ISO images for various platforms under different subdirectories (e.g. "ISO-IMAGES-i386" directory contains i386 platform ISO images). For a basic installation, the ISO image for first CD will suffice.

Once you have installed FreeBSD, you should also configure your network parameters to get connected to your existing network. This can be done during installation or later by modifying the /etc/rc.conf configuration file (covered in chapter 7).

Who is This Book for

For Network Administrators who would like to work with FreeBSD and are looking for skills beyond Installation and configuration of FreeBSD.

Conventions

In this book, you will find a number of styles of text that distinguish between different kinds of information. Here are some examples of these styles, and an explanation of their meaning.

There are three styles for code. Code words in text are shown as follows: "And finally, check the system's swap status using the following swapinfo(8) command."

A block of code will be set as follows:

```
flush
add check-state
add allow tcp from me to any setup keep-state
add allow tcp from 192.168.1.0/24 to me keep-state
add allow ip from 10.1.1.0/24 to me
add allow ip from any to any
```

When we wish to draw your attention to a particular part of a code block, the relevant lines or items will be made bold:

```
/dev/ad0s1a on / (ufs, local, noatime, soft-updates)
devfs on /dev (devfs, local)
procfs on /proc (procfs, local)
/dev/md1 on /tmp (ufs, local)
/dev/md2 on /mnt (ufs, local, read-only)
```

Any command-line input and output is written as follows:

```
# dd if=/dev/zero of=/swap0 bs=1024k count=256
```

New terms and **important words** are introduced in a bold-type font. Words that you see on the screen, in menus or dialog boxes for example, appear in our text like this: "Note that either the **userquota** or the **groupquota** can be specified for each partition in the **Options** column.".

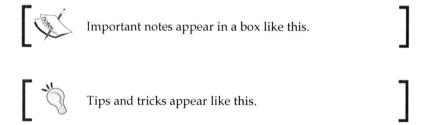

Important notes appear in a box like this.

Tips and tricks appear like this.

Reader Feedback

Feedback from our readers is always welcome. Let us know what you think about this book, what you liked or may have disliked. Reader feedback is important for us to develop titles that you really get the most out of.

To send us general feedback, simply drop an email to feedback@packtpub.com, making sure to mention the book title in the subject of your message.

If there is a book that you need and would like to see us publish, please send us a note in the **SUGGEST A TITLE** form on www.packtpub.com or email suggest@packtpub.com.

If there is a topic that you have expertise in and you are interested in either writing or contributing to a book, see our author guide on www.packtpub.com/authors.

Customer Support

Now that you are the proud owner of a Packt book, we have a number of things to help you get the most from your purchase.

Errata

Although we have taken every care to ensure the accuracy of our contents, mistakes do happen. If you find a mistake in one of our books—maybe a mistake in text or code—we would be grateful if you would report this to us. By doing this you can save other readers from frustration, and help to improve subsequent versions of this book. If you find any errata, report them by visiting http://www.packtpub.com/support, selecting your book, clicking on the **Submit Errata** link, and entering the details of your errata. Once your errata are verified, your submission will be accepted and the errata are added to the list of existing errata. The existing errata can be viewed by selecting your title from http://www.packtpub.com/support.

Questions

You can contact us at questions@packtpub.com if you are having a problem with any aspect of the book, and we will do our best to address it.

1
System Configuration—Disks

Disk I/O is one of the most important bottlenecks in the server's performance. Default disk configuration in every operating system is optimally designed to fit the general usage. However, you may need to reconfigure disks for your specific usage, to get the best performance. This includes choosing multiple disks for different partitions, choosing the right partition size for specific usage, and fine-tuning the swap size. This chapter discusses how to use the right partition size and tuning file system to gain better performance on your FreeBSD servers.

In this chapter, we will look into the following:

- Partition layout and sizes
- Swap, softupdates, and snapshots
- Quotas
- File system back up
- RAID-GEOM framework.

Partition Layout and Sizes

When it comes to creating disk layout during installation, most system administrators choose the default (system recommended) settings, or create a single root partition that contains file system hierarchy.

However, while the recommended settings work for most simple configurations and desktop use, it may not fit your special needs. For example, if you are deploying a mail exchanger or a print server you may need to have a /var partition bigger than the recommended size.

By default, FreeBSD installer recommends you to create five separate partitions as shown in the following table:

| Partition | Size | | Description |
	Minimum	Maximum	
Swap	RAM size / 8	2 * RAM size	Size of swap partition is recommended to be 2 or 3 times the size of the physical RAM. If you have multiple disks, you may want to create swap on a separate disk like other partitions.
/	256 MB	512 MB	Root file system contains your FreeBSD installation. All other partitions (except swap) will be mounted under root partition.
/tmp	128 MB	512 MB	Temporary files will be placed under this partition. This partition can be made either on the disk or in the RAM for faster access. Files under this partition are not guaranteed to be retained after reboots.
/var	128 MB	1 GB + RAM size	This partition contains files that are constantly "varying", including log files and mailboxes. Print spool files and other administrative files. Creating this partition on a separate disk is recommended for busy servers.
/usr	1536 MB	Rest of disk	All other files, including home directories and user installed applications, will be installed under this partition.

These values could change in further releases. It is recommended that you refer to the release notes of the version you are using, for more accurate information.

FreeBSD disklabel editor with automatically created partitions is shown in the following screenshots:

Depending on your system I/O load, partitions can be placed on different physical disks. The benefit of this placement is better I/O performance, especially on /var and /tmp partitions. You can also create /tmp in your system RAM by tweaking the tmpmfs variable in /etc/rc.conf file. An example of such a configuration would look like this:

```
tmpmfs="YES"
tmpsize="128m"
```

This will mount a 128 MB partition onto RAM using md(4) driver so that access to /tmp would be dramatically faster, especially for programs which constantly read/write temporary data into /tmp directory.

Swap

Swap space is a very important part of the virtual memory system. Despite the fact that most servers are equipped with enough physical memory, having enough swap space is still very important for servers with high and unexpected loads. It is recommended that you distribute swap partitions across multiple physical disks or create the swap partition on a separate disk, to gain better performance. FreeBSD automatically uses multiple swap partitions (if available) in a round-robin fashion.

When installing a new FreeBSD system, you can use disklabel editor to create appropriate swap partitions. Creating a swap partition, which is double the size of the installed physical memory, is a good rule of thumb.

Using swapinfo(8) and pstat(8) commands, you can review your current swap configuration and status. The swapinfo(8) command displays the system's current swap statistics as follows:

```
# swapinfo -h
    Device          1K-blocks    Used    Avail Capacity
    /dev/da0s1b     4194304      40K     4.0G    0%
```

The pstat(8) command has more capabilities as compared with the swapinfo(8) command and shows the size of different system tables, under different load conditions. This is shown in the following command line:

```
# pstat -T
    176/12328 files
    0M/4096M swap space
```

Adding More Swap Space

There are times when your system runs out of swap space, and you need to add more swap space for the system to run smoothly. You will have three options as shown in the following list:

- Adding a new hard disk.
- Creating a swap file on an existing hard disk and partition.
- Swapping over network (NFS).

Adding swap on a new physical hard disk will give better I/O performance, but it requires you to take the server offline for adding new hardware. Once you have installed a new hard disk, you should launch FreeBSD's disklabel editor and create appropriate partitions on the newly installed hard disk.

 To invoke the sysinstall's disklabel editor from the command line use `sysinstall diskLabelEditor` command.

If, for any reason, you cannot add new hardware to your server, you can still use the existing file system to create a swap file with the desired size and add it as swap space. First of all, you should check to see where you have enough space to create the swap file as shown as follows:

```
# df -h
```

Filesystem	Size	Used	Avail	Capacity	Mounted on
/dev/ad0s1a	27G	9.0G	16G	37%	/
devfs	1.0K	1.0K	0B	100%	/dev
procfs	4.0K	4.0K	0B	100%	/proc
/dev/md0	496M	1.6M	454M	0%	/tmp

Then create a swap file where you have enough space using the following command line:

```
# dd if=/dev/zero of=/swap0 bs=1024k count=256

256+0 records in
256+0 records out
268435456 bytes transferred in 8.192257 secs (32766972 bytes/sec)
```

In the above example, I created a 256MB empty file (256 * 1024k blocks) named `swap0` in the file system's root directory. Also remember to set the correct permission on the file. Only the root user should have read/write permission on file. This is done using the following command lines:

```
# chown root:wheel /swap0
# chmod 0600 /swap0
# ls -l /swap0
-rw------- 1 root wheel 268435456 Apr 6 03:15 /swap0
```

Then add the following `swapfile` variable in the `/etc/rc.conf` file to enable swap file on boot time:

```
    swapfile="/swap0"
```

To make the new swap file active immediately, you should manually configure `md(4)` device. First of all, let's see if there is any `md(4)` device configured, using `mdconfig(8)` command as shown as follows:

```
# mdconfig -l
    md0
```

Then configure `md(4)` device as shown here:

```
# mdconfig -a -t vnode -f /swap0
    md1
```

You can also verify the new `md(4)` node as follows:

```
# mdconfig -l -u 1

    md1      vnode      256M  /swap0
```

Please note that `-u` flag in the `mdconfig(8)` command takes the number of `md` node (in this case, 1). In order to enable the swap file, you should use `swapon(8)` command and specify the appropriate `md(4)` device as shown here:

```
# swapon /dev/md1
```

And finally, check the system's swap status using the following `swapinfo(8)` command:

```
# swapinfo -h
    Device        1K-blocks     Used    Avail    Capacity
    /dev/ad0s1b   1048576       0B      1.0G     0%
    /dev/md1      262144        0B      256M     0%
    Total         1310720       0B      1.3G     0%
```

Swap Encryption

Since swap space contains the contents of the memory, it would have sensitive information like **cleartext** passwords. In order to prevent an intruder from extracting such information from swap space, you can encrypt your swap space.

There are already two file system encryption methods that are implemented in FreeBSD 7 — gbde(8) and geli(8) commands. To enable encryption on the swap partition, you need to add .eli or .bde to the device name in the /etc/fstab file to enable the geli(8) command and the gbde(8) command, respectively. In the following example, the /etc/fstab file shows a swap partition encrypted using geli(8) command:

```
# cat /etc/fstab
    # Device            Mountpoint    FStype    Options       Dump    Pass#
    /dev/ad0s1b.eli     none          swap      sw            0       0
    /dev/ad0s1a         /             ufs       rw,noatime    1       1
    /dev/acd0           /cdrom        cd9660    ro,noauto     0       0
```

Then you have to reboot the system for the changes to take effect. You can verify the proper operation using the following swapinfo(8) command:

```
# swapinfo -h
    Device            1K-blocks    Used    Avail    Capacity
    /dev/ad0s1b.eli   1048576      0B      1.0G     0%
    /dev/md0          262144       0B      256M     0%
    Total             1310720      0B      1.3G     0%
```

Softupdates

Softupdates is a feature to increase disk access speed and decrease I/O by caching file system metadata updates into the memory. The softupdates feature decreases disk I/O from 40% to 70% in the file-intensive environments like email servers. While softupdates guarantees disk consistency, it is not recommended to enable it on root partition.

The softupdates feature can be enabled during file system creation (using sysinstall's disklabel editor) or using tunefs(8) command on an already created file system.

The best time to enable softupdates is before mounting partitions (that is in the super-user mode).

The following example shows softupdates enabled partitions:

```
# mount

   /dev/ad0s1a on / (ufs, local)
   devfs on /dev (devfs, local)
   /dev/ad0s1e on /tmp (ufs, local, soft-updates)
   /dev/ad0s1f on /usr (ufs, local, soft-updates)
   /dev/ad0s1d on /var (ufs, local, soft-updates)
```

In the above example, softupdates is enabled on /tmp, /usr, and /var partitions, but not on the root partition. If you want to enable softupdates on the root partition, you may use the tunefs(8) command as shown in the following example:

```
# tunefs -n enable /
```

Please note that you cannot enable or disable softupdates on an active partition (that is currently mounted partition). To do so, you should first unmount the partition or change it to read-only mode. In case you want to enable softupdates on root partition, it is recommended that you boot your system into single-user mode (in which your root partition is mounted as read-only) and then enable softupdates using the method mentioned in the above example.

Snapshots

A file system snapshot is a frozen image of a live file system. Snapshots are very useful when backing up volatile data such as mail storage on a busy mail server.

Snapshots are created under the file system that you are making snapshots from. Up to twenty snapshots can be created per file system.

The mksnap_ffs(8) command is used to create a snapshot from FFS partitions:

```
# mksnap_ffs /var /var/snap1
```

Alternatively, you can use the mount(8) command to do the same:

```
# mount -u -o snapshot /var/snap1 /var
```

Now that you have created the snapshot, you can:

- take a backup of your snapshot by burning it on a CD/DVD, or transfer it to another server using ftp(1) or sftp(1).
- Use dump(8) utility to create a file system dump from your snapshot.

The `fsck(8)` command is used on a snapshot file to ensure the integrity of the snapshot before taking backups:

```
# fsck_ffs /var/snap1

   ** /var/snap1 (NO WRITE)
   ** Last Mounted on /var
   ** Phase 1 - Check Blocks and Sizes
   ** Phase 2 - Check Path names
   ** Phase 3 - Check Connectivity
   ** Phase 4 - Check Reference Counts
   ** Phase 5 - Check Cyl groups
   464483 files, 5274310 used, 8753112 free (245920 frags, 1063399
   blocks, 1.8% fragmentation)
```

Remember the following, when working with snapshots:

- Snapshots will degrade the system's performance at the time of its creation and removal, but not necessarily while running.
- Remove snapshots as soon as you finish your work.
- Snapshots can be removed in any order, irrespective of the order in which they were created.

You can also mount a snapshot as a read-only partition to view or extract its contents, using the `mount(8)` command. To mount a snapshot, you should first create a `md(4)` node as follows:

```
# mdconfig -a -t vnode -f /var/snap1

   WARNING: opening backing store: /var/snap1 readonly
   md2
```

In the above case, `mdconfig(8)` command has attached `/var/snap1` to the first available `md(8)` node and returned the name of the created node. Now you can mount the `md(8)` node as a read-only file system:

```
# mount -r /dev/md2 /mnt
```

And verify the operation using the `mount(8)` command:

```
# mount

   /dev/ad0s1a on / (ufs, local, noatime, soft-updates)
   devfs on /dev (devfs, local)
   procfs on /proc (procfs, local)
   /dev/md1 on /tmp (ufs, local)
   /dev/md2 on /mnt (ufs, local, read-only)
```

To unmount the mounted snapshot, you should first use the umount (8) command, and then remove md(4) node using mdconfig(8) as shown here:

```
# umount /mnt
# mdconfig -d -u 2
```

Note that mdconfig(8) takes the number of md(4) node (in this case, md2) using -u parameter.

Finally, to remove a snapshot file, use rm(1) command. It may take a few seconds.

```
# rm -f /var/snap1
```

Quotas

Quotas enable you to limit the number of files or disk space for each user or group of users. This would be very useful on multiuser systems (like virtual web hosts, shell access servers) on which the system administrator should limit disk space usage, on a per-user basis.

Quota is available as an optional feature and is not enabled, by default, in FreeBSD's GENERIC kernel. In order to enable quotas in FreeBSD, you should reconfigure the kernel (explained in Chapter 2) and add the following line to the kernel configuration file:

```
options QUOTA
```

You should also enable quotas in the /etc/rc.conf file by adding the following line:

```
enable_quotas="YES"
```

Quotas can be enabled, either for a user or a group of users, according to the file system. To enable quotas on each partition, you should add the appropriate line in the /etc/fstab file. Each partition may have its specific quota configuration. The following example shows different quota settings in the /etc/fstab file:

 # cat /etc/fstab

# Device	Mountpoint	FStype	Options	Dump	Pass#
/dev/ad0s1b	none	swap	sw	0	0
/dev/ad0s1a	/	ufs	rw	1	1
/dev/ad0s1e	/tmp	ufs	rw	2	2
/dev/ad0s1f	/usr	ufs	rw, userquota	2	2
/dev/ad0s1d	/var	ufs	rw, groupquota	2	2
/dev/acd0	/cdrom	cd9660	ro,noauto	0	0

Note that either the **userquota** or the **groupquota** can be specified for each partition in the **Options** column. You can also combine both **userquota** and **groupquota** on one partition simultaneoulsy:

```
/dev/ad0s1f  /usr    ufs    rw,userquota,groupquota  2    2
```

Partition quota information is kept in the `quota.user` and `quota.group` files, in the root directories of their respective partitions.

Once you have performed the above steps, you need to reboot your system to load new kernel, and initialize the quota for appropriate partitions. Make sure `check_quotas` variable in the `/etc/rc.conf` file is not set to `NO`. Otherwise system will not create the initial `quota.user` and `quota.group` files. This can also be done by running the `quotacheck(8)` command, manually as follows:

```
# quotacheck -a

  quotacheck: creating quota file //quota.user
```

After rebooting, you can verify the quota activation by using the `mount(8)` command or use `quota(1)` utility to see the current quota statistics for each mount point:

```
# quota -v

  Disk quotas for user root (uid 0):
  Filesystem    usage quota limit grace files quota limit grace
        / 5785696     0     0     464037    0     0
```

Now that you have enabled quotas on your partitions, you are ready to set quota limits for each user or group.

Assigning Quotas

The `edquota(8)` utility is the quota editor. You can limit the disk space (block quota) and the number of files (`inode` quota) using this utility, on quota enabled partitions. Two types of quota limits can be set for both `inode` quota and block quota:

Hard limit is the implicit limit that cannot be exceeded. For example, if a user has a quota limit of 200 files on a partition, an attempt to create even one additional file, will fail.

Soft limit is the conditional limit that may be exceeded for a limited period of time, called **grace period**. If a user stays over the soft limit for more than the grace period (which is one week by default), the soft limit will turn into hard limit and the user will be unable to make any more allocations. However, if the user frees the disk space down to a soft quota limit, the grace period will be reset.

Running the edquota(8) command invokes your default text editor (taken from EDITOR environment variable), and loads current quota assignment status for the specified user:

```
# edquota jdoe

   Quotas for user jdoe:
   /: kbytes in use: 626, limits (soft = 0, hard = 0)
           inodes in use: 47, limits (soft = 0, hard = 0)
```

In the above case, user **jdoe** currently has forty seven files which use 626 kilobytes on the disk. You can modify the soft and hard values for either the block (first line) or the inode (second line). Once you finish setting quota limits, save and exit from your editor, and the edquota(8) utility will take care of applying new quota limits to the file system.

You can also change the default grace period using the edquota(8) utility. As in the previous example, edquota(8) invokes the default text editor to edit the current setting for the grace period:

```
# edquota -t0

   Time units may be: days, hours, minutes, or seconds
   Grace period before enforcing soft limits for users:
   /: block grace period: 0 days, file grace period: 0 days
```

The example, above, displays the current status of the grace period on a per-partition basis. You can edit the value of the grace period, save it, and exit from the editor to apply new grace period settings. For your new grace period settings to take effect, you should also turn quota off, for the relevant file system, and then turn it back on. This can be done using the quotaon(8) and quotaoff(8) commands.

And finally, repquota(8) is used to display the summary of quotas for a specified file system. The repquota(8) command can be used to have an overview of the current inode and block usage, as well as quota limits on a per-user or per-group basis (if -g flag on command line is specified).

When using quotas, always remember the following important notes:

- Setting a quota to zero means no quota limit to be enforced; this is the default setting for all users.

- Setting hard limit to one indicates that no more allocations should be allowed to be made.

- Setting hard limit to zero and soft limit to one indicates that all allocations should be permitted only for a limited time (grace period).

- Setting grace period to zero indicates that the default grace period (one week) should be used.

- Setting grace period to one second means that no grace period should be allowed.

- In order to use the edquota(8) utility to edit group quota setting, -g flag is specified.

File System Backup

There are different utilities in the FreeBSD base system to help system's administrators to take backups from their systems. But before starting to take backups, you should define your backup strategy.

Backups can be taken at the file-system-level, from the whole partition or physical disk, or on a higher-level. This enables you to select relevant files and directories t o be archived and moved to a tape device or a remote server. In this chapter, we will discuss different utilities and how to use them to create usable backups for your needs.

Dump and Restore

The dump(8) utility is the most reliable and portable backup solution to take backups on UNIX systems. The dump utility, in conjunction with restore(8), creates your basic backup toolbox in FreeBSD. The dump command is able to create full and incremental backups from the whole disk or any partition of your choice. Even if your file system that you want to take backups from, is live (which in most cases is), the dump utility creates a snapshot of your file system before the back up, to ensure that your file system does not change during the process.

By default, dump creates backups on a tape drive unless you specify another file or a special device.

A typical full backup using dump may look like the following example:

```
# dump -0auL -f /usr/dump1 /dev/ad0s1a

    DUMP: Date of this level 0 dump: Sat Apr 14 16:40:03 2007
    DUMP: Date of last level 0 dump: the epoch
    DUMP: Dumping snapshot of /dev/ad0s1a (/) to /usr/dump1
    DUMP: mapping (Pass I) [regular files]
    DUMP: mapping (Pass II) [directories]
    DUMP: estimated 66071 tape blocks.
    DUMP: dumping (Pass III) [directories]
    DUMP: dumping (Pass IV) [regular files]
    DUMP: DUMP: 66931 tape blocks on 1 volume
    DUMP: finished in 15 seconds, throughput 4462 KBytes/sec
    DUMP: level 0 dump on Sat Apr 14 16:40:03 2007
    DUMP: Closing /usr/dump1
    DUMP: DUMP IS DONE
```

In the above example, dump is used to take a full backup (note the -0 flag) of the /dev/ad0s1a file, which is mounted onto the / mount point to a regular /usr/dump1 file. The -L flag indicates that the partition is a live file system; so dump will create a consistent snapshot from the partition, before performing the backup operation.

 In case -L flag is specified, dump creates a snapshot in .snap directory in the root partition of the file system. The snapshot will be removed as soon as the dump process is complete. Always remember to use -L on your live file systems. This flag will be ignored in read-only and unmounted partitions.

And finally -u flag tells dump to record dump information in the /etc/dumpdates file. This information is used by dump for future backups.

The dump command can also create incremental backups using information recorded in the /etc/dumpdates file. In order to create an incremental backup, you should specify a higher backup-level from -1 to -9 in the command line. If backup-level is not specified, dump will assume a full backup (that is -0) should be taken.

```
# dump -1auL -f /usr/dump2 /dev/ad0s1a

    DUMP: Date of this level 1 dump: Sat Apr 14 15:00:36 2007
    DUMP: Date of last level 0 dump: Sat Apr 14 14:35:34 2007
    DUMP: Dumping snapshot of /dev/ad0s1a (/) to /usr/dump2
    DUMP: mapping (Pass I) [regular files]
    DUMP: mapping (Pass II) [directories]
    DUMP: estimated 53 tape blocks on 0.00 tape(s).
    DUMP: dumping (Pass III) [directories]
```

```
DUMP: dumping (Pass IV) [regular files]
DUMP: DUMP: 50 tape blocks on 1 volume
DUMP: finished in less than a second
DUMP: level 1 dump on Sat Apr 14 15:00:36 2007
DUMP: Closing /usr/dump2
DUMP: DUMP IS DONE
```

It also updates `/etc/dumpdates` with new backup dates:

```
# cat /etc/dumpdates

/dev/ad0s1a                        0 Sat Apr 14 14:35:34 2007
/dev/ad0s1a                        1 Sat Apr 14 15:00:36 2007
```

Once you have created dumps from your file system as regular files, you may want to move the dump file to another safe location (like a backup server), to protect your backups in case of a hardware failure. You can also create dumps directly on a remote server over SSH. This can be done by giving the following command:

```
# dump -0auL -f - /dev/ad0s1a | bzip2 | ssh admin@bkserver dd of=/usr/
backup/server1.dump
```

This will create a level 0 (or full) backup from the `/dev/ad0s1a` device over network using `ssh(1)` facility to host `bkserver` with username `admin` and uses `dd(1)` to create a file using input stream. And as we create a full backup, which may be a huge file, `bzip2(1)` is used to compress data stream to reduce the network load.

You can use your favourite compression program (for example, `gzip(1)`, `compress(1)`) with appropriate parameters, instead of `bzip2`.

 Using a compression program will reduce the network load at the cost of CPU usage during dump routine.

Now that you made your backup on a tape or a remote device, you may also have to verify or restore your backup in future.

The `restore(8)` utility performs the inverse function of what `dump` does. Using `restore`, you can simply restore a backup taken using the `dump` utility, or extract your files, deleted accidentally. It can also be used to restore backups over the network.

A simple scenario for using `restore` is restoring a full backup. It is recommended that you restore your backup to an empty partition. You have to format the destination partition, using `newfs(8)`, before restoring your backup. After you restore the full backup, you can proceed to restore the incremental backups, in the order in which they were created.

A typical restore procedure would look like the following command lines:

```
# newfs /dev/da0s1a
# mount /dev/da0s1a /mnt
# cd /mnt
# restore -r -f /usr/dump1
```

The `restore` command fully extracts the dump file to your current directory. So you have to change your current directory to wherever you want to restore the backup using the `cd` command.

Another interesting feature of the `restore` utility is the **interactive mode**. In this mode, you can browse through files and directories inside the dump file, and also mark the files and directories that should be restored. This feature is very useful in restoring the files and directories, deleted accidentally.

There are a number of useful commands in the interactive restore shell to help users choose what they want to extract. The `ls`, `cd`, and `pwd` commands are similar to their equivalents, and are used to navigate through the dump file. Using `add` and `delete` commands, you can mark and unmark files and directories that you want to extract. Once you finish selecting the files, you can use the `extract` command to extract the selected files.

```
# restore -i -f /usr/dump1
    restore > ls
    .:
    .cshrc      bin/      dev/      home@      mnt/      sbin/      var/
    .profile    boot/     dist/     lib/       proc/     sys@
    .snap/      cdrom/    entropy   libexec/   rescue/   tmp/
    COPYRIGHT   compat@   etc/      media/     root/     usr/
    restore > add sbin
    restore > add rescue
    restore > extract
    restore > quit
```

The `restore` command is also used to extract dump information from the dump file using the `what` command in the interactive mode:

```
    restore > what
    Dump    date: Sat Apr 14 16:40:03 2007
    Dumped from: the epoch
    Level 0 dump of / on server.example.com:/dev/ad0s1a
    Label: none
```

The tar, cpio, and pax Utilities

There may be scenarios when you may not have to take a full dump of your hard disk or partition. Instead, you may want to archive a series of files and directories to your backup tapes or regular files. This is where `tar(1)`, `cpio(1L)`, and `pax(1)` utilities come into play.

The `tar` command is UNIX's original tape manipulation tool. It was created to manipulate streaming archive files for backup tapes. It is not a compression utility and is used in conjunction with an external compression utility such as `gzip` and `bzip2`, and `compressd`, in case compression is required.

Besides tape drives, you can use `tar` to create regular archive files. The `tar` archive files are called **tarball**.

 Keep in mind that FreeBSD's `tar` utility, a.k.a `bsdtar(1)`, is slightly different from the GNU's tar. GNU tar or `gtar` is available in ports collection. Only BSD `tar` is covered in this chapter.

A tarball can be created, updated, verified, and extracted using the `tar(1)` utility.

```
# tar cvf backup.tar backup/
    a backup
    a backup/HOME.diff
    a backup/make.conf
    a backup/rc.conf
```

In the above example, `tar` is used to create a tarball called `backup.tar` from the `backup` directory. The c flag indicates `tar` should create a tar ball, v flag tells `tar` to be verbose and show a list of files on which the operation is being performed and f flag indicates the name of the output tarball (`backup.tar`) in the command.

To update a tarball, u flag is used:

```
# tar uvf backup.tar backup/
    a backup
    a backup/make.conf
    a backup/sysctl.conf
```

And x flag to extract the files from a tarball:

```
# tar xvf backup.tar
    x backup
    x backup/HOME.diff
    x backup/make.conf
    x backup/rc.conf
```

In all the above examples, the tarball archive was created as a regular file indicated by f flag. While omitting this flag, `tar` will use the default tape device on the `/dev/sa0` file. Other useful `tar` flags include z for `gzip` compression and j for `bzip2` compression.

> You can create tarballs over network with SSH using piping technique discussed in *Dump and Restore* section.

The `cpio` utility is another important archiving utility in the FreeBSD's base system. It is similar to the `tar` utility in many ways. It was also a POSIX standard until POSIX.1-2001 and was dropped due to the 8GB file size limitation.

The `pax` utility was created by IEEE STD 1003.2 (POSIX.2) to sort out incompatibilities between tar and cpio. Pax does not depend on any specific file format and supports a handful of different archive formats including `tar`, `cpio`, and `ustar` (POSIX.2 standard). Despite being a POSIX standard that is widely implemented, it is still not as popular as a `tar` utility.

The -w flag is used to create archive:

```
# pax -w -f backup.pax backup/
```

And -r to extract (or read) the archive to current directory:

```
# pax -r -f backup.pax
```

The `pax` utility is also able to read/write different archive types that can be specified by -x flag. The supported parameters of `pax` are shown in the following list:

- **cpio**: New POSIX.2 `cpio` format
- **bcpio**: Old binary `cpio` format
- **sv4cpio**: System V release 4 `cpio` format
- **sv4crc**: System V release 4 `cpio` format with CRC checksums
- **tar**: BSD `tar` format
- **ustar**: New POSIX.2 `tar` format

Snapshots

Actually, taking snapshots from a file system isn't a backup method, but is very helpful in restoring accidentally removed files. Snapshots can be mounted as regular file systems (even over network) and the system administrator can use regular system commands to browse the mounted file system and restore selected files and directories.

RAID-GEOM Framework

GEOM is an abstraction framework in FreeBSD that provides the infrastructure required to perform transformation on disk I/O operations. Major RAID control utilities in FreeBSD use this framework for configuration.

This section does not provide in-depth information about RAID and GEOM, but only discusses RAID configuration and manipulation using GEOM.

Currently GEOM supports RAID0 (Striped Set without parity) and RAID1 (Mirrored Set without parity) through geom(8) facility.

RAID0—Striping

Striping disks is a method to combine multiple physical hard disks into one big logical volume. This is done mostly using relevant hardware RAID controllers, while GEOM provides software support for RAID0 stripe sets.

RAID0 offers improved disk I/O performance, by splitting data into multiple blocks and performing simultaneous disk writes on multiple physical disks, but offers no fault tolerance for hard disk errors. Any disk failure could destroy the array, which is more likely to happen when you have many disks in your set.

Appropriate kernel module should be loaded before creating a RAID0 volume using the following command:

```
# kldload geom_stripe
```

This can also be done through the /boot/loader.conf file, to automatically load the module during system boot up, by adding this line:

```
geom_stripe_load="YES"
```

Normally, you will not need to load any GEOM module manually. GEOM related utilities automatically detect all modules that are required to be loaded, and will load it manually.

The gstripe(8) utility has everything you need to control your RAID0 volume. Using this utility you can create, remove, and query the status of your RAID0 volume.

There are two different methods to create a RAID0 volume using gstripe—manual and automatic. In the manual method, the create parameter is used, and volumes created using this method do not persist during reboots. The volumes should be created at boot time, if persistence is required:

```
# gstripe create stripe1 /dev/da1 /dev/da2
# newfs /dev/stripe/stripe1
```

The newly created and formatted device can now be mounted and used as shown here:

```
# mount /dev/stripe/stripe1 /mnt
```

In the automatic method, the metadata is stored on the last sector of every device, so that they can be detected and automatically configured during boot time. In order to create automatic RAID0 volume, you should use `label` parameter:

```
# gstripe label stripe1 /dev/da1 /dev/da2
```

Just like manual volumes, you can now format /dev/stripe/stripe1 using newfs and mount it.

To see a list of current GEOM stripe sets, gstripe has the list argument. Using this command, you can see a detailed list of devices that form the stripe set, as well as the current status of those devices :

```
# gstripe list

    Geom name: stripe1
    State: UP
    Status: Total=2, Online=2
    Type: AUTOMATIC
    Stripesize: 131072
    ID: 1477809630
    Providers:
    1. Name: stripe/stripe1
      Mediasize: 17160732672 (16G)
      Sectorsize: 512
      Mode: r1w1e0
    Consumers:
    1. Name: da1s1d
      Mediasize: 8580481024 (8.0G)
      Sectorsize: 512
      Mode: r1w1e1
      Number: 1
    2. Name: da0s1d
      Mediasize: 8580481024 (8.0G)
      Sectorsize: 512
      Mode: r1w1e1
      Number: 0
```

To stop a RAID0 volume, you should use the stop argument in the gstripe utility. The stop argument will stop an existing striped set ,but does not remove the metadata from the device, so that it can be detected and reconfigured after system reboots.

```
# gstripe stop stripe1
```

To remove metadata from the device and permanently remove a stripe set, the `clear` argument should be used;

```
# gstripe clear stripe1
```

RAID1—Mirroring

This level of RAID provides fault tolerance from disk errors and increased *READ* performance on multithreaded applications. But write performance is slightly lower in this method. In fact, RAID1 is a live backup of your physical disk. Disks used in this method should be of equal size.

The `gmirror(8)` facility is the control utility of RAID1 mirror sets. Unlike RAID0, all RAID1 volumes are automatic and all components are detected and configured automatically at boot time. The `gmirror` utility uses the last sector on each device to store metadata needed for automatic reconfiguration. This utility also makes it easy to place a root partition on a mirrored set.

It offers various commands to control mirror sets. Initializing a mirror is done using the `label` argument as shown here:

```
# gmirror label -b round-robin mirror1 da0 da1
```

In the above example, we created a mirror set named `mirror1` and attached the `/dev/da0` and `/dev/da1` disks to the mirror set.

The `-b` flag specifies the "balance algorithm" to be used in the mirror set. There are four different methods used as balance algorithms, which are listed as follows:

- **load**: Read from the device with the lowest load.
- **prefer**: Read from the device with the highest priority.
- **round-robin**: Use round-robin algorithm between devices.
- **split**: Split read requests that are bigger than or equal to slice size, on all active devices.

You may choose an appropriate algorithm depending on your hardware configuration. For example, if one of your hard disks is slower than the others , you can set higher priority on the fastest hard disk using `gmirror`'s `insert` argument and use the `prefer` method as the balance algorithm.

Once you finish initializing your mirror set, you should format the newly created device using `newfs` command and mount it to relevant mount point:

```
# newfs /dev/mirror/mirror1
```

```
# mount /dev/mirror/mirror1 /mnt
```

The `stop` argument stops a given mirror.

Using the `activate` and `deactivate` arguments you can active and deactivate a device that is attached to a mirror, which would be useful in removing or replacing a hot-swappable hard disk. When a device is `deactivated` inside a mirror set, it will not attach itself to the mirror automatically, even after a reboot, unless you re-activate the device using the `activate` argument.

To add a new device to the mirror set, or to remove a device permanently, the `insert` and `remove` arguments can be used, respectively. The `remove` argument also clears metadata from the given device. This is shown in the following command lines:

```
# gmirror insert mirror1 da2
# gmirror remove mirror1 da1
```

If you want to change the configuration of a mirrored volume (for example, changing balance algorithm on the fly), the `configure` argument can be used:

```
# gmirror configure -b load mirror1
```

In case of disk failure, when a device is faulty and cannot be reconnected to the mirror, the `forget` argument will tell `gmirror` to remove all faulty components. Once you replace the faulty disk with a brand new one, you can use the `insert` argument to attach a new disk to the array, and start synchronizing data.

Disk Concatenation

This method is used to concatenate multiple physical hard disks to create bigger volumes, beyond the capacity of one hard disk. The difference between this method and RAID0 's is that, in this method, data is written to the disk sequentially. This means that the system will fill the first device first, and the second device will be used only when there is no space left on the first device. This method does not offer any performance improvements or redundancy.

To create a concatenated volume, the `gconcat(8)` facility is available. As in RAID0, there are two methods to create a concatenated volume—manual and automatic.

Using the `create` parameter, you can create a manual concatenated volume and attach the desired physical disks. In this method, as no metadata will be written on the disk, the system will not be able to detect and reconfigure the volume after system reboots.

In order to create an automatic concatenated volume, the `label` parameter should be used:`# gconcat label concat1 da0 da1 da2`

Once a volume is created using either the manual or the automatic method, it should be formatted using `newfs` as shown as follows:

```
# newfs /dev/concat/concat1
# mount /dev/concat/concat1 /mnt
```

There is no way to remove a device from a concatenated volume. However, you can add new disks to an existing volume, and grow the size of the file system on the volume:

```
# gconcat label concat1 da3 da4
# growfs /dev/concat/concat1
```

To stop a concatenated volume, the `stop` argument is used. However this will not remove the volume permanently. The `clear` argument will remove the concatenated volume permanently, and also remove the GEOM metadata from the last sector of the attached devices.

Summary

The impact of disk I/O should not be overlooked when performance is a concern. A well configured storage will dramatically improve the system's overall performance. This chapter introduces the necessary tips and information a system administrator needs, to tweak the storage setup on a FreeBSD server. We have also seen how to take backups, weed out system redundancy and improve performance using RAID arrays, and ways and means of creating and managing virtual memory partitions, effectively.

2
System Configuration— Keeping it Updated

As a system administrator, you would definitely know the importance of keeping the system up-to-date to work around the security holes and bug fixes while keeping the highest service availability. Moreover, as FreeBSD gets upgraded round the clock, it is very important to know the right time and the need for an update.

Upgrading a system requires updating the local source tree from a server and compiling specific parts of a system such as a library, the FreeBSD kernel, or in some cases, the whole operating system. For those who are not interested in dealing with the source code and recompiling, there are other ways to perform the binary updates. The professionals can customize the binary updates generated for their systems by changing the source code and recompiling, to gain better performance.

For the developers and end users the source code is available on the project's CVS servers. Hence, the FreeBSD system administrator must have a basic knowledge of CVS. Developers use CVS to record the updates to the source tree and the end users check out the latest changes to their system, to update it as required. This chapter discusses different ways of tracking the security-related updates. Further, it discusses rebuilding the kernel, and the world (except the kernel), for those who prefer to create their customized and optimized systems from scratch.

In this chapter we will look into the following:

- CVSup as the synchronizing source— tracking –STABLE and –CURRENT
- Ports collection
- Security advisories
- Customizing and rebuilding kernel
- Rebuilding world
- Binary update
- Recovering from a dead kernel

CVSup—Synchronizing the Source Code

The FreeBSD project makes a heavy use of CVS to make the source tree available for different releases of the operating system on the development servers. The FreeBSD project also uses the Perforce version control system for various other (mostly experimental) projects. However, as a system administrator, there is no need to deal with the Perforce system. It is highly recommended that you keep track of the latest changes by subscribing to the appropriate mailing lists and checking the CVS tree. A list of FreeBSD project's mailing list is available at `http://lists.freebsd.org/`.

There are various tags available for different releases of FreeBSD, on the CVS server. Depending on the `revision` tag that you are tracking, you may see different volumes of traffic on the CVS server. There are two types of tags—the `branch` and `release` tags.

The `branch` tags refer to a particular line of development, while the `release` tags refer to the FreeBSD release in a specified time.

For example, the `RELENG_7` tag indicates the line of development for FreeBSD - 7.x (also known as FreeBSD 7-STABLE or –STABLE for short). Alternatively, `RELENG_7_1` is a release branch for FreeBSD-7.1, which will only be updated for the security advisories and other critical updates.

An example of `release` tags is `RELENG_7_0_0_RELEASE`, which is the release point of FreeBSD 7.0-RELEASE.

The `HEAD` tag is the main line of development and all new features are imported to this tree. This tree contains the codes that are necessary for the test reasons and may break your running system down, due to the library updates or changes in the memory structure.

 It is not advisable to track –CURRENT tree on a production server as some of the new updates may render your system unstable.

It is important to choose the `revision` tag, which you want to track, to keep your servers up-to-date and stable. It is also recommended to keep track of the `release` tag of your currently installed FreeBSD version. For example, if your server is running FreeBSD 7.0 (which was installed from 7.0-RELEASE CD-ROM), it is advisable to keep it synchronized with `RELENG_7_0` tag, which contains only the critical updates. By tracking the –STABLE branch (in this case `RELENG_7`), you will have all the features and updates made to your FreeBSD release development line (FreeBSD 7.x in this case). This means that once the 7.1-RELEASE is released, you can check it out on the `RELENG_7` branch and update your system.

After choosing to track the `revision` tag, you will need appropriate tools to update your local source tree from the project's CVSup server. The most convenient way to do this is to use the `cvsup(1)` or the `csup(1)` tool.

CVSup is a CVS file synchronization tool that is used in FreeBSD, to synchronize source trees (including the system source codes and ports system) with the master CVS repositories.

The CVSup, which is available from the source tree as `net/cvsup` or `net/cvsup-without-gui`, is the standard tool for CVS synchronisation and has been available for a long time. Despite being a crucial tool, it is never imported to the base system because it was written in Modula-3 language. This is where the `csup` comes into life. In fact `csup` is a rewrite of the original `cvsup` in C language, and being a lightweight tool, was found suitable to be included in the FreeBSD base system (as of FreeBSD 6.2). However, `csup` is not exactly the same as `cvsup` (currently `csup` supports only the checkout-mode, while `cvsup` supports the `cvs-mode` also). But they share the same command-line, syntax, and supfile format.

In most cases, you won't need to install CVSup on FreeBSD 7.0, unless you are a CVSup fanatic or need a feature that is not available in `csup` (like CVSup server mirroring).

If you install `cvsup` using the source code, it takes a long time. Instead, you can add the `cvsup-without-gui` package using the `pkg_add(1)` utility from an online repository as shown here:

```
# pkg_add -r cvsup-without-gui
```

Tracking –STABLE

To synchronize your current source tree with –STABLE of the same branch, you need to create a supfile. A supfile is a configuration file describing a collection of files to be synchronized from the server. You need to create a supfile before running `cvsup` (or `csup`). A sample supfile is shown in the following code:

```
*default host=cvsup7.freebsd.org
*default base=/var/db
*default prefix=/usr
*default release=cvs
*default delete use-rel-suffix compress
src-all tag=RELENG_7
```

In the above supfile, we are tracking the `src-all` tree from the RELENG_7 branch tag. This is the –STABLE for the 7.x line of development, which contains the latest code of this release, including the critical fixes, security updates, and other new features that are merged from –CURRENT branch. Merged from - Current (MFC) means that the code that was committed to –CURRENT for testing is approved to be imported to –STABLE branch.

In the above example, the server `cvsup7.freebsd.org` is used. There are numerous CVSup mirrors available for the end users. So you don't have to spam the main CVSup server.

The updated list of the CVSup mirrors is available in the FreeBSD handbook at `http://www.freebsd.org/doc/en_US.ISO8859-1/books/handbook/cvsup.html`. You may choose the geographically nearest mirror for a better performance. You can also use the `fastest_cvsup(7)` utility (available under `sysutils/fastest_cvsup` in ports collection), which helps you to find the fastest CVSup server depending on your geographical location and network behavior:

```
# fastest_cvsup -Q -r -c all
```

cvsup.uk.freebsd.org

In the above example, it fetches the list of CVSup mirrors from the handbook and tries to connect to all servers (actually connects to server and does not rely on ping), and makes decisions based on the servers' response time. In the case above, the UK-based mirror of FreeBSD is the best. This could however be different for your location.

> The `fastest_cvsup` would take a few minutes to figure out which mirror is most suitable. The time depends on your internet connection speed. On a typical dsl internet connection, it would take up to ten minutes.

You can take the supfile samples from `/usr/share/examples/cvsup`, copy it to `/etc`, and modify it to match your preferences.

After creating your first supfile, you can use CVSup or `csup` to synchronize your local copy of repository with the latest online version. If you are using a narrow band internet link, you can enable the compression, to gain better performance.

```
# csup /etc/cvsupfile

    Connected to cvsup.uk.freebsd.org
    Updating collection src-all/cvs
     Edit src/Makefile.inc1
```

```
Edit src/UPDATING
...
Finished successfully
```

 The csup maintains syntax similar to that of cvsup. For all the examples in this book, csup and cvsup can be used interchangeably.

Tracking the –STABLE branch is a very good idea for the production systems, only if you are aware of the latest changes in the branch. You should be aware of the minor software upgrades and changes in the systems libraries that will affect the operation of your server, in addition to the critical bug fixes and security updates.

 As compression takes more CPU resources from the server, using compression in CVSup is not recommended, unless you really need it.

There are a number of ways to know about the latest important changes made to the branch. One of the methods is by reading the /usr/src/UPDATING file. This file contains all the latest important changes made to the current branch in the reverse chronological order. However, not all the changes are documented in the UPDATING file. The FreeBSD -STABLE mailing list has the latest information about the –STABLE branch including the users' experience, problem reports, and developers announcements. You can subscribe to the list or view its archives at http://lists.freebsd.org/mailman/listinfo/freebsd-stable.

Tracking –CURRENT

The HEAD tag on the CVS tree contains the latest development code. All the new features, major library updates, and fundamental changes are tested in this branch. This branch is mainly targeted for developers and enthusiasts who are interested in using the cutting-edge features, testing the functionality, hunting bugs, and developing software for FreeBSD. This branch, which is also known as –CURRENT, is not recommended for the production environment and day to day usage. Hence you don't track this branch, unless you need a new feature which is not available in –STABLE.

 An operating system built from –CURRENT code is not stable and may break down frequently. Do not use this branch on your servers, unless you know what you are doing and ready to face the consequences.

The only difference between the supfiles from the –STABLE and –CURRENT branch lies in the `tag` attribute:

```
*default host=cvsup7.freebsd.org
*default base=/var/db
*default prefix=/usr
*default release=cvs
*default delete use-rel-suffix compress
src-all tag=.
```

As there would be several major changes each time you synchronize your local source repository, it would be a good idea to check the `/usr/src/UPDATING` file more frequently.

There is also a mailing list dedicated to the –CURRENT issues where people discuss the latest changes, bug reports, and possible fixes, which is called **freebsd-current** and is available for subscription at `http://lists.freebsd.org/mailman/listinfo/freebsd-current`..

Ports Collection

If you are relying on the ports collection (which is discussed in detail in the next chapter) to install the new software and keep the existing software up-to-date, you will need to keep your ports repository updated.

There are a number of ways to keep the ports tree updated, of which, the most popular are, updating using `cvsup(1)` and `portsnap(8)`.

Tracking Ports

Using CVSup to keep the ports tree up-to-date is like synchronizing with source tree, with a few minor differences. The first difference is that you need to track `ports-*` repository (where * is the ports collection names) instead of `src-all`. And the second difference is that there is only one `branch` tag for ports collection which is always the `HEAD` branch. It means that the ports collection is the same among different releases of FreeBSD.

A sample ports supfile is shown as follows:

```
*default host=cvsup7.freebsd.org
*default base=/var/db
*default prefix=/usr
*default release=cvs
*default delete use-rel-suffix compress
ports-all tag=.
```

Running CVSup brings your ports collection located at /usr/ports to the latest available revision. This is shown here:

```
# csup /etc/cvsupfile

   Connected to cvsup7.freebsd.org
   Updating collection ports-all/cvs
    Edit ports/devel/qt4/Makefile
    Edit ports/mail/thunderbird/Makefile
    Edit ports/mail/thunderbird/distinfo
    ...
   Finished successfully
```

You can also run csup periodically, using cron to make sure that your ports tree is always up-to-date. For this, you should run csup with appropriate arguments from cron and redirect the output to a log file, for further inspection. The sample cron line that runs csup everyday at 4:30 is shown as follows:

```
30 4 * * * root /usr/bin/csup /etc/cvsupfile 2>&1 > /var/log/csup.log
```

 The csup updates the live /usr/ports directory. Hence, if you have changed anything within the /usr/ports sub tree, your changes will be overwritten by csup.

Portsnap

Although-using CVSup, to make the ports tree updated, is quite straightforward, some people choose to use the portsnap. The portsnap is a relatively new system for updating the ports tree, securely. It has been included in the FreeBSD's base system, since FreeBSD 6.2. Hence, there is no need to install the software from the ports tree.

The snapshots from the ports tree are updated every hour. It is signed to prevent any malicious modifications and can be downloaded using the HTTP protocol.

The portsnap has some advantages over the csup, which make life easier for the system administrator. The advantages are listed as follows:

- All updates are cryptographically signed and are hence secure.
- It requires zero configuration, and takes a couple of commands to update the whole ports tree.
- It is included in the FreeBSD's base system. No third-party software is required to be installed.
- It uses less network and disk I/O resources as compared to the CVSup protocol.

Just like `csup`, the portsnap updates are incremental, and there is no need to fetch the whole ports tree every time you want to update it. When you run portsnap for the first time, it downloads a compressed copy of a ports tree to `/var/db/portsnap`. The next time you update the tree, one or more binary diffs of the tree will be downloaded.

> Binary diffs are created using Colin Percival's bsdiff tool. The bsdiff is the same as the original `diff(1)` utility, except for the fact that it uses sophisticated algorithms to compare two binary files and creates small binary patch files that can be applied later, using `bspatch` utility. These tools were created with the intention of providing security patches to the FreeBSD binaries rather than for re-compiling the binaries from the source code. The `freebsd-update(8)` utility also uses the same tools to apply security patches to the system's binaries.

You should first download the ports tree. To do this, you should run `portsnap` with the `fetch` argument as shown here:

```
# portsnap fetch
```

Once the ports tree is downloaded, you can update the live ports tree (that lives in `/usr/ports`) with recently downloaded ports snapshot, using the following portsnap's `update` command:

```
# portsnap update
```

> If this is the first time you are updating the ports tree using the portsnap, you should run the `portsnap extract` before running the `portsnap update`. The `portsnap` cannot update the ports tree that was not created using `portsnap` (for example, it cannot be updated using CVSup)

Security Advisories

An important part of the day to day life of a system administrator is to track the latest security issues and bug fixes for the operating systems that he runs on his servers. There are a number of well-known security related mailing lists in which you can find the latest update of the security issues in different operating systems and softwares. The FreeBSD project also has a mailing list dedicated to the security updates and advisories for the end users. The `freebsd-security-notifications` is a low traffic mailing list that contains the latest security information related to the FreeBSD operating system and the included softwares. If you are concerned about the security of your systems, you are strongly advised to subscribe to the `freebsd-security-notifications` mailing list at `http://lists.freebsd.org/mailman/listinfo/freebsd-security-notifications`.

The FreeBSD security officer provides security advisories for several branches of FreeBSD. A list of all the recent security advisories for different releases is available at http://www.freebsd.org/security/.

VuXML—Vulnerability Database

Vulnerability and eXposure Markup Language (VuXML) is a method to document the vulnerabilities and security issues that affect the FreeBSD operating system and ports collection. The FreeBSD's VuXML is available online at http://www.vuxml. org/freebsd/ as well as in ports collection (which you, hopefully, keep updated) in the ports/security/vuxml/vuln.xml file.

Different software packages rely on the VuXML information to check the installed software packages for security issues. The most important software in this area is portaudit(1).

The portaudit utility should be installed from the security/portaudit directory of the ports collection and helps the system administrator check the installed packages for known security issues and vulnerabilities, based on the VuXML information:

```
# portaudit -Fda

    auditfile.tbz                  100% of    41 kB    26 kBps
    New database installed.
    Database created: Sat Apr 21 23:40:01 IRST 2007
    0 problem(s) in your installed packages found.
```

In the above example, portaudit downloads the latest vulnerability database and checks all installed packages against the VuXML database.

CVS Branch Tag

If you are not interested in tracking –STABLE, then you need to track the branch tags that are used only for the security advisories and other critical fixes. When tracking the branch tags, you don't need to worry about breaking a production system as there is no major new software upgrade, or a major functionality change in this tree. A sample release tag used in the supfile is like RELENG_7_1 which sticks to the FreeBSD 7.1 release and updates, only when a security advisory or a critical fix is issued.

Customizing and Rebuilding Kernel

The default FreeBSD GENERIC kernel is good enough for a typical installation. It contains support for the most commonly used hardware including network interfaces, USB ports, SCSI disk, and other commonly used hardware that are most likely to exist on any computer or server. However, there is no guarantee that all your installed hardware is supported by this kernel. It is also not the ideal kernel for the high performance servers. There is a lot of hardware support compiled into this kernel that you probably won't ever need.

Creating a custom kernel for your server has many advantages that include (but not limited to) the following:

- Removing support for unnecessary hardware from the kernel will lead to smaller memory footprint and faster system boot up process.
- Custom kernel would only support your currently installed hardware that was unavailable in the default GENERIC kernel.
- Custom kernel may include support for some features that are not available in GENERIC kernel, such as Firewall and NAT support.

 Removing unnecessary modules from the statically built kernel does not mean that you are completely removing the feature. Most modules can be loaded dynamically during system run time when needed.

The kernel configuration files can be found under the /usr/src/sys/i386/conf directory. This is the default directory for the i386 platform. However, if you are not on i386 platform, you should use the relevant subdirectory to your platform as listed in the following table:

Subdirectory in /usr/src/sys	Platform
amd64	AMD's AMD64 and Intel 64 platform
i386	Intel 32bit Platform
ia64	Intel IA-64 (Itanium) Platform
pc98	NEC PC-98x1 Platform
powerpc	PowerPC platform
sparc64	Sun Microsystems' UltraSPARC Platform

The configuration file is a text-based configuration file that contains information about the modules and options that are supposed to be statically compiled into the kernel.

If there is no `/usr/src/sys/i386/conf` directory on your machine, you are unlikely to have the FreeBSD source tree on your hard disk. You may want to install the source tree from your installation media (most likely the CD-ROM from which you install the FreeBSD) and then use CVSup to update the source tree to the latest revision.

The system's default kernel configuration file is called GENERIC, which is found in the same directory.

Reading the GENERIC file gives you a complete picture of what a kernel configuration file would look like. However, the GENERIC file does not contain all the possible options and modules.

There are two files that contain almost all the possible kernel modules and options definitions. The file `/usr/src/sys/i386/conf/NOTES` contains machine-dependent configuration notes (for the i386 architecture in this example) while the `/usr/src/sys/conf/NOTES` file has machine-independent notes. It is recommended that you have a thorough look at these two files before you create a new custom kernel file.

To create a custom kernel file, you can copy the GENERIC file to a new name and make the appropriate modifications to the new file. Do not modify the GENERIC kernel. You will need the GENERIC kernel in case of an emergency.

```
# cd /usr/src/sys/i386/conf
# cp GENERIC MYSERVER
```

This will make a copy of the default GENERIC kernel for the i386 platform with a new name, so that you can create a new kernel based on the GENERIC configuration.

After removing the unnecessary modules and adding the appropriate ones to support your hardware, and after tweaking the options according to your hardware configuration, you should build and install the kernel.

To build a custom made kernel, a few steps should be taken. First, change the directory to the sources directory:

```
# cd /usr/src
```

Then build the new kernel as shown here:

```
# make buildkernel KERNCONF=MYSERVER
```

It will take several minutes to compile a new kernel depending on your hardware. Sometimes, if it breaks here, you should re-check your kernel configuration file for a syntax error or missing module dependencies. Consult the appropriate NOTES file when needed.

After finishing the kernel building process, you are ready to install the new kernel. This is shown in the following command:

```
# make installkernel KERNCONF=MYSERVER
```

The recently compiled kernel and associated modules will be installed in the `/boot/kernel` and `/boot/modules` respectively. You may notice that there is a `/boot/GENERIC` directory, which is kept for the worst case scenario.

Rebooting the system will load your new customized kernel. You can verify this by seeing the boot messages or `uname(1)` command after system boot up:

```
# uname -v
```

FreeBSD 7.0-STABLE #2: Mon Jan 15 13:35:36 BST 2007   root@server.example. net:/usr/obj/usr/src/sys/MYSERVER

Creating a custom kernel may look pretty straightforward, there are a few notes that you should always consider, before building your new custom kernel. These notes are listed here:

- Make sure that you have read the `/usr/src/UPDATING` file. This file contains important notes that may affect your system behavior.

- Make sure that your source tree is up-to-date and has all the necessary critical updates.

- Revise your kernel configuration file. Missing modules may halt your system during boot up process. Make sure that all the necessary modules are present in the kernel configuration file.

- Read the notes for modules that you use in the respective NOTES file. There are a number of important notes that may have a major effect on your newly compiled kernel.

Rebuilding World

Rebuilding the kernel does not mean that everything is made up-to-date. Rebuilding world (mostly referred to as `buildworld`) is a method to recompile the whole system (except the kernel part) using the source code. This includes all the system utilities and libraries.

This would be useful when a major library is updated from the base system or when you want to upgrade your system (for example, from 7.0 to 7.1).

Rebuilding world does not need any specific configuration and is possible by running a few commands. However, sometimes, there could be unpredictable consequences.

To avert such consequences, you could take the following precautions :

- Take backups of your system.
- Never do it on a production server unless you have already tested it on your test box.
- Try it on a trivial machine before deploying such an update on a production server.

Now that you are given the boring warnings, you may proceed to rebuild the whole operating system, ground up. Remember to update your source tree to get the latest updates and critical fixes and read the `/usr/src/UPDATING` file.

To begin building the world, use the following commands:

```
# cd /usr/src
# make buildworld
# make buildkernel
# make installkernel
```

This would take a few hours to complete, depending upon your hardware. Now it's time to sit back and enjoy your coffee. Most UNIX people love to watch the scrolling lines while drinking their coffee.

When it is over, you should reboot your system into a single-user mode:

```
# nextboot -o "-s" -k kernel
# reboot
```

The system will boot using your recently compiled kernel. Now you should install the compiled world and update the configuration files:

```
# mergemaster -p
# make installworld
# mergemaster -Ui
# reboot
```

The `mergemaster(8)` utility helps you update your configuration files. In the above example, the configuration files that you have never modified are automatically updated (`-U` flag), and you are also prompted for the configuration files that you have changed (`-i` flag). You can merge your modifications into a new configuration file using `mergemaster`'s interactive shell and commit the merged configuration file.

When you have finished installing the world and merging the configuration files, it's time to reboot into normal mode and enjoy your updated operating system.

If everything goes fine, you can remove the stale remains of the build process from the /usr/obj directory, as well as the unnecessary libraries from the previous version.

This can be achieved by running the make check-old command in the same directory where you built the world. This will display a list of currently obsolete files, directories, and shared libraries. In order to remove all the obsolete files, use the make delete-old command.

Rebuilding the world is a lengthy process but you can reduce the build time using a few tricks shown here:

- If you have a SMP machine or a HyperThreading feature enabled, you can take advantage of the parallel make. The -j flag in the make utility tells the make to run n simultaneous processes to gain better performance. The n can be equal to a number of installed processors. For example, the make -j2 buildworld makes the build process two times faster.

- Rebuilding world in the single-user mode, instead of the normal mode, will be faster (and safer) as the system has more resources available in the single-user mode. You can turn off profiling, by adding NO_PROFILE=YES in /etc/make.conf.

 There are cases in which some ports may stop working after a system upgrade. It is recommended that the ports should be rebuilt after performing a major system upgrade.

Binary Update

Updating a system from the source is a time and resource consuming process. Many system administrators prefer to use binary updates for faster and safer upgrades. However, binary updates have their own disadvantages. You cannot customize your system binaries for your specific hardware configuration.

There are two methods to get the binary updates. The first method is getting a monthly snapshot of FreeBSD in the ISO CD-ROM image format. The snapshots are available from http://www.freebsd.org/snapshots/ and are updated every month. You can get –STABLE or –CURRENT snapshots for the latest releases, based on your hardware architecture (for example. i386, sparc, amd64, and so on). However, this method is not recommended if you want to update a production server.

The FreeBSD 6.2 imports a useful utility called freebsd-update(8) to the FreeBSD's base system. This utility examines your currently installed binaries, and contacts portsnap server mirror to fetch the latest binary update for your system components.

The `freebsd-update` utility does not update –STABLE and –CURRENT. It can be used only when you are tracking a release tag like 7.0-p9.

Updates are not actual binaries but are the binary diffs between original and updated binaries. Consequently, the updates are smaller in size and take less bandwidth and time to download. These updates are made by the FreeBSD's security team and are cryptographically signed for more security. The digital signature is checked, once they are downloaded. This is shown in the following code:

```
# freebsd-update fetch

    Fetching updates signature...
    Fetching updates...
    Fetching hash list signature...
    Fetching hash list...
    Examining local system...

    Fetching updates...
    /boot/kernel/sppp.ko...
    Updates fetched
```

To install the updates, run the following commands:

```
# freebsd-update install

    Backing up /boot/kernel/sppp.ko...
    Installing new /boot/kernel/sppp.ko...
```

The `freebsd-update` utility is a safe method to update the system's binaries. Always make sure that you have the backup of your configuration files. However, if you are not happy with the updates and they break or overwrite something that they shouldn't, then you can find a friend in `freebsd-update rollback`.

Recovering from a Dead Kernel

There are occasions when your newly compiled kernel does not boot. This may happen due to a driver mismatch (with a non-existing or wrong hardware). In such cases, you can still boot your system with GENERIC kernel and fix the problem with your customized kernel. In fact, when you install a new kernel (which will be installed in the `/boot/kernel` subdirectory), the previous kernel will move to the `/boot/kernel.old` directory. Hence, if the machine cannot boot with the new kernel, it will likely to boot with the older one.

The loader menu during the boot-up process of your current kernel is shown in the following screenshot:

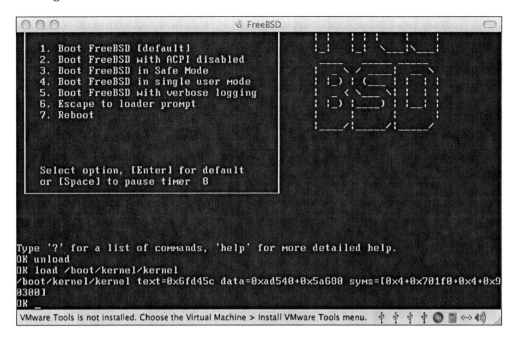

To load the previous kernel, you should stop the system from booting the current kernel by choosing the Escape to loader prompt from the loader menu during the boot up process. Once the loader prompt appears, you should unload the existing modules and load the previous kernel, and then continue the boot process:

```
# unload
# load /boot/kernel.old/kernel
# boot
```

Summary

When it comes to keeping the production or test systems up-to-date, every system administrator has his or her own strategy for upgradation. The FreeBSD gives a fine-level of control over this process and covers almost every taste.

This chapter explains the different methods such as synchronizing the source code using CVSup, so that you can selectively build and install or upgrade any part of the FreeBSD. This includes rebuilding a single system binary from the source code, to rebuilding the customized kernels, and even rebuilding all nuts and bolts of the system from the source code. This will also let you perform major system upgrades (for example, from 7.x to 8.x) on the same system, without re-installing from the installation media or losing system configuration.

You can also keep your ports tree up-to-date, by using the same technique that is used to keep the source tree updated.

As you have also seen the binary update methods, you do not need to go through the lengthy process of rebuilding the different parts of the system from the source code. The binary updates let you download and apply the binary patches against the running system.

3
System Configuration— Software Package Management

FreeBSD is well-known for its efficient package management system. From a system administrator's point of view, these features are extremely time-saving. Using the FreeBSD ports and package management tools, system administrators do not have to deal with the manual software installation and hence avoid the dependency pitfall. Using software package management facilities available in FreeBSD, installing and upgrading software has turned from a painful process into an entertaining task.

FreeBSD also has a rich library of available software applications and utilities. With these ready–to-install software packages (about 17,000 (and counting)), you will hardly find a *nix-based software which is not available in the FreeBSD's ports system.

Basically, FreeBSD offers two different ways to install a package. **Package system** offers an easy way to get and install precompiled software packages in the binary form. **Ports system** is a method to download the software source code and build the final package from the source on your computer. Each method has its pros and cons, which are discussed in this chapter.

In this chapter, we will cover the following:

- Ports and packages
- Packet management tools—`portupgrade` and `portmaster`

Ports and Packages

Almost every modern *nix distribution supports its own definition for software packaging. However, the goal of all distributions is to simplify the process of software installation for that specific platform.

Different platforms are bundled with various versions of the common libraries and build tools. Each of those libraries and build tools uses its own directory hierarchy and philosophy of the software package management. FreeBSD also has its own rules and philosophy. For example, all user software should be installed relative to the /usr/local directory.

Using the FreeBSD's built-in tools, the system administrator doesn't have to worry about the details. The software is built using the right libraries, and installed at the proper location along with the documentation and configuration files. You can also remove the software that is not needed, or even upgrade it without harming the other installed applications.

The Legacy Method

There is a common method to install an application from the source code in Unix-like operation systems—fetching tarball, extracting, running configure, running make to compile the program, and finally installing it. An example of such a scenario is given as follows:

```
# tar zxvf tcpreplay-3.0.0.tar.gz

   x tcpreplay-3.0.0/
   x tcpreplay-3.0.0/aclocal.m4
   x tcpreplay-3.0.0/autogen.sh
   x tcpreplay-3.0.0/config/
   [...]

# cd tcpreplay-3.0.0

# ./configure

   checking whether to enable maintainer-specific portions of
   Makefiles... no
   checking if malloc debugging is wanted... no
   checking build system type... i386-unknown-freebsd7.0
   [...]
```

```
# make

    Making all in scripts
    gcc -DHAVE_CONFIG_H -I. -I../src        -Wall -O3 -std=gnu99 -Wextra    -
    I/usr/include -MT man2html.o -MD -MP -MF .deps/man2html.Tpo -c -o
    man2html.o man2html.c
    mv -f .deps/man2html.Tpo .deps/man2html.Po
    [...]
```

Finally run the `make install` command to install the software. This is a simple example as it has no dependencies and hence does not complain about anything. Now if this package had dependencies upon other packages that are not installed, then the `build` process will face problems. Therefore you must find the appropriate version for each package and go through the same process for each library.

This method may work for small applications, but is definitely not suitable for larger applications with more dependencies and complexities. It is also not recommended to install the applications in FreeBSD as the program may not respect the FreeBSD rules for compilation and installation.

Software Directories

As you have decided now to install your application as a native package or from the FreeBSD ports system, you have to find out if that specific application is already ported to FreeBSD. There are various resources available to search your application:

- **FreshPorts**: It is a website (available online at `www.freshports.org`) maintained by Dan Langille as an online directory of the FreeBSD ports and the latest changes made to each port.

  You can search for the available software by name, description, or other properties.

- **FreeBSD website**: There is a list of available software ports on this website located at `http://www.freebsd.org/ports`. Just like FreshPorts, this is also able to list the ports in each category, and search based on different criteria.

- **Local ports repository**: If you have a local ports repository, you can search the repository using `make search` command running from `/usr/ports` directory. This feature will be discussed in detail, later in this chapter.

Packages

A package is an archive file (mostly with `.tgz` or `.tbz` extension) that contains precompiled binaries of a specific software application, documentation, sample configurations files, and other related files. It also contains a few other metafiles that contain information describing how the software is installed or removed.

Metafiles also include information about dependencies, and where each file or folder is installed. The package may optionally include any script that is needed during the installation and the removal of the package.

The `pkg_add(1)` command takes a package, extracts the contents, and installs the package according to the instruction in the bundled metafiles. Optionally, if the package is not available in the current directory, you can specify `-r` argument in the command line to tell `pkg_add` to download the appropriate package from the package repository on the FreeBSD project's FTP server:

```
# pkg_add -r tcpreplay

   Fetching ftp://ftp.freebsd.org/pub/FreeBSD/ports/i386/packages-7-
   stable/Latest/tcpreplay.tbz... Done.
```

You can see how to install a package with a single command. The `pkg_add` command uses the metafiles to find out the packages that are needed for the dependency of this package and install them if they are not already installed.

Note that using `-r` switch tells `pkg_add` to download a package from an online FreeBSD package repository. The `pkg_add` utility connects to the FreeBSD project's FTP server and downloads the latest available package based on the currently installed version of FreeBSD.

You can also download any third-party FreeBSD packages and use the `pkg_add` to install the downloaded package files. While most of the packages are available online from the public repositories, there are certain packages that are not available due to licensing restrictions. Such software should be installed using the ports system that instructs users to retrieve software, manually, for installation.

Packages that are available on the FreeBSD online repository have passed several tests to ensure that they are compatible with the FreeBSD's guidelines. It is always recommended that you download packages from the FreeBSD's repository instead of any third-party sources.

In order to remove an installed package, you can use `pkg_delete(1)`. This is shown in the following command:

```
# pkg_delete -ix tcpreplay

   delete tcpreplay-2.3.5_1? Y
```

The `pkg_delete(1)` needs the exact name of the installed package including the version number. You can find the exact name of the installed package using `pkg_info(1)` utility. However, to make your life easier, you can use the `-x` argument which treats the given package name parameter as a regular expression, and deletes all the packages that match the expression. This would obviously be dangerous. So use of the `-i` argument to prompt for your input, before actually removing anything, is highly recommended.

When the packages are installed, they are registered on the packages database. You can look through the registered package database using the `pkg_info(1)` utility. Using the `pkg_info` utility, you can see a complete list of all the installed packages, and also search in the database using regular expressions. The most popular usage of `pkg_info` is, grepping its output to find out whether a package is installed or not:

```
# pkg_info | grep -i ssl

    openssl-0.9.8e     SSL and crypto library
    php5-openssl-5.2.1_3 The openssl shared extension for php
```

Ports

Unlike the packages that come in a precompiled binary form, ports are a set of metafiles that describe how a specific application should be built for FreeBSD. In fact, packages are built from ports.

A port contains instructions needed to download, patch, compile, and install according to the FreeBSD's guidelines. Using the ports system, the system administrator does not need to worry about the specific build issues and dependencies for each application.

Besides, the user can specify build-time options to customize the application. This may include adding or removing features, as well as compiler options for your specific hardware.

The ports collection is a set of directories and files located under `/usr/ports`. There are several categories listed under the ports collection. Each of them contains a number of ports related to that category.

If there is no ports collection in `/usr/ports`, you probably haven't installed the collection during installation. Please refer to Chapter 2, *System Configuration – Keeping it Updated*, for more information about updating the local ports collection repository using `cvsup`.

A category is a directory that contains several ports that are directories themselves. For example, `sjitter` is located under `net-mgmt/sjitter`.

To find a specific port in ports collection, you can use `make search` facility as shown here:

```
# cd /usr/ports

# make search name=sjitter
    Port:    sjitter-0.14b
    Path:    /usr/ports/net-mgmt/sjitter
    Info:    A client/server jitter measurement utility
    Maint:   farrokhi@FreeBSD.org
    B-deps:  gettext-0.16.1_1 gmake-3.81_1 libiconv-1.9.2_2
    R-deps:
    WWW:     http://www.alcasat.net/dev/sjitter/
```

The search result gives all basic information about the port—the port's full name, version, and the path is found under the ports tree. A brief description of the port, email address of the port's maintainer, dependencies which are required to build and run this port, and finally the URL where you can find more information about the port, are also thrown up in the search.

The `search` facility in ports system uses the `/usr/ports/INDEX-7` (as in FreeBSD 7) file as its reference. You should always make sure that your INDEX file is up-to-date in order to get an accurate result. The INDEX file can be downloaded using `make fetchindex` command or automatically rebuilt using `make index` commands.

Almost everything you can do with ports is possible using the `make` utility. A list of `make` targets with description for each is found in the following table:

Target	Description
config	Asks user for port-specific build options, if available.
config-recursive	Runs config for all dependencies of a specific port.
fetch	Downloads necessary files and patches.
checksum	Verifies checksum for the downloaded files.
depends	Builds and installs dependencies for a specific port.
extract	Extracts the downloaded files into a work directory.
patch	Applies patches to the extracted files, if available.
configure	Runs configure script for the port, if available.
build	Builds the port.
install	Installs the port and registers the installation in the packages database.
showconfig	Shows the current configuration for the port.
showconfig-recursive	Shows the configuration for the port and its dependencies.

Target	Description
rmconfig	Removes any configuration saved by the config option.
rmconfig-recursive	Runs rmconfig for the port and its dependencies.
config-conditional	Runs config only if the port is not already configured (save the configured that does not exist).
fetch-list	Shows a list of files that needs to be downloaded for the port.
fetch-recurisve	Runs fetch for the port and all dependencies.
fetch-recursive-list	Runs fetch-list for the port and its dependencies.
missing	Prints a list of missing dependencies that should be installed.
clean	Cleans up the work directory.
distclean	Cleans the downloaded files for the port.
deinstall	Removes and installs port and unregisters it from the packages database
package	Creates a package tarball from the build port.
package-recursive	Creates a package of the port and all its dependencies.
search	Finds the ports based on specific criteria.
quicksearch	Runs search but shows reduced output (only portname and path is shown).

Once you find the port you want to install, you should change the current directory to the ports directory and run the make install command:

```
# cd /usr/ports/net-mgmt/sjitter/
# make install

   => sjitter-0.14b.tgz doesn't seem to exist in /usr/ports/distfiles/.
   => Attempting to fetch from http://www.alcasat.net/dev/sjitter
          sjitter-0.14b.tgz                 100% of 8070  B 5910   Bps
   ===>  Extracting for sjitter-0.14b
   => MD5 Checksum OK for sjitter-0.14b.tgz.
   => SHA256 Checksum OK for sjitter-0.14b.tgz.
   ===>  Patching for sjitter-0.14b
   ===>   sjitter-0.14b depends on executable in : gmake - found
   ===>  Configuring for sjitter-0.14b
   ===>  Building for sjitter-0.14b
   [...]
```

That is all you need to do, to install a port. In the above example, the ports system looked for the required files, downloaded the files which were not available locally, checked the downloaded files against the local checksums, extracted tarball into the `work` directory, looked for required dependencies, and finally built the software from the source code. Once the build process is done, the ports system installs the application in the appropriate path under the `/usr/local` hierarchy.

 When you run `make install`, the ports system automatically runs all steps required to install the port, including `fetch`, `extract`, `patch`, and so on. In fact you do not need to run all the steps every time you install a port. In most cases, running `make install` will be enough to install a port.

When you install a port, the ports system creates a directory called `work` under the `port` directory, where all the build processes are done. Once the port is installed, you do not need this directory anymore. You should run `make clean` in order to cleanup the `work` directory.

 You can combine several different arguments into a single command, like `make install clean`, which installs the package and then removes the stale `work` directory after installation.

Removing an installed package is possible using `make deinstall` command. You should change your current directory to the port's directory that you want to remove and run `make deinstall`:

```
# cd /usr/ports/net-mgmt/sjitter/
# make deinstall

    ===>   Deinstalling for net-mgmt/sjitter
    ===>   Deinstalling sjitter-0.14b
```

 Using `make deinstall`, you can remove all the files that are installed by the application during the installation, excluding the files that were created by the application after the installation. You may want to get a backup from the configuration, or the data files of a specific port, before actually removing that port for your future reference.

Some ports may let you choose various build-time options, before it is built. In this case, you will be presented a dialog box that offers you a few items to choose from. Once you finish selecting the options, the port will start the build procedure based on the options you have specified. These options will also be saved and used the next time you want to install this port (perhaps for upgrade reasons). If for any reason you decide to change the options, you can do this by running the `make config` command. This will actually ignore any saved option for the port and present the port configuration dialog again.

In order to see what options (if available) are specified for a port, use the `make showconfig` command to give you a list of the options configuration:

```
# cd /usr/ports/irc/irssi
# make showconfig

    ===> The following configuration options are available for irssi-
    0.8.11:
        PERL=on "Enable perl support"
        PROXY=off "Enable proxy support"
        SOCKS=off "Enable socks proxy support"
        IPV6=on "Enable IPv6"
        BOT=off "Enable bot"
    ===> Use 'make config' to modify these settings
```

Package Management Tools

While FreeBSD comes bundled with all the necessary tools that you need to manage packages, there are several other third-party tools too. These tools aim to make life easier with ports, especially while upgrading the installed packages.

Without the third-party tools, you may have to remove the packages manually, and install a newer version, to upgrade an installed package. You may also need to upgrade the other packages that are needed for the new package. While being straightforward for smaller applications, it leads to headaches for larger packages with more dependencies and dependants. Package management tools are created to solve this issue, as well as other deficiencies and missing features in the native ports and package tools.

The two most important tools in this area include **portupgrade** and **portmaster**. Each of these comes with its own set of unique features.

This chapter is not supposed to go into the details of package management utilities. It is recommended to refer the FreeBSD Handbook and appropriate management pages for more in-depth information about the package management tools.

Portupgrade

The portupgrade (can be found at `ports-mgmt/portupgrade` in ports system) is a widely used set of twelve utilities that are designed to overcome some deficiencies in native package management utilities. A list of the utilities, and a short description of what they do, can be found in the following table:

Utility	Description
portinstall	A useful utility to install ports.
portcvsweb	Lets users browse online CVS history on web.
portupgrade	A handy utility to upgrade the installed packages.
portversion	A fast replacement for `pkg_version(1)` utility.
portsclean	Cleans unnecessary work directories and **distfiles**.
portsdb	Manages a binary database of ports INDEX file.
ports_glob	Expands the ports globs.
pkg_deinstall	A wrapper to `pkg_delete(1)` utility with more features.
pkg_fetch	A utility to download the package files.
pkg_glob	Expands the package globs.
pkg_which	Checks packages contents for a specific file.
pkgdb	Manages binary database of the installed packages.

portinstall

The `portinstall(1)` utility offers an easy way to install a software from the ports collection. While using `portinstall`, you do not need to know where a port is actually located.

```
# portinstall -i sjitter

    --->   Session started at: Tue, 01 May 2007 23:21:36 +0330
    Install 'net-mgmt/sjitter'? [yes] y
    --->   Fresh installation of net-mgmt/sjitter started at: Tue, 01 May
    2007 23:21:41 +0330
    --->   Installing 'sjitter-0.14b' from a port (net-mgmt/sjitter)
    --->   Build of net-mgmt/sjitter started at: Tue, 01 May 2007 23:21:46
    +0330
    --->   Building '/usr/ports/net-mgmt/sjitter'
    [...]
    --->   ** Install tasks 1: 1 done, 0 ignored, 0 skipped and 0 failed
    --->   Listing the results (+:done / -:ignored / *:skipped / !:failed)
           + net-mgmt/sjitter
    --->   Packages processed: 1 done, 0 ignored, 0 skipped and 0 failed
    --->   Session ended at: Tue, 01 May 2007 23:21:58 +0330 (consumed
    00:00:22)
```

In the above example, the `sjitter` utility is installed with a single command. The `-i` switch turns on the interactive mode, in which the user will be prompted before building and installing the package.

If you prefer to install a package instead of building an application from the source code, you can use the `-P` flag to tell `portinstall` to look for a package file in the local repository. If a package is not locally available, `portinstall` will try to fetch the package from the online package repository. And finally if a package file cannot be fetched for some reason, `portinstall` will build it from the source (the port method).

The `portinstall` utility (which is the same as `portupgrade` utility) is a complicated tool with many different arguments that are not covered in this chapter. It is highly recommended to take a look at the management pages to review all the possibilities while using this utility.

pkg_deinstall

Basically, the `pkg_deinstall` utility is a wrapper for the original `pkg_delete` utility with two advantages. They are:

- The utility understands wildcards. So you do not have to know the full package name.
- The utility supports recursion through dependencies.

```
# pkg_deinstall -ri wget

    --->   Deinstalling 'rkhunter-1.2.9'
    delete rkhunter-1.2.9? y
    --->   Deinstalling 'wget-1.10.2_1'
    [Updating the pkgdb <format:bdb_btree> in /var/db/pkg ... - 427
    packages found (-1 +0) (...) done]
    delete wget-1.10.2_1? y
    [Updating the pkgdb <format:bdb_btree> in /var/db/pkg ... - 426
    packages found (-1 +0) (...) done]
    --->   Listing the results (+:done / -:ignored / *:skipped / !:failed)
            + rkhunter-1.2.9
            + wget-1.10.2_1
    --->   Packages processed: 2 done, 0 ignored, 0 skipped and 0 failed
```

In the above example, `pkg_deinstall` was called to remove `wget` and all the packages that depend on it (note that `-r` switch is for recursion). It goes through the package database and finds that the `rkhunter` package depends on `wget` and asks if it should be removed.

portupgrade

The main utility in this collection is `portupgrade(1)`. As the name suggests, it is used to upgrade the installed packages. Using `portupgrade`, you can simply upgrade a package as well as its dependencies (the packages that this package depends upon) and dependent packages (the packages that depend upon this package). You can upgrade single or multiple packages based on the criteria you specify:

```
# portupgrade -r sjitter
```

This command will upgrade the `sjitter` port to the latest available version that it can find in the ports system.

```
# portupgrade -ri 'php*'
```

This command will upgrade all the installed packages whose name starts with "php" as well as all the dependant ports, that need to be upgraded. You will also be asked before each upgrade, thanks to the `-i` parameter.

You can also choose to update from the packages rather than rebuild the port from the source code, which might be less time consuming in some cases. This may include upgrading KDE, which takes hours while building from the source, but only a few minutes to upgrade using the packages.

```
# portupgrade -rP 'mysql*'
```

This command tries to upgrade all the installed packages whose name starts with "mysql" and their dependent ports using packages. The `portugprade` tries to find relevant packages locally or from the online repository. However, if a package is not available, `portupgrade` proceeds to build the package from source. You can override this behavior by specifying `-PP`. In this case, the upgrade process will fail, if a pre-built package is not available.

```
# portupgrade -a
```

Using `-a` parameter, you can upgrade all the installed packages to the latest version. This is time consuming but it would be a very good idea to give it a try, once in a while. You may also want to specify the `-i` parameter, so that you will be asked before any package is being upgraded.

portversion

The `portversion(1)` utility is used to compare the version of installed packages with the ports available in the ports repository. By running `portversion` after synchronizing your local ports repository, you can find out, which of the installed packages is out-of-date and needs to be updated.

```
# portversion -voL =

   thunderbird-1.5.0.10    <  needs updating (port has 2.0.0.0)
   vlc-0.8.5_12            <  needs updating (port has 0.8.6.b,2)
```

The above command checks all the installed packages against the equivalent ports available in the repository. Only the packages, whose version is not equal to the version available in the ports, are shown (-o -L = argument). The latest available version is also shown for your reference (-v argument).

pkg_which

The pkg_which(1) utility is very useful in finding out which package has installed a specific file. If the given file is installed by any of the installed packages, the name of the package will be returned:

```
# pkg_which visudo

   sudo-1.6.9.14
```

portsclean

The portsclean(1) helps a system administrator to clean the garbage remaining from the ports build process, stale package files, and duplicated or orphaned, shared libraries. It is good practice to run portsclean once in a while to clean up the garbage and free some disk space.

```
# portsclean -CDL

   Cleaning out /usr/ports/*/*/work...
   Delete /usr/ports/databases/mysql50-client/work
   Delete /usr/ports/devel/t1lib/work
   Delete /usr/ports/www/eventum/work
   done.
   Detecting unreferenced distfiles...
   Delete /usr/ports/distfiles/asterisk-1.4.2.tar.gz
   Delete /usr/ports/distfiles/avahi-0.6.17.tar.gz
   Delete /usr/ports/distfiles/dnspython-1.4.0.tar.gz
```

 Portsclean does not actually remove the orphaned and duplicated, shared, libraries but moves them to /usr/local/lib/compat/pkg, just in case you want to restore them.

Portmaster

The `portmaster(8)` utility (available in `ports-mgmt/portmaster` in ports tree) has been created to address some deficiencies in the `portupgrade`. The benefits are listed here:

- `portmaster` does not depend on the external languages, unlike `portupgrade` that heavily depends on Ruby and Perl languages. It relies only on the system shell. In fact `portmaster` is a huge shell script.

- Unlike `portupgrade`, `portmaster` does not rely on external databases. Rather, it relies on the system's package database that is available in `/var/db/pkg`.

- `portmaster` downloads **distfiles** in the background, while updating packages in the foreground, which saves a lot of time.

```
# portmaster vlc

  ===>>> Gathering distinfo list for installed ports
  ===>>> Update vlc-0.8.5_12? [n] y
  ===>>> Port to upgrade: vlc-0.8.5_12
  ===>>> Port directory: /usr/ports/multimedia/vlc
  ===>>> Launching 'make checksum' for multimedia/vlc in background
  ===>>> Gathering dependency list for multimedia/vlc from ports
  ===>>> Starting recursive 'make config' check
  [...]
```

Summary

In this chapter you have learnt how to install and update software packages using systems native tools, and third-party tools such as the `portupgrade` and `portmaster`.

The system administrator can choose to use any of the package management tools. If you are already happy with `portupgrade`, you won't need to switch to `portmaster` or any other management tool, and vice versa. Basically all of the package management tools are doing the same job but using different methods.

Before you use any set of tools to manage your software packages, just make sure that you have already been through the available documentation and man pages. It gives you more insight on how your favorite utility is working, and how it can make your life easier.

Another thing to remember is that, not all package updates are trivial. I've seen many system administrators who do not bother to update their installed software, even when faced with security issues. The `portaudit` tool would be a great help in this subject. It will help you find which of the installed packages has security advisory, and is awaiting updation.

It is recommended that you keep your ports tree up-to-date with your preferred method, which is explained in Chapter 2. With the updated ports repository, you can easily upgrade the installed packages to the latest version, using the tools explained earlier in this chapter.

Finally, always consult `/usr/ports/UPDATING` before carrying out any major upgrade on your package installation. Doing massive updates may lead to a break down in a running system. The UPDATING file will keep you aware of the latest important changes to any single port or the entire ports infrastructure.

System Configuration—
System Management

In this chapter, you will learn how to deal with processes as well as manage and monitor system resources. Knowing how the system resources are being allocated and how each process is performing will help you tune the system to get the most out of it. To run an efficient server is only possible by doing efficient resource management. FreeBSD comes with a complete set of resource monitoring and management tools that let the system administrators get the most out of their systems, when used wisely.

In this chapter, we will look into the following:

- Process management and control
- Resource management and control
- Process accounting.

Process Management and Control

This chapter goes through some basic (but necessary) information about processes and daemons and will tell you in a nutshell, what a system administrator should know. You need to spend some time knowing your system's running processes and see how they are performing and how much resource each of them needs. Knowing this information will help you figure out whether your system is running efficiently and smoothly. It is also important to detect any abnormal system behavior, by looking at the output of any relevant process management utility output.

Processes and Daemons

Each running program is called a **process**. Your server has a number of processes running all the time, including the other background processes that keep your system running. Each process has a unique Process ID (PID) that is assigned by the system. The first system process, init, always has PID 1. This process is launched by the system kernel during boot process. Any other process that is launched after init has a unique PID between 2 to 99999. Once a process gets completed, the PID will be returned to the system. When the system reaches PID 99999, it starts assigning available PIDs starting from 2 over and over again. The processes are identified by their PIDs.

A **daemon** is a process that runs in the background, detached from the terminal, and waits for a system or a network event to act upon. For example, a web server (That is httpd) is a daemon that runs in the background and listens on TCP port 80 for any incoming connection. As soon as it receives a request to serve a page, it performs the necessary steps to load the object from the disk and transfer it via network to the client. Another example of a daemon is the cron scheduler. The cron daemon is always running in the background waiting for the specific time to run appropriate commands.

 Many daemons have a trailing "d" in their name that means the process is a daemon. This includes httpd, snmpd, pop3d, moused, sshd, and so on.

There are several tools available in the base system that gives you full control over processes. Using these tools, you can see which processes are running and how much CPU time or memory they are using, what their PID number is, and so on. You can also control the behavior of the running processes by sending them signals.

A **signal** is a message that is sent to a running process by the system. Processes have different reactions based on the received signals. A list of the most commonly used signals are found in the following table:

Signal	Signal name	Description
1	HUP	Causes process to reload its configuration
2	INT	Interrupt
3	QUIT	Quit
6	ABRT	Abort
9	KILL	Non-catchable, non-ignorable, implicit kill
15	TERM	Software termination signal

Sending signals to processes are explained later in this chapter.

Getting Information about Running Processes—ps, top, and pgrep

To see a list of currently running processes, you can use the ps (1) command. The ps utility shows a list containing information about the running processes, their PIDs, current process status, the process owner, and other information based on the command line arguments you specify.

```
# ps
     PID        TT     STAT     TIME        COMMAND
     893        v0     Is+      0:00.00     /usr/libexec/getty Pc ttyv0
     894        v1     Is+      0:00.00     /usr/libexec/getty Pc ttyv1
     895        v2     Is+      0:00.00     /usr/libexec/getty Pc ttyv2
     896        v3     Is+      0:00.00     /usr/libexec/getty Pc ttyv3
     908        p0     I        0:00.01     su -
     909        p0     S        0:00.14     -su (csh)
    5638        p0     R+       0:00.00     ps
```

The above output shows a list of currently running processes, which are owned by the current user. To see a list of all the processes running on the system, you can use -a flag. The popular combination of argument for ps is -auxww. The -u argument shows the owner, the name for each process, -x shows processes that are not attached to any terminals (mostly daemons), and -ww shows the output in wide format, including the complete command line with arguments of the running process.

Using the ps command, you can see only the process list and its status, the moment you invoke the ps command. Instead, top (1) command shows an interactive and live list of running processes, sorted by their PID. The top can be used to identify the active processes and see how much of the system resources they use. The top (1) also shows the current memory allocation and processor(s) status for the system and each process.

The output generated by the `top` command is shown in the following screenshot:

```
● ● ●                    Terminal — ssh — 80x25
last pid:  5664;  load averages:  0.00,  0.00,  0.00    up 0+00:32:42  20:04:57
22 processes:  1 running, 21 sleeping
CPU states:  0.0% user,  0.0% nice,  0.0% system,  0.0% interrupt,  100% idle
Mem: 65M Active, 45M Inact, 54M Wired, 240K Cache, 56M Buf, 294M Free
Swap: 1024M Total, 1024M Free

  PID USERNAME    THR PRI NICE   SIZE    RES STATE    TIME   WCPU COMMAND
  825 mysql         5  20    0 60104K 55320K kserel   0:01  0.00% mysqld
  905 farrokhi      1  96    0  8240K  3744K select   0:01  0.00% sshd
 5645 root          1  96    0  3524K  1692K RUN      0:00  0.00% top
  909 root          1  20    0  4436K  3036K pause    0:00  0.00% csh
  826 root          1   8    0 10312K  8256K nanslp   0:00  0.00% perl5.8.8
  903 root          1   4    0  8240K  3704K sbwait   0:00  0.00% sshd
  668 root          1  96    0  3188K  1160K select   0:00  0.00% syslogd
  906 farrokhi      1  20    0  4176K  2736K pause    0:00  0.00% tcsh
  908 farrokhi      1   8    0  3572K  1532K wait     0:00  0.00% su
  777 mysql         1   8    0  3488K  1360K wait     0:00  0.00% sh
  855 root          1   8    0  3188K  1236K nanslp   0:00  0.00% cron
  848 root          1  96    0  5532K  2976K select   0:00  0.00% sshd
  893 root          1   5    0  3188K  1028K ttyin    0:00  0.00% getty
  896 root          1   5    0  3188K  1032K ttyin    0:00  0.00% getty
  895 root          1   5    0  3188K  1032K ttyin    0:00  0.00% getty
  894 root          1   5    0  3188K  1032K ttyin    0:00  0.00% getty
  175 root          1  20    0  1388K   756K pause    0:00  0.00% adjkerntz
  582 root          1  99    0  1888K   496K select   0:00  0.00% devd
```

The `pgrep(1)` helps you to find PID(s) of running processes by their names. It takes a pattern in the command line and returns PID for any match of the process. The output of `pgrep` can be used in conjunction with the other utilities to perform batch tasks on running processes:

```
# pgrep httpd

    1755
    1754
    1753
    1752
    1751
    1750
```

The above example returns any PIDs for processes whose names matches with the `httpd` string.

The `pgrep` command can also return process names in addition to the `PID`s as shown here:

```
# pgrep -l sh

    1719 csh
    1716 tcsh
    1715 sshd
    1713 sshd
     839 sshd
     768 sh
```

Sending Signals to Running Processes—kill, killall, and pkill

The `kill(1)` command is used to send signals to a running process by the `PID` specified on the command line. Obviously the `PID` of a running process can be found using `ps(1)` command. The default signal, if nothing is specified, is `TERM` signal. The `TERM` signal causes the process to terminate gracefully:

```
# ps ax | grep vim

   95934  p1  T        0:00.08 vim
# kill 95934
```

There are cases when the software is unable to process a `TERM` signal, or does not terminate normally. The `KILL` signal can be used to implicitly kill a process and free the allocated resources back to the system as shown here:

```
# kill -KILL 95934
```

The `kill(1)` can also be used to send any other signal to a process. A good example of the non-killing actions would be the `HUP` signal. The hang-up (`HUP`) signal will cause a process to reload its configuration as follows:

```
# ps ax | grep sshd

   837  ??  Ss       0:00.02 /usr/sbin/sshd

# kill -HUP 837
```

The `kill(1)` utility takes `PID` in the command line. Hence you need to find out the `PID` for each process that you want to send a signal to ,using the `ps(1)` command. Instead, `killall(1)` takes the process name instead of `PID`. Using `killall` you can send a signal to one or more running process:

```
# killall httpd
```

There might be more than one process running with the same name. For example, multiple `getty` processes or multiple `httpd` processes. Using `killall` will send the specified signal to all these processes, which may not be what you had intended to do.

The `pkill(1)` is another variant of the kill family that kills or sends signals to one or more processes that match the pattern given on the following command line:

```
# pkill -KILL tcsh
```

 Use `pkill(1)` with even more care as you kill the processes that you don't actually intend to kill.

Prioritizing Running Processes—nice and renice

Running processes may have different scheduler priorities and consequently have more CPU time assigned. The priority-level is called `nice`. You can see the nice-level of the current process using the `ps(1)` or `top(1)` commands as follows:

```
# ps -l
```

```
UID    PID   PPID  CPU PRI NI VSZ  RSS   MWCHAN STAT TT TIME     COMMAND
1001  61737 61736  0   20  0  4172 2500  pause  Is  p0 0:00.03  -tcsh (tcsh
1001  98391 98390  0   20  0  4176 2604  pause  Ss  p1 0:00.03  -tcsh (tcsh
1001  98479 98391  0   96  0  3256 804   -      R+  p1 0:00.00   ps -l
```

The default nice-level for programs that you run is set to zero. The `nice(1)` utility will let you run a program with altered scheduling priority.

```
# nice -n 5 gzip file
```

In the above example, the command `gzip file` is called using `nice` with the default `nice` value incremented by 5. This means that if the current shell is running with `nice` value 0 (which is the default), the nice value for the called utility will be 5.

 If you are running **csh** or **tcsh**, calling nice will actually invoke shell's built-in `nice` function. In order to run the actual `nice` utility, you should call it using the actual path: `/usr/bin/nice`

In order to change the `nice` value for an already running process, you may use the `renice(8)` utility. The `renice(8)` utility lets you to change the `nice` value of a process by its `PID` or a group of processes that are owned by a specific user:

```
# renice -n 5 335
```

The above example will increase the nice-level of `PID` 335 by 5.

```
# renice -n 5 -u 101
```

The above example will increase the nice-level of all programs owned by UID(extracted from `/etc/passwd` file)101.

To decrease the `nice` value of a process, you can use `renice` with a negative value:

```
# renice -n -3 335
```

 Any user can increase the `nice` value of his own processes, but only the root user can decrease the `nice`-level of any process, even if he was the one who had increased the nice value.

Resource Management and Control

FreeBSD offers various utilities to monitor the current status of the resources and how they are used. You saw a few of these utilities earlier in this chapter that were mostly process related. There are also other utilities that monitor the other behaviors of the system—disk I/O, network, virtual memory, buffers, and so on.

System Resource Monitoring Tools—vmstat, iostat, pstat, and systat

The `vmstat(8)` is a utility used to report various system statistics. It shows statistics about process, virtual memory, disk, and CPU activity. This utility is very useful in gathering live statistics on a running server. The following example shows the live statistics on a FreeBSD server, every five seconds:

```
# vmstat -w 5
```

procs			memory		page				disk			faults			cpu		
r	b	w	avm	fre	flt	re	pi	po	fr	sr	ad0	in	sy	cs	us	sy	id
1	1	0	166740	217276	7	0	0	0	7	0	0	4	49	266	0	0	100
1	0	0	166740	217204	4852	0	0	0	4521	0	79	81	10755	798	69	8	23
1	0	0	166740	237948	3653	0	0	0	6092	0	240	243	8197	1484	38	19	42
1	0	0	167120	236952	4801	0	0	0	4359	0	77	79	10741	789	58	15	27
1	0	0	166740	236184	4743	0	0	0	4338	0	82	84	10732	814	69	15	15
1	0	0	169368	235184	4649	0	0	0	4225	0	77	79	10485	784	62	19	19

By default, `vmstat` shows the detailed information about the processes (**procs** column), system memory (**memory** column), page faults and paging activity (**page** column), disk operations (**disk** column), trap and interrupt rates (**faults** column), and the processor activity (**cpu** column).

While some statistics are updated every five seconds, running any of the utilities mentioned above, with a faster than five seconds (-w5) update, will be ineffective.

The `iostat(8)` specifically reports the I/O statistics in the sense of KB/t (Kilobytes per transfer), Tps (Transaction per second), and MB/s (Megabytes per second) as per the storage device. The `iostat` also shows **tty** statistics including "**tin**" and "**tout**" (which are characters read from or write to terminals, respectively).

```
# iostat -w 5

        tty                     ad0                       cpu
  tin   tout     KB/t    tps    MB/s    us   ni   sy   in   id
    0      5     5.86      3    0.02     2    0    0    0   97
    0     26    63.12     29    1.80    88    0    9    3    0
    0      9    63.89     30    1.84    89    0    6    5    0
    0      9    46.60     42    1.89    85    0    8    8    0
```

The above examples show the statistics for **ad0** (the only available physical disk on the sample platform).

The `pstat(8)` utility displays information about open files, swap utilization, and terminals status.

To see the current swap utilization you may use `-s` argument:

```
# pstat -s

    Device               1K-blocks     Used       Avail       Capacity
    /dev/ad0s1b.eli       1048576        0        1048576         0%
```

The `pstat` command also displays the open files table status by using the `-f` argument:

```
# pstat -f

    227/16424 open files
       LOC       TYPE    FLG    CNT    MSG    DATA         OFFSET
    c4032dc8    inode    RW      28     0    c4286600       1b6e2
    c4032dc8    inode    RW      28     0    c4286600       1b6e2
    c4032dc8    inode    RW      28     0    c4286600       1b6e2
    [...]
```

In the above example, the system has 227 open files out of the maximum 16424 (maximum possible open files in this case).

Moreover, to see the brief status of the current system swap and file table usage, the -T argument is helpful:

```
# pstat -T

   93/16424 files
   0M/1024M swap space
```

And finally the systat(1) is the all-in-one tool for the system resource monitoring. It does almost anything that the other utilities, mentioned so far in this chapter, can do. The systat command can display information about network—icmp, icmp6, ip, ip6, and tcp as well as the netstat and ifstat that show network socket activity status and network interface statistics, respectively.

To display any of the statistics information mentioned above, systat takes a command line argument. For example, systat -tcp command shows the detailed information about any tcp packet that was sent or received by the system every 5 seconds. The example output of the systat -tcp command is shown in the following screenshot:

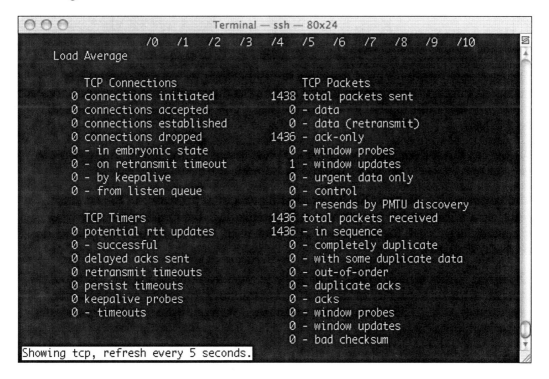

Process Accounting

Process accounting is a method to control the systems's resource allocation as well as tracking users' commands and system monitoring.

Once you enable process accounting functionality in FreeBSD, all the information about the processes launched by different users will be logged into an accounting file. The log database can be used later for statistical and administrative reasons.

To enable security accounting, you need to add the following variable to the `/etc/rc.conf` file:

```
accounting_enable = "yes"
```

After the system reboots, it creates a log file called `/var/account/acct` (if it does not already exist) and updates the log file on every process executed. The process accounting functionality will be enabled after the system reboots.

If you do not want to reboot the system, you can create the log file and enable the process accounting manually as follows:

```
# touch /var/account/acct
# accton /var/account/acct
```

The `accton(8)` utility is used to enable or disable the process accounting. The `accton(8)` accepts only one argument and that is the log file that you want to record the accounting information. If no parameter is given, the process accounting will be disabled.

As soon as the system starts to record the process accounting information, you can use the `lastcomm(1)` or `sa(8)` utilities to examine the accounting records.

The `lastcomm(1)` displays the list of recently executed processes in the reverse order. In addition to the process name, it also displays the name of the user who executed the process, the amount of CPU time used, and when the time process has started and exited.

The `sa(8)` utility is used to manipulate the process accounting log file. Using `sa(8)`, you can extract a summary of the executed commands, the number of times the process was called, CPU time taken in minutes, average number of I/O operations, and other statistics:

```
# sa
        132     16.11re     0.01cp      0avio       6882k
          3      0.01re     0.01cp      0avio       2155k       perl5.8.8
          2      0.05re     0.00cp      0avio       8987k       php
```

2	0.00re	0.00cp	14avio	5440k	troff
6	0.04re	0.00cp	0avio	41300k	***other
2	0.00re	0.00cp	0avio	12400k	col
2	0.04re	0.00cp	0avio	0k	ron*
15	0.00re	0.00cp	0avio	0k	cut
3	0.00re	0.00cp	0avio	14000k	fmt
2	0.00re	0.00cp	2avio	6100k	groff
2	0.00re	0.00cp	0avio	0k	grotty
3	0.01re	0.00cp	0avio	27200k	head
5	0.00re	0.00cp	0avio	15600k	lastcomm
2	3.29re	0.00cp	9avio	21000k	man
2	3.29re	0.00cp	0avio	0k	more
2	0.00re	0.00cp	0avio	0k	sa
8	3.34re	0.00cp	0avio	30800k	sh
62	0.03re	0.00cp	0avio	0k	sh*
3	6.00re	0.00cp	0avio	0k	sleep
2	0.00re	0.00cp	0avio	0k	tbl
4	0.00re	0.00cp	0avio	25000k	zcat

You can modify the sa(8) output using different command line arguments, like -c to sort by the number of times each process was called, or -b to sort by the sum of CPU time taken for each process.

Summary

With more information about your current system resource usage, you can improve the system's performance and identify the bottlenecks in your server. Experienced UNIX administrators use such tools to constantly monitor server behavior and optimize its performance.

In this chapter, you were introduced to the basic toolbox for monitoring the system's performance and security. By combining these tools, you will have a better control over your processes and users.

To get the most out of these basic but powerful system utilities, it is recommended that you have a look over the manual pages for the commands discussed in this chapter.

5
System Configuration—Jails

FreeBSD offers built-in virtualization features that cannot be found in most other operating systems. **Jails** let the system administrator create one or more isolated environments on a host FreeBSD system to run different services and applications. There are many scenarios where jails can help improve the security and scalability of the system, which are discussed in this chapter. Jails also provide valuable opportunities for service providers to minimize their hardware expenses and get the best out of their hardware by running multiple instances of FreeBSD operating environment on the same hardware.

In this chapter, we will look at the following:

- Concept
- Introduction
- Setting up a jail
- Configuring the host system
- Starting the jail
- Automatic startup
- Shutting down and managing jails
- Jail security and limitations

Concept

The concept of **chroot** environment has been in BSD-like operating systems since the 4.2BSD version. Using the chroot(8) utility, the system administrator can change the root directory from the point of view of the specific processes. This will make the application assume the specified directory as the root directory of the system. System administrator needs to replicate the required directory hierarchy (for example, /etc or /lib) under the specified chroot directory in order to make the application work.

This helps to limit the scope of file system of the process. The process cannot access files and directories outside the chrooted environment and consequently keeps the other parts of the system safe from potential security compromises. However, when it was introduced, several security vulnerabilities were found (and fixed) that would let an attacker escape from the chrooted environment and get access to the host file system. While `chroot(8)` only limits the scope of the file system visibility, the processes will still pretty much share everything else in the operating environment.

Introduction

Jails were introduced with several security and functionality improvements over the traditional chroot. While chroot was used to limit the scope of the file system for processes, jail is used to develop more complex virtualization scenarios, including running an almost full operating system inside a jail. This type of jail is commonly referred to as the **Virtual Server**. You can set up multiple jails on a host system (the actual operating system you installed on the physical hardware) that runs multiple, complete, FreeBSD systems running different software.

A virtual server is used when you want to test a new software or service in a test environment, without actually engaging the physical hardware. Another scenario is to set up jails for other people who want to have root access to the system. Giving root access of a jail, gives super-user power to users, without giving them full access to the host system. For example, different web hosting companies create jails and virtual dedicated servers, and give full access of the jails to their customers.

Each jail has its own files, processes, and users (including its own root user). However, there are also certain limitations in using jails. For example, they prevent you from doing low-level system operations. These are discussed later in this chapter.

There is another type of jail, called the **Service Jail**. A service jail does not have all the components of the operating system (including all the libraries, manuals, and configurations). Rather, it contains only the required components that are needed to run a specific service such as a web server. However, if you want to run only one or two services in a jail environment, then service jails are much smaller in size and offer more security.

Jails are lightweight, have low overheads, and are easy to deploy and manage. A system administrator may have several jails running on a single host system with minimum headache, offering different network services, which is similar to running multiple physical servers.

Jails do not offer complete virtualization which the VMWare or other virtualization software do. There are several limitations in jails that would be discussed later in this chapter.

Setting Up a Jail

Creating a jail is almost as easy as doing a buildworld, as explained in Chapter 2, (*System Configuration – Keeping it updated*), and installing it in a different directory other than the system's actual root directory.

First you need to decide where you want to deploy the jail directory. A good place to do so would be the /usr/jail subdirectory as there is always plenty of free space available on the /usr partition. You may want to choose a different directory based on your system's disk configuration. Define a variable that contains your jail subdirectory address. If you are running C shell or its variants, run the command shown here:

```
# setenv D /usr/jails/webserver1
```

If you are using bourne shell, run the following command:

```
# export D=/usr/jails/webserver1
```

In the above example, we chose webserver1 as the jail's home directory name. This is also used as the jails' hostname.

Then you should rebuild the whole system (assuming you already have system sources installed in /usr/src) and install it in the jails subdirectory:

```
# mkdir -p $D
# cd /usr/src
# make buildworld
# make installworld DESTDIR=$D
# make distribution DESTDIR=$D
```

In the above example, we have created the jail subdirectory and built a complete system from the source code and installed the result in the jail's subdirectory. This process would take a few hours, depending on your host hardware.

If you have already built the world, replace you can skip the make buildworld part to save a lot of time. This would also be a good idea when you are creating multiple jails and you don't want to rebuild the whole system for each jail.

The make installworld installs the whole system except for /etc subdirectory. This is actually what make distribution does for you. Use this command with caution—any typing error may lead to overwriting the host system's /etc directory and will cause loss of your system configuration.

 You do not need to compile a kernel for your jails as they will use the running system's kernel.

If you plan to set up multiple jails, you may repeat the process for the other jail directory hierarchies, except the `buildworld` part. For example, to install a new jail under the `/usr/jails/anotherjail` directory, run the following commands:

```
# setenv D /usr/jails/anotherjail
# mkdir -p $D
# cd /usr/src
# make installworld DESTDIR=$D
# make distribution DESTDIR=$D
```

You can set up as many jails depending on how many resources your host hardware can handle.

You should also manually `mount devfs` under the jail before configuring the jail as follows:

```
# mount -t devfs devfs $D/dev
```

Once the initial setup of the jail is finished, there are several steps to be taken in order to make the jail usable.

Configuring the Host System

Jails make use of the host systems network stack, for their network subsystem. The IP address that you use for the jail should be already configured on the host system's network interface.

For example, if your system uses `10.0.0.1` as IP address on `bge0` network interface, and you want to use `10.0.0.2` on the jail, you should add the following line to your `/etc/rc.conf`:

```
    ifconfig_bge0_alias0="inet 10.0.0.2/32"
```

You may run `/etc/rc.d/netif start` command to apply the changes to the network interface.

Then you should look for the network services running on the host system and bound to all IP addresses:

```
# sockstat -41
```

USER	COMMAND	PID	FD	PROTO	LOCAL ADDRESS	FOREIGN ADDRESS
root	inetd	1450	5	tcp4	*:21	*:*
root	inetd	1450	6	udp4	*:69	*:*
root	sendmail	1031	3	tcp4	*:25	*:*
root	sshd	1025	3	tcp4	*:22	*:*
root	syslogd	970	6	udp4	*:514	*:*

The local address field has `*:[port number]` which means the service is listening on all the available IP addresses. All these services should be modified so that they only listen to the host's IP address. All the above programs have their own method to change the IP address binding.

To force **inetd** to listen to a specific IP address, you should modify the `inetd_flags` variable in `/etc/rc.conf`:

```
inetd_flags="-wW -C 60 -a 10.0.0.1"
```

You should run `/etc/rc.d/inetd reload` for the changes to take effect.

The next process that you should look into is sendmail. If your host system is not a mail server, you can modify the `sendmail_enable` in `/etc/rc.conf` so that the sendmail process listens only to the localhost:

```
sendmail_enable="NO"
```

Then you should run `/etc/rc.d/sendmail restart` in order to apply the changes.

The next process you should look into is `sshd`. To force the `ssh` daemon to listen to a specific IP address, you should modify the `sshd` configuration file located at `/etc/ssh/sshd_config`:

```
ListenAddress 10.0.0.1
```

In order to enforce the changes to take place, you should run `/etc/rc.d/sshd reload`. Use this command with caution if you are connected to your server via SSH. This may cause you to lock yourself out of the server. If you don't want to take a trip to your data center to restart `sshd` from the system's console, double-check your configuration!

Finally, the daemon to look into is `syslogd`. Unless you are logging into the `syslog` messages over the network, you don't want the `syslog` daemon to listen to a network socket. In this case, you may disable remote logging by adding this line to `/etc/rc.conf`:

```
syslogd_flags="-ss"
```

Running the `/etc/rc.d/syslogd` restart will enforce the changes to take effect immediately.

If there is any other process that is listening on all interfaces for the incoming connections, consult the appropriate manual pages for instructions to change the interface binding.

The big exception is the RPC `portmapper`, which is used for the NFS protocol. Since there is no easy way to enforce `portmapper` to listen only on one IP address, this protocol should be completely disabled on the host server. This means that your host operating system cannot act as the NFS server or the client. In order to disable the RPC `portmapper`, the following line should be added to `/etc/rc.conf`:

```
rpcbind_enable="NO"
```

Once you finish modifying daemon configuration, you should verify the network daemons are bound to a single address using the `sockstat(1)` utility:

```
# sockstat -41
```

USER	COMMAND	PID	FD	PROTO	LOCAL ADDRESS	FOREIGN ADDRESS
root	sendmail	1611	3	tcp4	127.0.0.1	*:*
root	inetd	1562	5	tcp4	10.0.0.1:21	*:*
root	inetd	1562	6	udp4	10.0.0.1:69	*:*
root	sshd	832	3	tcp4	10.0.0.1:22	*:*

Starting the Jail

Now your system is ready to perform the initial configuration of jail. This can be done using the `jail(8)` utility. The `jail(8)` utility requires at least four parameters in the command line — jail path on file system, jail's hostname, jail's IP address, and the command that you want to run in jail.

In order to start the jail manually the first time, you should run the following command:

```
# jail /usr/jails/webserver1 webserver1 10.0.0.2 /bin/sh
```

This command runs the bourne shell inside your jail. From here, whatever you do affects your jail only. To verify that you are actually inside the new jail, use the following command:

```
# uname -a
```

```
webserver1
```

There are a few steps that should be taken before the jail is ready to roll:

- Set up `/etc/rc.conf` so the jail does not configure the network interface. The following line should be added to `/etc/rc.conf`:

  ```
  network_interfaces=""
  ```
- Set up your DNS servers in `/etc/resolve.conf` to name resolution works correctly inside the jail.
- Set the time zone using the `tzsetup(8)` utility.

- Set root password using the `passwd(1)` utility.
- Create an empty `/etc/fstab` file.
- Enable basic network services in `/etc/rc.conf` for remote access. You may want to add `sshd_enable="YES"` to `/etc/rc.conf` file.
- Create user accounts.
- Perform other tunings that you do on your new servers.

Many of the initial tasks can be done by running the `sysinstall(8)` utility from inside the jail.

Once you have finished the basic setup, you may use the `exit` command to return to the host OS.

Automatic Startup

Now you are almost ready to start the jail. You can run the jail using the `jail(8)` utility as mentioned earlier. However, you can set up `/etc/rc.conf` on the host system and let the system start and stop jails automatically. First of all you should enable the jails and also tell the name of your jails in `/etc/rc.conf`:

```
jail_enable="YES"
jail_list="webserver1 theotherjail anotherone"
```

In the above example, you can define multiple jails in the `jail_list` variable, separated by space.

There is also a short configuration for each jail to be specified in the `jail_list` variable that should be added to `/etc/rc.conf`:

```
jail_webserver1_rootdir="/usr/jails/webserver1"
jail_webserver1_hostname="webserver1"
jail_webserver1_ip="10.0.0.2"
jail_webserver1_exec="/bin/sh /etc/rc"
jail_webserver1_devfs_enable="YES"
jail_webserver1_fdescfs_enable="YES"
jail_webserver1_procfs_enable="YES"
```

So we have introduced all the necessary information about each jail in the `/etc/rc.conf` file. Note the `jail_webserver1_exec` variable that tells the command to be invoked when jail starts. Running the `/etc/rc` script will simulate a system boot up for jail.

Now, in order to start the jail, you may use the `/etc/rc.d/jail` script:

```
# /etc/rc.d/jail start webserver1
```

This command will start the jail named `webserver1`. In order to start all the jails that are specified in `/etc/rc.conf`, you should run the following command:

```
# /etc/rc.d/jail start
```

This command will start all the jails.

Note that all the jails you specified in `/etc/rc.conf` will be automatically started at system boot up.

Shutting Down Jails

The typical system commands that you use, to shutdown or reboot the system — `shutdown(8)`, `halt(8)`, and `reboot(8)` are not jail-friendly and cannot be used from inside a jail. In fact, shutting down or rebooting the jail cannot be done from inside the jail and should be done by the system administrator on the host system. The best way to stop a jail is to use jail rc script:

```
# /etc/rc.d/jail stop webserver1
```

This command will stop (or shutdown) the jail named `webserver1`.

To restart a jail, you can invoke the `jail rc` script with the `restart` argument as shown here:

```
# /etc/rc.d/jail restart webserver1
```

 Running the `/etc/rc.shutdown` rc script from inside the jail may simulate a system shutdown. This should be used as the last resort to restrain access, to stop the jail from the host system. However, this may lead to leaving some jailed processes running. Also, this is not a technically clean method to shutdown a jail.

Managing Jails

In addition to the standard utilities that you use to control the processes (`ps`, `kill`, and so on), there are two more utilities available for jails.

The `jls(8)` utility displays a list of currently running jails. This is shown as the following command:

```
# jls
```

JID	IP Address	Hostname	Path
1	10.0.0.2	webserver1	/usr/jails/webserver1

As you have noticed from the above example, each active jail is identified by a Jail Identifier (**JID**) number. The **JID** number is used to refer to the running jails in the various utilities.

As the host system's administrator, you don't need to log into each jail to run a specific command. This is possible using the `jexec(8)` utility. This utility lets the host system's administrator run any command in an active jail (identified by **JID**) from the host.

```
# jexec 1 ls
```

```
.cshrc        bin      etc    libexec    proc      sbin    usr
.profile      boot     home   media      rescue    sys     var
COPYRIGHT     dev      lib    mnt        root      tmp
```

While running jails on a system, you may see different outputs in various process management utilities. Using `ps(1)`, the most important change you will see is `J` flag in the STAT column of the imprisoned processes. You can easily identify whether a process is running in jail using the `ps` command. This is shown in the following command:

```
# ps ax | grep ssh
```

```
    821   ??  Is     0:00.00 /usr/sbin/sshd
   1044   ??  IsJ    0:00.00 /usr/sbin/sshd
```

In the above example, the process with `PID` 821 is `sshd` that is running on the host system while the second instance (`PID` 1044) is the one running inside a jail.

You can also send signals to the imprisoned processes using `pkill(1)` and `killall(1)` commands. In order to signal an imprisoned process, the **JID** of jail should be specified by the `-j` argument:

```
# pkill -HUP -j 1 sshd
```

This will send the HUP signal to the `sshd` process, which is running, to the jail with **JID** 1.

```
# pkill -HUP -j any sshd
```

The above example sends the HUP signal to the imprisoned `sshd` processes in any running jail.

And to kill any process running inside a specific jail, you may use the following command:

```
# killall -j 1
```

Jail Security

Security is one of the main concerns while running the jails. A jail is supposed to be limited and completely harmless for the host system as well as the other jails. If an attacker gains access to a jail, he should not be able to escape from the jail and the scope of vulnerability has to be limited to the compromised jail. The system administrator should take special care, while running the jails. Also, as all the jails share the same running kernel with the host system, having uncontrolled access from inside a jail to the kernel will cause major security problems. For example, a misconfigured jail can be used to access the resources on the other jails (or host system), or interfere with the operations of the other jails.

While the jail's infrastructure does not let the imprisoned process access outside the scope of jails, a misconfigured system may unintentionally provide direct access to the devices (via /dev device nodes), which could affect the whole system (for example, network interface or memory).

The devfs(5) mount is the jail's achilles heel. Jails should have a /dev mount point which contains device nodes from the device file system. The major security issues are caused due to the full access to the host system's devfs(5) namespace. For example, a user inside a jail can read the console's message buffer or access the physical hardware connected to the host system, which is not desirable in most cases.

Luckily, devfs supports **rulesets** that can control the attributes of the device nodes in each devfs mount point. A devfs ruleset is a set of rules that specifies access permissions as well as visibility of each and every device node that lives in the devfs namespace. For example, you can hide certain device nodes (such as disk nodes, console, or terminals) from being shown in the /dev mount point inside a jail.

If you are starting a jail using /etc/rc.d/jail rc script, a default devfs ruleset is applied to the /dev mount point of the jail. The /dev mount inside the jail will look like the following:

```
# ls /dev

   fd      null    ptyp1   random  stdin   ttyp0   ttyp2   zero
   log     ptyp0   ptyp2   stderr  stdout  ttyp1   urandom
```

You can define your own devfs ruleset in the /etc/devfs.rules file. However, if nothing is specified, settings from the /etc/defaults/devfs.rules will be used. You can find default jails ruleset under the devfsruleset_jail section.

Revealing inappropriate device nodes under a jail environment may lead to major security issues for your host system, when a jail is being compromised. Reveal device nodes with caution.

Jail Limitations

The FreeBSD jails do not provide true virtualization as all the jails running on a host system are using the same kernel and sharing a lot of resources. This will lead to some security issues that may affect all the jails on a system. For example, if a root user in a jail has the ability to put the network interface in the promiscuous mode, the user will be able to tap the network traffic for all the other jails running on the system.

Also, due to the fact that all the jails as well as the host system are sharing the same kernel, the root user inside a jail cannot load or unload any kernel module. Moreover, it has very limited access to `sysctl` variables. The administrator cannot modify network configuration such as the IP address, or any other network interface configuration, or the routing table. The imprisoned root user also has no access to the firewall rules and always obeys the host system's firewall setup.

There are also a few limitations from the perspective of the file system, such as the prohibition of mounting or unmounting the file system inside a jail, because the environment is chrooted. Moreover, a root user inside a jail cannot create the device nodes, as we had discussed earlier in the section—*Jails security.*

Summary

Jails offer very low overheads, lightweight virtualization features for FreeBSD. You may run multiple jails on a host system, creating multiple virtual servers, each of which acts almost like a real server with a few limitations. Jails can be used for content hosting, software development, and testing new features without harming the host system.

Jails can be installed in a few steps, and removed by simply removing the jail's directory.

Like other features, jail subsystem is under constant development. The best resource available on the latest updates on jail subsystem is `jail(8)` manual pages. It is recommended that a system administrator, who plans to make serious use of jails, reads through this.

6
System Configuration—Tuning Performance

FreeBSD was designed and is being developed, with performance in mind. It has proved to be a very high performance operating system for the network applications as well. There are millions of sites running FreeBSD as their hosting platform (according to Netcraft). Many users use FreeBSD as their gateway router and firewall, while many others run their network services (for example, WWW, Mail, FTP, and so on) over FreeBSD.

When you set up a new installation of FreeBSD on your server, the default configuration is designed to be conservative to offer more stability over various hardware configurations. However, you may want to tweak a few parameters to get the most out of your powerful hardware and advanced FreeBSD features. This chapter helps you to tweak many of the important parameters required to run a high performance FreeBSD server.

In this chapter, we will look at the following:

- Tweaking Kernel variable using SYSCTL
- Kernel
- SMP
- Disk
- Network
- The /etc/make.conf file
- The /boot/loader.conf file.

Tweaking Kernel Variables using SYSCTL

The `sysctl(8)` utility allows system administrator to read or modify certain kernel variables during system run time. There are more than a thousand variables out of which, some of them are read-only and cannot be changed during the run time, while some others can be modified to change the kernel's behavior.

 Some variables are read-only while the system is running, but can be set up during system boot from `/boot/loader.conf` or by hard coding the variable into the kernel configuration, which is discussed later in this chapter.

All the variables are divided into different categories. The most important categories include:

- **dev**: This catogory contains device node related variables.
- **hw**:This category contains hardware related variables.
- **kern**: This category contains kernel related variables.
- **net**: This category contains network stack related variables.
- **security**: This category contains security related variables.
- **vfs**: This category contains file system related variables.
- **vm**: This category contains virtual memory related variables.

You can see a complete list of `sysctl` variables by running the `sysctl -a` command. However, the output of this command can be very long. Combining the `grep(1)` to search for certain variables can be very useful:

```
# sysctl -a | grep recvspace

    net.local.stream.recvspace: 8192
    net.local.dgram.recvspace: 4096
    net.inet.tcp.recvspace: 65536
    net.inet.udp.recvspace: 42080
    net.inet.raw.recvspace: 8192
```

The current value of a `sysctl` variable can be examined by using the following `sysctl(8)` command:

```
# sysctl net.inet.ip.forwarding

    net.inet.ip.forwarding: 0
```

If you are curious to know what a specific variable is, you can use `sysctl` with `-d` argument and `sysctl` will show a short description for the variable as follows:

```
# sysctl -d net.inet.ip.forwarding

    net.inet.ip.forwarding: Enable IP forwarding between interfaces
```

And finally, to modify a variable run the following command:

```
# sysctl net.inet.ip.forwarding=1

    net.inet.ip.forwarding: 0 -> 1
```

You may want to modify a few variables permanently. To achieve this, you should add variable definitions to the `/etc/sysctl.conf` file, and the system will load your variables upon boot up process.

> It is recommended that you do not play with `sysctl` variables on a production system. Applying inappropriate modifications may render your system unstable or pave the way for other unprecedented behaviors. Use this utility with caution. Always try your changes on a test machine before rolling out the actual changes on a production server.

There are a few variables that cannot be set during system run time. A good example of this is `kern.maxusers` variable:

```
# sysctl kern.maxusers=512

    sysctl: oid 'kern.maxusers' is a read only tunable
    sysctl: Tunable values are set in /boot/loader.conf
```

Adding this variable to the `/etc/sysctl.conf` file also won't help. These types of variables should either be added to the `/boot/loader.conf` file or hardcoded in the kernel configuration file.

Later is this chapter, only a few of the important `sysctl` that would be useful in tweaking your system's performance variables are introduced. You may use the combination of `grep` and `sysctl` to find many interesting variables that may help you get more information about your system or identify change in its behavior.

Kernel

As discussed in Chapter 2, you can recompile the systems kernel from source to add or remove certain features. Beside adding or removing modules, you can optimize your kernel performance in several ways.

The first is to reduce the size of the kernel by removing any unnecessary stuff. Since the kernel should be completely loaded into the memory during boot process, reducing kernel size will reduce memory usage and consequently more memory will be available for other processes. This will also result in a faster system boot up process.

You can remove many unnecessary hardware support entries as well as debug information from your kernel to reduce its size.

As good practice, you can make a copy of the stock kernel (can be found at `/sys/i386/conf/GENERIC`) and remove (or comment out) all unnecessary hardware support. Depending on your hardware, this may include unnecessary SCSI, RAID, Network Card, etc.

[Depending on the hardware architecture you use to run FreeBSD, your kernel configuration file may be located at a different location such as `/sys/sparc64/conf` or `/sys/amd64/conf`.]

Another important tweak is to remove all debugging options from kernel configuration. Kernel configuration file is well documented so that these entries can be easily spotted:

```
makeoptions     DEBUG=-g
```

Alternatively, if you are tracking the `-current` CVS tag, you may have these lines in the kernel configuration file as well:

```
# Debugging for use in -current
options   KDB
options   DDB
options   GDB
options   INVARIANTS
options   INVARIANT_SUPPORT
options   WITNESS
options   WITNESS_SKIPSPIN
```

You may need to edit the kernel configuration file and recompile the kernel to find your optimized kernel configuration. During optimization, pay special attention to the comments in the kernel configuration file. There are some modules that cannot be removed from the kernel.

When you recompile the kernel, the system does not use compiler optimizations for various reasons. You may want to try compiler optimizations which, in most cases, result in faster binary code. However, depending on which compiler optimization you use, the kernel's binary size may also increase.

To enable compiler optimizations, you should add the following line or a similar line, depending on your preferences, to the kernel configuration file:

```
makeoptions     COPTFLAGS="-O2 -pipe -funroll-loops -ffast-math"
```

Always use these types of modifications with caution, as it may render your system unstable. It is advised that you don't use the -O3 flag, as it has proven to result in an unstable binary output.

SMP

If you are using a multi-processor (SMP) hardware, you should know that the SMP features are optional in the FreeBSD 7 stock kernel. However, as the SMP is enabled (by default) in the GENERIC kernel, you need to always ensure that you have the following lines in your kernel configuration when building a new kernel:

```
options         SMP
device          apic
```

Once you have compiled and rebooted with a new kernel, you would see multiple processors being detected during boot time. Alternatively, you can read the dmesg(8) output:

```
# dmesg | grep -i cpu

  CPU: Intel(R) Xeon(TM) CPU 3.20GHz (3200.14-MHz 686-class CPU)
    Logical CPUs per core: 2
  FreeBSD/SMP: Multiprocessor System Detected: 4 CPUs
   cpu0 (BSP): APIC ID:   0
   cpu1 (AP): APIC ID:   1
   cpu2 (AP): APIC ID:   6
   cpu3 (AP): APIC ID:   7
  cpu0: <ACPI CPU> on acpi0
  cpu1: <ACPI CPU> on acpi0
  cpu2: <ACPI CPU> on acpi0
  cpu3: <ACPI CPU> on acpi0
  SMP: AP CPU #2 Launched!
  SMP: AP CPU #1 Launched!
  SMP: AP CPU #3 Launched!
```

You can also take advantage of SMP, while building world from the source. The make(1) utility lets you run multiple simultaneous jobs. Using this feature will save tons of time while rebuilding world. For example in a quad-processor environment you may use:

```
# make -j4 buildworld
```

This will run a maximum of four simultaneous processes, which is most likely to use all available CPU resources, and consequently speed up the build process.

> It is advised that you do not to use this feature while building a kernel as it could break the build procedure.

Traditionally FreeBSD uses 4BSD scheduler as the default scheduler. However, an alternative scheduler called ULE has been also available since FreeBSD 5 and it has improved tremendously since then. It is now recommended to use ULE scheduler instead of 4BSD scheduler in FreeBSD 7, and it will be the default scheduler in the next release of FreeBSD. To use ULE scheduler, you should replace the `SCHED_4BSD` option in your configuration file with following line:

```
options         SCHED_ULE
```

Disk

In some cases, you may find the kernel's default limits very annoying. Especially when you are running a busy server, you are likely to run out of "file descriptors" or face I/O limits.

File limits

Infact everything, including actual files, network sockets, and so on, is treated as a file in UNIX. On a busy server, which has many network sockets or disk files open, the file descriptor tables will be exhausted and you will see `file: table is full` in system's message buffer. The `kern.maxfiles` kernel variable contains the maximum number of file descriptor limit.

```
# sysctl kern.maxfiles

   kern.maxfiles: 8192

# sysctl kern.maxfiles=16384

   kern.maxfiles: 8192 -> 16384
```

I/O Performance

The new UFS2 file system which is available in FreeBSD 7 offers higher performance as compared to the legacy UFS file system. However, you can still tweak your file system by using different mount options.

There are actually four different modes that you can use to mount a UFS file system:

- **Sync**: In this mode all I/O to file will be done synchronously. This means that both data and metadata will be written synchronously to the disk. Although this will slow down the disk I/O performance, this makes the system immune to crashes.

- **Noasync**: In this mode, data is written to disk asynchronously while metadata is written synchronously. This will greatly enhance performance, as compared to the sync mode, and is also almost safe from system crashes.

- **Softupdates**: This method properly orders the metadata writes and ensures consistency of data on disk. The performance in this mode is somewhat like noasync mode. This feature has been explained in Chapter 1.

- **Async**: This is the fastest, but the most dangerous method. All writes in this mode are done asynchronously and there is a high risk of data loss in case of power failure.

Noasync is the default mode, if nothing else is specified.

Modes can be set by using `mount(8)`'s -o option . You should also update the "options" column in the `/etc/fstab` file, for the changes take effect upon a system boot up.

> Do not use async mode for root partition. Corrupting of this partition may prevent your system from booting up correctly.

By default, the system updates the last access time of any file that is being accessed. This will produce I/O overhead on the busy file systems. If you do not want to know when a file was accessed the last time, you may want to turn this feature off, to improve the disk I/O performance. To turn this feature off, you should set the `noatime` option on any partition. During run time, you must use the following command:

```
# mount -u -o noatime /usr
```

This will turn the `noatime` flag on, on the `/usr` partition. To make these changes permanent, the `/etc/fstab` file must be updated accordingly.

RAID

RAID (explained in Chapter 1, *System Configuration – Disks*), will also help you reduce I/O overheads and improve the disk read/write times. You should select a RAID strategy based on your application and the performance or redundancy your application requires. Different levels of RAID offer different levels of I/O performance.

The various levels of RAID are described in the following list:

- **RAID 0 (Striped Set)**: This method will improve the read and write speed slightly, as read and writes span across multiple physical disks.
- **RAID 1 (Mirrored set)**: This method improves the read performance as data will be read from multiple physical disks, but the write performance is almost the same as non-RAID scenario.
- **RAID 5 (Striped set with Parity)**: This method improves both read and write performance, especially on the SMP hardware, if the software RAID is in use.

You should choose a good RAID strategy that will help you improve the I/O performance as well as the system's reliability for I/O intensive applications.

Network

Despite having performance in mind, FreeBSD has conservative defaults for the TCP/IP network stack that can be tuned to get a performance better than from the default configuration.

There are a few `sysctl` variables that can be changed in order to gain better network performance. However, you should examine each feature to see whether it is suitable for your environment, before deploying it on a production machine.

The network related `sysctl` variables are stored under the net category. You can collect the complete list of these variables along with a short description using `sysctl(8)` utility:

```
# sysctl -d net
```

A number of important variables are explained in this chapter.

TCP Delayed ACK

By default, the network stack applies 10-100 milliseconds delay before sending TCP ACK message. This may lead to low performance on busy file servers (SMB protocol) or busy web servers. You can override this delay by turning off the `net.inet.tcp.delayed_ack` using `sysctl` variables:

```
# sysctl net.inet.tcp.delayed_ack=0
    net.inet.tcp.delayed_ack: 1 -> 0
```

Disabling TCP delayed ACK will greatly improve TCP performance, especially when using SAMBA. But this violates RFC1122 guidelines (RFC1122 – "Requirements for Internet Hosts – Communication layers" can be found at `http://tools.ietf.org/html/rfc1122`). You may not want to disable this feature unless you really have to.

RFC 1323 Extensions

RFC 1323 specifies guidelines (specifically, TCP window scaling) for gaining high TCP/IP performance over large bandwidth*delay paths. This extension is enabled in FreeBSD 7 by default. However, you may want to disable these extensions in some cases to experience network connection stalls.

```
# sysctl net.inet.tcp.rfc1323=0

    net.inet.tcp.rfc1323: 1 -> 0
```

TCP Listen Queue Size

The incoming connection queue size is limited to 128 connections by default. This is very low for busy servers that may need to handle some thousand new connections per second. The default value can be changed by modifying the `kern.ipc.somaxconn` variable:

```
# sysctl kern.ipc.somaxconn=1024

    kern.ipc.somaxconn: 128 -> 1024
```

TCP Buffer Space

The `net.inet.tcp.sendspace` and `net.inet.tcp.recvspace` variables control the send and receive buffer size allowed for any TCP connection.

```
# sysctl net.inet.tcp.sendspace=65536

    net.inet.tcp.sendspace: 32768 -> 65536
```

The default value for `sendspace` and `recvspace` are 32768 and 65536 respectively. It is advised not to increase the default buffer sizes, if you are running a busy server that is serving many network connections simultaneously. Increasing buffer sizes will cause more kernel memory usage. In the case of too many concurrent connections, your system may end up out of memory, due to inactive TCP connections. However, if you were serving a server with a few clients and high-speed network connectivities, increasing buffer sizes would lead to great performance improvements.

If you are increasing the buffer spaces to a number larger than 65536, make sure the other ends of connection also support TCP window scaling options according to the RFC1323. Otherwise, you will not see any performance improvement over your connections.

Network Interface Polling

Device polling lets system poll devices, instead of waiting for hardware devices, to generate hardware interrupts. Device polling will greatly enhance the NIC performance on FreeBSD. However, this feature is not enabled in the FreeBSD's GENERIC kernel and needs manual kernel reconfiguration, to be enabled.

To enable device polling support to kernel, the following two lines should be added to your kernel configuration file:

```
options         DEVICE_POLLING
options         HZ=1000
```

Please note that we have also slowed down the system clock ticks to prevent the system from spending a lot of time on poll devices.

Once you have recompiled the kernel with the above options in your kernel configuration files, the device polling feature will be enabled in your kernel. The polling behavior can be controlled by the kern.polling set of variables. To see a list of available variables along with a short description, you may use:

```
# sysctl -d kern.polling
```

The ifconfig(8) utility offers a few options to control the polling feature on network interfaces. To enable polling on a specific interface, you may use the following command:

```
# ifconfig bge0 polling
```

This will enable polling on the bge0 network interface. This can be verified by using ifconfig again:

```
# ifconfig bge0

  bge0: flags=8843<UP,BROADCAST,RUNNING,SIMPLEX,MULTICAST> metric
0 mtu 1500
          options=48<VLAN_MTU,POLLING>
          ether 00:0c:6e:7b:74:42
          inet 192.168.0.5 netmask 0xffffff00 broadcast 192.168.0.255
          media: Ethernet autoselect (100baseTX <full-duplex>)
          status: active
```

You do not have to enable the `kern.polling.enable` sysctl variable that is obsolete. Setting this variable to 1 will enable polling on all capable interfaces.

The /etc/make.conf file

When you compile something from the source code in FreeBSD, the default set of parameters will be passed to the compiler. As you can change some of these parameters globally, they can be applied to most applications that you compile on your machine.

A good example of this would be the CPU optimizations and hardware specific parameters that may lead your compiler to produce more efficient and optimized binary code. This is especially useful when using ports or rebuilding world.

Most of these settings can be controlled from the `/etc/make.conf` file. There are a few variables that can be set in this file, which have a direct effect on your compiler behavior.

CPUTYPE

The `CPUTYPE` variable specifies your processor type so that the compiler will produce the optimized binary code for your specific processor. A list of supported processors can be found in the `/usr/share/examples/etc/make.conf` file.

If you are using an Intel Core Duo processor, you will want to set this variable to "core2" in the `/etc/make.conf` file:

```
CPUTYPE?=core2
```

Make sure you choose the correct processor type by reviewing boot messages (or `dmesg(8)` output). Otherwise, the binary code may not run properly on your system.

A list of currently supported processor optimizations that are available can be found in the following table:

Processor Family	CPUTYPE value
Intel IA32	core2, core, Nocona, pentium4m, pentium4, prescott, pentium3m, pentium3, Pentium-m, pentium2
Intel IA64	itanium, itanium2
AMD	opteron, athlon64, athlon-mp, athlon-xp, athlon-4, athlon-tbird, athlon, k8, k6-3, k6-2, k6, k5

CFLAGS and COPTFLAGS

The CFLAGS variable specifies any additional compiler options that you want to pass to the compilers. These additional settings mostly deal with the performance of the compiling process or that of the output binary code. A typical CFLAGS variable would look like this:

```
CFLAGS=          -O2 -pipe
```

In the above example, two parameters are passed to the compiler. The -O2 flag sets the optimization-level to 2, which is acceptable for most applications. Another optimization flag that you will use is -Os that optimizes the output binary for smaller size.

It is advisable not to use the -O3 option (the highest level of gcc binary optimization) as it is likely to break the output binary code.

Ports system also respects the variables you set in the /etc/make.conf file. However, some of the ports need to have the WITH_OPTIMIZED_CFLAGS variable set in order to enable optimization during compile process.

Another important variable that you may want to set in your make.conf is WITHOUT_DEBUG variable. Some ports build with the debug information, unless this variable is set. It is recommended that you set this variable in your make.conf in order to ensure that these ports are not compiled with debug information:

```
WITHOUT_DEBUG = yes
```

The /boot/loader.conf file

Some variables cannot be modified during the system run time and consequently in the sysctl.conf file. These variables can either be compiled in a kernel or set from the /boot/loader.conf file. A list of such variables is listed in the /boot/defaults/loader.conf file.

Do not modify the /boot/defaults/loader.conf file. This file contains some default values. You may modify the /boot/loader.conf file instead.

A good example of these variables is the kern.maxusers variable. Setting this variable magically scales up some other kernel variables, including the number of maximum open files, sizing of network buffers, and so on.

If nothing is specified, FreeBSD automatically tunes this variable during boot up, based on the system's physical memory.

In order to compile this variable statically into a kernel, the following line should be added to the kernel configuration file:

```
maxusers  512
```

Alternatively, you can set this variable in the `/boot/loader.conf` file:

```
kern.maxusers="512"
```

Summary

There are many parameters that you can tweak to get better performance on your server. Depending on the services that you are running on your server, you may need to overcome different bottlenecks. For example, mail server deals with a large number of open files as well as a high I/O rate. Busy web servers are very network intensive and tweaking network parameters will greatly enhance performance on a web server.

The freeBSD-performance mailing list (located at `http://lists.freebsd.org/mailman/listinfo/freebsd-performance`) is a good place to discuss performance issues and the different methods to improve your system's performance.

7

Network Configuration— Basics

FreeBSD gives you an in-depth control over your network configuration. This is done using a few simple but powerful tools such as ifconfig(8).

This chapter explains interface configuration using ifconfig(8) utility and a number of related configuration files, as well as some connectivity test and debugging tools.

In this chapter, we will look at the following:

- Ifconfig utility
- Advanced ifconfig options
- Network testing tools.

Ifconfig Utility

The ifconfig(8) utility is your all-in-one utility to configure a network interface's layer2 and layer3 characteristics.

From an operating system's point of view, your system has a number of physical and logical network interfaces attached.

Physical network interfaces include the following:

- Ethernet interfaces with different physical ports (that is electrical or optical)
- Wireless network interface (802.11 a/b/g/n)
- Bluetooth interface
- Printer (PLIP) interface.

Logical network interfaces include the following:

- Loopback interface
- Tunnel interfaces (for example GRE, PPP, GIF, and FAITH,)
- VLAN interfaces
- Bridge interfaces.

The Ifconfig utility is used to display the current status of any interface that is installed on the system. For example, to figure out what interfaces are available on your system, you may use the following command:

```
# ifconfig -l
    fxp0 xl0 plip0 lo0
```

The system in the above example has four network interfaces, out of which two (fxp0 and xl0) are physical while the other two (plip0 and lo0) are logical interfaces.

 In FreeBSD, network interfaces are named after their driver. For example, Intel NICs are identified as fxp, Broadcom Gigabit NICs as bge, and so on.

The Ifconfig utility can also be used to display the detailed status of an interface as shown here:

```
# ifconfig fxp0
    fxp0: flags=8843<UP,BROADCAST,RUNNING,SIMPLEX,MULTICAST> mtu 1500
          options=b<RXCSUM,TXCSUM,VLAN_MTU>
          inet6 fe80::20c:29ff:fefd:f61d%em0 prefixlen 64 scopeid 0x1
          inet 198.168.0.5 netmask 0xffffff00 broadcast 198.18.0.255
          ether 00:0c:29:fd:f6:1d
          media: Ethernet autoselect (100baseTX <full-duplex>)
          status: active
```

The above interface summary displays an fxp (Intel family) network interface that has both IPv4 (inet) and IPv6 (inet6) addresses configured. Other information including MAC address (ether) and media specific options are also displayed.

A list of important interface **flags** is listed in the following table:

Flag name	Description
UP	Indicates that the interface's Layer3 protocol is up.
BROADCAST	Indicates that the broadcast address is valid. Not used for point-to-point interfaces.

Flag name	Description
LOOPBACK	Indicates that this interface is a loopback interface.
POINTTOPOINT	Indicates that this is a point-to-point (for example tunnel) interface.
RUNNING	Indicates that the resources are allocated for this interface and driver is running.
NOARP	Indicates that ARP is disabled on this interface (inet family specific).
PROMISC	Indicates that the interface is in the promiscuous mode. In this mode, interface receives all packets, regardless of whether the packets are destined for this host or not.
ALLMULTI	Indicates that this interface receives all multicast traffic.
ACTIVE	Indicates that TX hardware queue is full.
SIMPLEX	Indicates that the interface cannot hear its own transmissions.
SMART	Indicates that this interface automatically manages its own routes.
LINK0 , LINK1 , LINK2	Per link layer defined attribute.
MULTICAST	Indicates that this interface supports multicast.
PPROMISC	Indicates that the user-requested promiscuous mode has been enabled on this interface.
MONITOR	Indicates that this interface is in monitor mode and does not transmit anything on the wire. In this mode the interface drops packets after being processed by bpf(4).
STATICARP	Indicates that this interface only replies to requests from statically defined ARP entries and does not send any ARP request.
DEBUG	Indicates that the debugging code is enabled and extra error logs will be displayed on the console.

Besides the interface flags, there are also a few interface **options** (capabilities) that are specific to the installed NIC hardware. A list of available NIC options can be found in the following table:

Option Name	Description
RXCSUM	NIC can offload checksum on RX
TXCSUM	NIC can offload checksum on TX
HWCSUM	NIC can offload checksum on both TX and RX
NETCONS	Can be used as network console
VLAN_MTU	VLAN-compatible MTU is supported
VLAN_HWTAGGING	Hardware VLAN tagging support
JUMBO_MTU	Jumbo frames (9000 bytes MTU) are supported

Option Name	Description
POLLING	Drivers supports POLLING (explained in chapter 6)
VLAN_HWCSUM	RX and TX checksum offloading on VLANs is supported
TSO4	TCP Segmentation Offloading is supported
TSO6	TCP6 Segmentation Offloading is supported
TSO	Both TSO4 and TSO6 are supported
LRO	TCP Large Receive Offloading is supported

In `ifconfig(8)` output, the **media** field displays the current media options for the network interface card. In the previous example, the NIC was set to **autoselect** and has negotiated **100Base-TX full-duplex** with the switch that it was connected to.

Your NIC may support different media options depending on its hardware capabilities. These capabilities may differ from one NIC to other. To see a list of NIC capabilities you may consult driver's manual pages (for example `man fxp`) or use `ifconfig` with `-m` flag and `ifconfig` displays a list of supported media options after the interface status:

```
# ifconfig fxp0

    fxp0: flags=8843<UP,BROADCAST,RUNNING,SIMPLEX,MULTICAST> mtu 1500
            options=b<RXCSUM,TXCSUM,VLAN_MTU>
            inet6 fe80::20c:29ff:fefd:f61d%em0 prefixlen 64 scopeid 0x1
            inet 198.168.0.5 netmask 0xffffff00 broadcast 198.18.0.255
            ether 00:0c:29:fd:f6:1d
            media: Ethernet autoselect (100baseTX <full-duplex>)
            status: active
            supported media:
                    media autoselect
                    media 100baseTX mediaopt full-duplex
                    media 100baseTX
                    media 10baseT/UTP mediaopt full-duplex
                    media 10baseT/UTP
                    media 100baseTX mediaopt hw-loopback
```

Once you configure a network interface with an IP, IPX, or AppleTalk address, the interface will be automatically marked as up, the routing entry will be added to the routing table, and system starts transmitting and receiving traffic on the configured interface.

The interface can be disabled using the `ifconfig`'s down option:

```
# ifconfig bge0 down
```

When an interface is marked as `down`, the system stops transmitting traffic on the interface. If possible, the system also resets the interface so that it does not receive any incoming traffic.

You can bring an interface up again with the `ifconfig`'s up option:

```
# ifconfig bge0 up
```

 Marking an interface down does not necessarily deactivate the physical layer. This is why you will see your switch port active, even when the interface is down. On the other hand, after seeing an interface status as up does not indicate that the physical layer link is active. The `status` field in `ifconfig` output indicates the actual physical layer status.

In order to make the interface configuration persistent and configure network interfaces automatically after system reboot, you should add appropriate lines to the `/etc/rc.conf` configuration file. Your `rc.conf` file may contain several interface configuration lines for each physical interface installed on your system and in accordance with the address you configure on an interface. A typical interface configuration line looks like the following sample:

```
ifconfig_fxp0="inet 10.2.0.1  netmask 255.255.255.192"
ifconfig_fxp0_alias0="inet 10.2.0.5  netmask 255.255.255.255"
```

The first part of the parameter is `ifconfig_fxp0` which indicates that this is an `ifconfig` statement for the `fxp0` interface. You should replace this with the interface name that you want to configure. The second part of the statement inside the double quotation mark indicates the `ifconfig` configuration parameters you want to use for that specific interface. For example, the first configuration line assigns IPv4 address `10.2.0.1` with subnet mask `255.255.255.192` to interface `fxp0`.

The second line is the same as the first line, but it assigns a secondary address (alias) to the same interface. Assigning secondary addresses to an interface is explained later in this chapter.

During system start up, the `/etc/rc.d/netif` script takes care of network interface configuration. This `rc` script is also useful in loading network configuration without actually rebooting the server. For example, if you've added a few aliases to an existing interface or configured a new interface in the `/etc/rc.conf` file, you can apply the new settings by calling the `netif` rc script:

```
# /etc/rc.d/netif restart
```

This will reload the network configuration and apply your changes. However, you may want to verify this to see whether all changes are applied, or not, using the `ifconfig` utility.

Once you run the `netif` rc script, you should then run the `routing` rc script to tell the system to install appropriate routing entries into the system's routing table as follows:

```
# /etc/rc.d/routing restart
```

 The `netif` rc script may remove default route (and other routes) from the routing table. Based on this fact, manually running these `rc` scripts over a network connection (For example SSH and Telnet) is not recommended as you may lose your remote access to the device. However, there is less risk of losing connectivity to the host if you are on the same subnet as the server.

Configuring IP Address

To assign an IP address to a network interface, you may use `ifconfig` with the following syntax:

```
# ifconfig fxp0 inet 192.168.0.10 netmask 255.255.255.0
```

This will assign IPv4 address `192.168.0.10` with netmask `255.255.255.0` to network interface `fxp0`. The `ifconfig` utility also supports CIDR notation while assigning IP addresses to an interface. For example, you may use the following command which has the same result as the previous example:

```
# ifconfig fxp0 inet 192.168.0.10/24
```

The `inet` keyword (called **address family**) indicates that we want to assign an IPv4 address to the interface. The `ifconfig` utility supports different address families as shown in the following list:

- `inet` for IPv4 address family.
- `inet6` for IPv6 address family.
- `atalk` for AppleTalk protocol.
- `ipx` for Novell IPX/SPX protocol suite.
- `link`, `ether`, and `lladdr` for Layer2 (Ethernet) protocol.

If no address family is defined, the `ifconfig` assumes the `inet` address family by default.

To assign an IPv6 address to the interface, you may use the following syntax:

```
# ifconfig fxp0 inet6 2001:db8:bdbd::123 prefixlen 48
```

You can also shorten the syntax by using CIDR notations instead of using the `prefixlen` keyword. The equivalent of the previous example, using CIDR notation, would look like the following command line:

```
# ifconfig fxp0 inet6 2001:db8:bdbd::123/48
```

Configuring Layer2 Address

You may want to modify the MAC address on your network interface for any reason. This is possible using `ifconfig` with the `ether` address family to modify the layer2 addresses.

For example, you can set the MAC address on `xl0` interface to `00:01:02:ae:13:57` using the following command:

```
# ifconfig xl0 ether 00:01:02:ae:13:57
```

 Changing Ethernet address will briefly reset the interface in order to ensure that the MAC address is correctly set. If you are remotely connected to the server, changing the MAC address on the interface that you are connected to, may result in your connection getting dropped.

Configuring IPX

The support for IPX protocol is not enabled by default in GENERIC kernel, and a custom kernel with IPX option should be compiled (explained in Chapter 2) to support the IPX address family.

To enable IPX support, the following line should be added to the kernel configuration file:

```
options         IPX
```

The IPX protocol functionality will be available after the system is rebooted with newly compiled custom kernel.

In order to assign an IPX address to a network interface card, you may use `ifconfig(8)` with `ipx` as the address family parameter as shown here:

```
# ifconfig xl0 ipx 0x101
```

The above example assigns IPX address `0x101` to `xl0` interface.

The IPX address can be assigned in the `netnum[.nodenum]` format, where `netnum` is one to eight hexadecimal digit IPX network number and optional `nodenum` parameter is twelve hexadecimal digit link-level address.

To make the above changes permanent, you should add the following line to `/etc/rc.conf`, so that the address is assigned to the interface after system bootup:

```
ifconfig_xl0="ipx 0x101"
```

You can also verify the IPX address assignment using `ifconfig` and specifying the IPX address family. This will omit display of information about other protocols that are enabled on this interface:

```
# ifconfig xl0 ipx

xl0: flags=8843<UP,BROADCAST,RUNNING,SIMPLEX,MULTICAST> metric 0 mtu 1500
        options=9<RXCSUM,VLAN_MTU>
        ipx 101H.102ae1357
```

The system does not act as the IPX gateway by default and does not forward the IPX traffic between interfaces. In order to enable this functionality, you may want to add the following line to the `/etc/rc.conf` file:

```
ipxgateway_enable="YES"
```

If you do not want to reboot the system to give effect to the changes, you can enable IPX forwarding using the `sysctl` utility:

```
# sysctl net.ipx.ipx.ipxforwarding=1

net.ipx.ipx.ipxforwarding: 0 -> 1
```

FreeBSD also has IPX routing daemon in the base system. The `IPXrouted(8)` command is a Routing Information Protocol (RIP) daemon for IPX protocol. To enable this daemon, you should add the following line to your `/etc/rc.conf` file, so that daemon will be automatically started upon system reboot:

```
ipxrouted_enable="YES"
```

To start the IPX routing daemon manually, you should run the appropriate rc script:

```
# /etc/rc.d/ipxrouted start

Starting ipxrouted.
```

Configuring AppleTalk

Like IPX protocol, the AppleTalk protocol is not enabled in the default system kernel. The support for this protocol should be compiled into a custom kernel by adding the following line to the kernel configuration file and rebooting the system with a new kernel:

```
options         NETATALK
```

Once your new kernel with AppleTalk protocol is running, you can assign AppleTalk addresses to your interface using the ifconfig(8) utility:

```
# ifconfig fxp0  atalk 725.40 range 725-727
         atalk 725.40 range 725-727 phase 2
```

You have to add the following line to your /etc/rc.conf file to make the changes permanent, and to automatically assign the address to interface after system bootup:

```
ifconfig_fxp0="atalk 725.40 range 725-727"
```

To verify AppleTalk address assignment, you should use ifconfig again:

```
# ifconfig fxp0 atalk
    fxp0: flags=8843<UP,BROADCAST,RUNNING,SIMPLEX,MULTICAST> metric
    0 mtu 1500
            options=9<RXCSUM,VLAN_MTU>
            atalk 725.40 range 725-727 phase 2 broadcast 0.255
```

 For "File and Printer Sharing" using AppleTalk protocol, you should use *netatalk* software, which is available from ports system and is located under the /usr/ports/net/netatalk subdirectory.

Configuring Secondary (alias) IP Addresses

There are different scenarios where you need multiple IP addresses (called aliases) on the same network interface. These may include running virtual web hosts on a single machine using different IP addresses, or being a gateway for different subnets. Theoretically, you may have an unlimited number of alias addresses on an interface.

Aliases can be added and removed using the ifconfig(8) utility.

The following example shows assigning an IP address to the fxp0 interface and then adding multiple aliases to the same interface:

```
# ifconfig fxp0 192.168.0.11/24
# ifconfig fxp0 10.0.1.33/24 alias
# ifconfig fxp0 10.0.21.1/25  alias
```

In the above example, three IP addresses are assigned to the fxp0 interface. The first IP address, 192.168.0.11/24 is assigned as the primary IP address while two others are added as aliases or secondary addresses. In order to make these changes permanent, you should add the following lines (Note the _alias suffix) to the /etc/rc.conf file:

```
ifconfig_fxp0="inet 192.168.0.5/24"
```

```
ifconfig_fxp0_alias0="inet 10.0.1.33/24"
ifconfig_fxp0_alias1="inet 10.0.21.1/25"
```

To remove an alias, the `-alias` flag is used. You can remove aliases in any order using the `ifconfig` utility. For example, to remove the second address in the previous example, you may use the following command:

 # ifconfig x10 10.0.1.33/24 -alias

The above command removes a specific address from the interface, regardless of the order in which the aliases were added.

There is one thing you must take care of while adding aliases to an interface – the calculation of the subnet mask for the aliases that are from the same subnet.

If you are adding aliases from the same subnet to an interface (for example 192.168.10.1, 192.168.10.2 and 192.168.10.3 from a /24 subnet), you should assign the correct netmask to one of the IP addresses of this subnet, and the other addresses should take the /32 subnet masks.

The following example shows how to add multiple IPs from the same subnet to a network interface, and also adding addresses from other networks to the same interface:

 # ifconfig bge0 192.168.10.1/25

 # ifconfig bge0 192.168.10.2/32 alias

 # ifconfig bge0 192.168.10.3/32 alias

 # ifconfig bge0 172.16.31.12/24 alias

As you may have noted, the first IP address has the correct subnet mask for its network, but the secondary addresses which are from the same subnet are using the /32 (or 255.255.255.255) subnet mask. And the last alias uses the correct subnet mask as it is from a different subnet.

Configuring Media Options

Different network interfaces have different capabilities based on hardware features and driver implementation. A list of currently supported network interface cards with their corresponding driver name can be found in the `/sys/i386/conf/GENERIC` kernel configuration file.

To find out the capabilities of an interface, you may either read related manual pages (for example, `man fxp`) or use `ifconfig` with `-m` flag:

```
# ifconfig -m xl0

   xl0: flags=8843<UP,BROADCAST,RUNNING,SIMPLEX,MULTICAST> metric
0 mtu 1500
           options=9<RXCSUM,VLAN_MTU>
           capabilities=49<RXCSUM,VLAN_MTU,POLLING>
           ether 00:01:02:ae:13:57
           inet 192.168.14.1 netmask 0xffffff00 broadcast 192.168.14.255
           media: Ethernet autoselect (100baseTX <full-duplex>)
           status: active
           supported media:
                   media autoselect
                   media 100baseTX mediaopt full-duplex
                   media 100baseTX
                   media 10baseT/UTP mediaopt full-duplex
                   media 10baseT/UTP
                   media 100baseTX mediaopt hw-loopback
```

In the above example, the hardware capabilities of `xl0` interface are shown. The interface is able to offload RX checksums, support VLAN MTUs, and interface polling. It is also capable of supporting 10baseT and 100baseT in both half-duplex and full-duplex modes. Configuring certain interface capabilities and options is explained later in this chapter.

By default, if no media type is specified, system sets media type for network interfaces to `autoselect`. This setting would be fine for interface speed, but there are certain cases where the media duplex is not correctly negotiated. Generally, it is not advisable to configure ports to auto-negotiate in production environment. Port speed and duplex should be explicitly configured on both host and switch sides.

To configure `xl0` interface for 100baseT full-duplex, the following command should be used:

```
# ifconfig xl0 media 100baseTX mediaopt full-duplex
```

Changing interface media options when you are connected through a network connection, for example ssh, may lock you out of the host. It is recommended that you use physical console or any other non-network method to change these network settings.

Configuring VLANs

FreeBSD supports IEEE 802.1Q VLAN protocol. This means that you can configure VLAN tagging on network interfaces.

In order to configure VLANs, you must create VLAN pseudo-interfaces first as shown here:

```
# ifconfig vlan0 create
```

This will create a virtual interface called `vlan0`. Note that the interface name should begin with the `vlan` keyword and should have an arbitrary number attached. If you do not specify the interface number, the `ifconfig` will create a VLAN device, automatically assigns first free device number and prints the name of the created device.

Once the VLAN pseudo-interface is created, you should assign two parameters to the interface at the same time – VLAN number and Parent Interface.

VLAN number is actually the VLAN ID that will be inserted into the 802.1q frame header. **Parent Interface** is the name of the physical interface that is supposed to act as the trunk port. This is shown in the following command:

```
# ifconfig vlan0 vlan 10 vlandev fxp0
```

Then you should configure layer3 parameters on the VLAN configuration, just like a normal physical interface, as shown here:

```
# ifconfig vlan0 10.0.2.1/24
```

Since you do not assign IP address to the physical trunk interface (parent interface), the system does not bring the interface up and you should do this step manually:

```
# ifconfig fxp0 up
```

The above example configures the `vlan0` device with `vlan` tag 10 and assigns it to the `fxp0` interface. Since the VLAN interface is a virtual interface, it makes a copy of the parent interface's attribute, including hardware address and device capabilities as shown here:

```
# ifconfig vlan0

    vlan0: flags=8842<BROADCAST,RUNNING,SIMPLEX,MULTICAST> metric
0 mtu 1500
            ether 00:01:02:ae:13:57
            media: Ethernet 100baseTX <full-duplex>
            status: active
            vlan: 10 parent interface: fxp0
```

From now on, the parent interface (in this case, `fxp0`) is the trunk port, and you can initialize and configure more VLAN interfaces and assign them to the trunk interface.

Once you finish the VLAN port configuration, the trunk port (parent interface) accepts the 802.1q frames and forwards the frames to the appropriate VLAN interface based on the VLAN tag number from frame header. On the other side, every packet that is transmitted via VLAN interface, will encapsulate in the 802.1q frame and divert it to the parent interface for transmission on the wire.

If you want to change the interface binding of a VLAN interface from one physical interface to another, you should remove the binding from the first interface manually using `ifconfig`'s `-vlandev` option. Then assign it to another interface with the `vlandev` option.

```
# ifconfig vlan0 -vlandev
```

The above command will disassociate `vlan0` interface from its parent interface. And to re-assign VLAN port to another interface, you should go through the same process that you did while configuring the VLAN interface:

```
# ifconfig vlan0 vlan 10 vlandev bge1
```

If you do not need the VLAN interface anymore, you can completely remove the interface using the `ifconfig`'s `destroy` option:

```
# ifconfig vlan0 destory
```

To initialize the VLAN interfaces and assign them to physical interfaces during system boot time, you should add appropriate configurations to the `/etc/rc.conf` file. To create VLAN interfaces, the following lines should be added:

```
cloned_interfaces="vlan0 vlan1 vlan2"
ifconfig_vlan0="inet 10.0.2.1/24 vlan 10 vlandev fxp0"
ifconfig_vlan1="inet 192.168.3.1/24 vlan 20 vlandev fxp0"
ifconfig_vlan2="inet 172.16.0.1/24 vlan 30 vlandev fxp0"
ifconfig_fxp0="up"
```

The first line tells the system to create three virtual interfaces called `vlan0`, `vlan1`, and `vlan2`. The next three lines configure the VLAN pseudo-interface, assign IP address to each interface, as well as define VLAN tag number and parent interface (trunk port). The last line in the configuration brings the trunk port up manually.

Advanced ifconfig Options

The `Ifconfig` utility has a few options to fine tune some advanced setting on network interfaces.

Hardware Offloading

You can offload some processor-intensive tasks to your network interface cards, if your network interface can support it. Offloading increases the network performance by releasing more CPU resources for applications and performs some network tasks in the network interface hardware-level.

This includes offloading TCP/IP checksum calculations, TCP segmentation, VLAN tagging, and TCP Large Receive offloading.

You can use `ifconfig -m` to find out which options are supported by your network interface.

For example, on a `bge` interface, it would look like following:

```
# ifconfig -m bge0 | grep cap
```

capabilities=9b<RXCSUM,TXCSUM,VLAN_MTU,VLAN_HWTAGGING,VLAN_HWCSUM>

In the above example, the `bge` supports RXCSUM and TXCSUM, that are checksum offloading for RX and TX traffic respectively. To enable RXCSUM on this interface you may use the following command:

```
# ifconfig bge0 rxcsum
```

Or to disable RXCSUM you may use the following command:

```
# ifconfig bge0 -rxcsum
```

The same applies to TXCSUM. You can also enable or disable both RXCSUM and TXCSUM, together, using the `hwcsum` flag. For example, the following command enables both RXCSUM and TXCSUM on the `bge0` interface:

```
# ifconfig bge0 hwcsum
```

TCP Segmentation Offloading (TSO) and Large Receive Offloading (LRO) are also two Intel-specific hardware offloading features that allow some layer4 segmentation to be offloaded to the network interface hardware. Currently only the `em(4)` driver supports these features. In order to enable TSO and LRO on an interface, you may use the following commands respectively:

```
# ifconfig em0 tso
# ifconfig em0 lro
```

You have to use the `tso4` and `tso6` options for offloading TCPv4 and TCPv6 segmentations, respectively, as some cards do not support `tso` for both IPv4 and IPv6. You can also use these options when you do not want to enable offloading for a certain protocol stack.

If your hardware supports it, you can also offload VLAN tagging to your network interface card, if your physical interface is associated with a `vlan(4)` interface. To enable hardware VLAN tagging, you may use the following command:

```
# ifconfig bge0 vlanhwtag
```

This enables VLAN tagging on the physical interface-level. To disable hardware-based VLAN tagging, you may use the following command:

```
# ifconfig bge0 -vlanhwtag
```

Promiscuous Mode

By enabling the promiscuous mode, interface does not filter incoming Ethernet frames based on the destination MAC address. It actually passes all incoming traffic to the upper layer in the TCP/IP stack, regardless of the destination address in layer2 and layer3 headers.

This feature is especially useful while wiretapping on a network interface. Certain software such as `tcpdump`, enable this mode on the network interface to allow us to see the passing traffic on the interface. For example, while running `tcpdump(1)` on `xl0` interface, you may see the interface status, which looks like this:

```
# ifconfig xl0

    xl0: flags=8843<UP,BROADCAST,RUNNING,PROMISC,SIMPLEX,MULTICAST> metric
0 mtu 1500
          options=9<RXCSUM,VLAN_MTU>
          capabilities=49<RXCSUM,VLAN_MTU,POLLING>
          ether 00:01:02:ae:13:57
          inet 192.168.14.1 netmask 0xffffff00 broadcast 192.168.14.255
          media: Ethernet autoselect (100baseTX <full-duplex>)
          status: active
```

There are certain cases where you want to manually disable the promiscuous mode on a physical interface. In this case, you may use the following command:

```
# ifconfig xl0 -promisc
```

MTU

You can adjust MTU size on network interfaces using `ifconfig`. Default MTU for an interface depends on your interface characteristics and varies in different interfaces, but the default MTU size on an Ethernet interface is 1500 bytes.

MTU is used to limit the size of frames that are transmitted on a physical interface. Packets larger than the MTU size will be fragmented into smaller frames if allowed according to the `df` bit in the packet's header.

In a gigabit network, you may want to increase the default MTU size to a larger number to gain better performance.

 Before enabling jumbo-frames, make sure all the hosts on the subnet are able to receive packets with large MTUs.

For example, to set MTU size on `ti0` interface to 9000 (jumbo frame), you may use the following command:

```
# ifconfig ti0 mtu 9000
```

Once you change the MTU on an interface, it is recommended that you reset the interface by using `ifconfig`'s `down` and `up` commands. This will ensure that all connections use the new MTU settings.

ARP

The default behavior of an Ethernet interface is to use `arp(4)` for mapping between layer2 (Ethernet) and layer3 (IP) addresses. The mapping is kept in the "ARP table". If an entry does not exist for a specific destination address, the system broadcasts an `arp` query to find the Ethernet address of the host.

To disable talking Address Resolution Protocol (ARP) on an interface, you may use the following command:

```
# ifconfig fxp0 -arp
```

This will completely disable ARP on the `xl0` interface and you will see the `NOARP` flag on the interface when ARP is disabled:

```
# ifconfig xl0 | grep flag

    xl0: flags=88c3<UP,BROADCAST,RUNNING,NOARP,SIMPLEX,MULTICAST> metric 0
    mtu 1500
```

There may be some rare circumstances when you want to disable ARP on an interface- for example when a special device is connected to your network that cannot handle ARP requests. Otherwise, it is advised that you do not disable ARP on Ethernet interfaces.

Static ARP

There are several methods by which a host can poison the ARP tables of other hosts on the network by transmitting fake `arp` advertisements. When this happens, other hosts are disabled from receiving traffic, or worse, traffic is redirected to another host instead of the actual network gateway.

In order to prevent such attacks on an untrusted Ethernet network, you may want to change the default behavior of ARP and prevent the host from learning ARP information from network.

In this case you have to manually set up an ARP table for trusted hosts on your network and instruct the system to not learn ARP advertisement from the wire. This method is known as setting up static ARP.

In order to set up static ARP entries, you should use the `arp(8)` utility. This utility is covered in more detail later in this chapter. However, in order to simply add a static arp entry to the system's ARP table, you may use the following command:

```
# arp -s 192.168.0.151 00:c0:91:30:ab:cd
```

The above example shows how to statically map the IP address `192.168.0.151` to MAC address `00:c0:91:30:ab:cd`.

Once you finish setting up your trusted MAC address table, you should configure your network interface to exclusively permit traffic for static ARP entries as shown here:

```
# ifconfig xl0 staticarp
```

This will disable sending ARP requests to unknown addresses on the `xl0` interface and relies on static ARP entries in the ARP table.

To verify the operation, you should check the interface flags using `ifconfig` as shown in the following command:

```
# ifconfig xl0 | grep flags
    xl0: flags=88843<UP,BROADCAST,RUNNING,SIMPLEX,MULTICAST,STATICARP>
    metric 0 mtu 1500
```

To disable Static ARP on an interface, you may use `ifconfig` with the `-staticarp` option.

Monitor Mode

Putting an interface in monitor mode means that the interface should not transmit anything over the physical interface. This is mostly the case on the passive sniffing port. You do not want anything to be transmitted and the host to be stealth on the network.

Enabling monitor mode on an interface prevents transmitting traffic on the interface. Consequently the interface cannot be used to transmit or forward traffic as long as the monitor option is enabled.

To enable monitor option on an interface, you may use ifconfig with the monitor flag:

```
# ifconfig fxp0 monitor
```

This command puts the fxp0 interface into the monitor mode. To verify if an interface is in monitor mode, you should look for the monitor flag in the interface flags:

```
# ifconfig xl0 | grep flags

    xl0: flags=48843<UP,BROADCAST,RUNNING,SIMPLEX,MULTICAST,MONITOR>
    metric 0 mtu 1500
```

Configuring Fast EtherChannel

Fast EtherChannel (FEC) allows grouping of multiple (up to eight) interfaces to create a high capacity virtual interface. Creating FEC interfaces can be done through the netgraph(4) subsystem, and you can easily create and maintain interfaces using the /etc/rc.conf configuration file.

A sample configuration of a FEC interface, which is created by bonding two physical interfaces (bge0 and bge1), is shown in the configuration here:

```
    fec_interfaces="fec0"
    fecconfig_fec0="bge0 bge1"
    ifconfig_fec0="inet 192.168.21.4/24"
```

The first line in the example tells the system to initialize a virtual interface called fec0. You can specify multiple fec interfaces by separating the interface names using space. In the above example, FEC members are specified in the second line. You do not need to configure the IP address on the physical interface, and configure the address on fec virtual interface instead.

Default Routing

If an outgoing packet is not destined for a local subnet (that is taken from the IP address and subnet mark configured on network interfaces), the packet will be forwarded to a default router (gateway) for further routing decision making and delivery.

The default gateway address should be installed in the host's routing table. This can be done manually using the route(8) utility. You can add the default route entry in the routing table by using the following command:

```
# route add default 192.168.0.1

   add net default: gateway 192.168.0.1
```

In the above example 192.168.0.1 is the IP address (or hostname) of your gateway. Obviously, the default gateway should be in the same IP subnet as your host.

If a routing entry for default gateway is already installed in your routing table and you want to modify the entry, you should use the route change command instead:

```
# route change default 192.168.0.21

   change net default: gateway 192.168.0.21
```

And to verify the installation of the default route in the routing table, the route get command will be used as shown in the following commands:

```
# route get default

     route to: default
  destination: default
         mask: default
      gateway: 192.168.0.21
    interface: fxp0
        flags: <UP,GATEWAY,DONE,STATIC>
  recvpipe  sendpipe  ssthresh  rtt,msec    rttvar  hopcount      mtu
  expire
        0         0         0         0         0         0      1500        0
```

The route(8) command and FreeBSD's routing capabilities are explained in more detail in Chapter 10, *Network Configuration – Routing and Bridging*.

Name Resolution

There are various sources that a host may use to translate hostnames to IP addresses. The most common methods are the DNS and hosts file. FreeBSD looks in the `/etc/host.conf` configuration file to find out which method(s) should be used to resolve the hostnames.

A typical `host.conf` file would look like following:

```
# cat /etc/host.conf

    hosts
    dns
```

This is how a typical system translates host names to IP addresses:

1. The system looks for matching host names in the `/etc/hosts` file. If a matching pattern was found, it will use the returned IP address.

2. If the host cannot be resolved using the hosts file, the system then queries the DNS servers as defined in the `/etc/resolv.conf` configuration file.

 You can change the order of lines in this file or remove any of them, if necessary. For example, if you want to disable DNS lookups and rely on the `/etc/hosts` file, you should remove (or comment out) the DNS line in this file.

The `/etc/hosts` file contains a few default entries that are created during system setup. A typical host file may look like the following command:

```
# cat /etc/hosts

    ::1                         localhost.example.net localhost
    127.0.0.1                   localhost.example.net localhost
    192.168.0.1                 myhost.example.net myhost
    192.168.0.1                 myhost.example.net.
```

You can add your own host to the IP mapping entries to the file or modify existing mappings. It is also recommended that you update this file after changing your hostname or IP address in order to reflect the correct information.

FreeBSD's DNS resolver client uses the `/etc/resolv.conf` configuration file to determine which DNS servers should be used and in what order. You can define as many DNS servers as you require, in this file, and they will be used in the same order as configured in the `resolv.conf` file. As soon as one of the servers returns the answer to the DNS query, the search will stop.

The following is a sample `resolv.conf` file that contains several DNS servers:

```
# cat /etc/resolv.conf

    search example.net
    nameserver 192.168.21.3
    nameserver 192.168.21.4
    nameserver 172.18.9.21
```

The first line of `resolv.conf` in the above example indicates the search domain using the "search" keyword. Basically, this indicates the local domain name of our host. When looking up a host name which is not found, this domain name is appended to the hostname and turns it into a Fully Qualified Domain Name (FQDN) and tries looking up the FQDN.

The next three lines indicate the three different name servers. System queries each name server in the order they are listed in `resolv.conf`. A maximum of three **nameserver** lines can be defined in this file.

> If `resolv.conf` is not present, or no **nameserver** field is set in `resolv.conf`, the system will automatically look for a **nameserver** running on localhost.

Network Testing Tools

FreeBSD has a number of important network test and troubleshooting tools in the base system. Hence, you have most of the necessary tools that you need to troubleshoot network connectivity issues. These tools can perform very simple connectivity tests as well as very complicated traffic capture and analysis, to help the administrator spot the potential network issues in the minimum timeframe.

Ping

Ping is the most widely used tool to test network connectivity that can be found in almost every operating system that contains a TCP/IP network stack. While looking simple, the `ping(8)` command is actually a very advanced network test tool that can be used to solve complex network problems.

The simplest usage of the `ping` command is to transmit ICMP echo-request packets to a host and show connectivity status to the host, based on the received ICMP echo-reply packets from the host:

```
# ping -c3 192.168.0.20

    PING 192.168.0.20 (192.168.0.20): 56 data bytes
    64 bytes from 192.168.0.20: icmp_seq=0 ttl=64 time=0.794 ms
```

```
64 bytes from 192.168.0.20: icmp_seq=1 ttl=64 time=0.990 ms
64 bytes from 192.168.0.20: icmp_seq=2 ttl=64 time=0.972 ms
--- 192.168.0.20 ping statistics ---
3 packets transmitted, 3 packets received, 0.0% packet loss
round-trip min/avg/max/stddev = 0.794/0.919/0.990/0.088 ms
```

In the above example, the ping utility is used to transmit 3 ICMP packets (note -c3 option) to host the IP address 192.168.0.20. If the packet count is not specified, ping will continue to transmit ICMP packets until it receives a TERM signal (or simply the CONTROL-C key combination on the console).

Once it finishes, ping prints two lines of statistics including the number of packets transmitted, the number of packets received, which should normally be equal to the number of packets that were sent and the percentage of lost packets. In the second line, the packet round-trip time is minimum, average, and maximum. Finally the standard deviation is printed.

The default ICMP packet size that ping transmits is 56 bytes data (which will become 64 bytes when lower layer headers are inserted).

Using these statistics, you can simply find out the connectivity quality to the destination host from delay, packet loss, and the jitter point of view.

> Despite the simplicity, ping has several options that can be combined to get different types of results. It is recommended that you see the ping(8) manual page for more detailed information.

Traceroute

While the ping(8) utility can be used for end-to-end connectivity test, the traceroute(8) is used to find out the route between source host and destination host and discover all the layer3 hosts between two nodes.

The traceroute utility uses the TTL feature to discover routers between two nodes. It transmits packets (UDP or ICMP) towards destination host with a TTL of 1. Once the first router in path receives the packet, it decrements the TTL and returns an ICMP TIME_EXCEEDED message back to the source host. The traceroute command sends as many packets as it discovers, to all interim hosts and reaches the destination host.

```
# traceroute freebsd.org

    traceroute to freebsd.org (69.147.83.40), 64 hops max, 40 byte packets
    1  208.79.80.97 (208.79.80.97)  1.831 ms  1.976 ms  2.000 ms
```

```
 2  8.14.32.209 (8.14.32.209)  3.006 ms  2.992 ms  2.992 ms
 3  208.79.80.1 (208.79.80.1)  13.000 ms  7.983 ms  10.005 ms
 4  ge-6-3-224.car2.Raleigh1.Level3.net (64.158.228.13)  134.997 ms
199.983 ms  36.009 ms
 5  ae-6-6.ebr2.Washington1.Level3.net (4.69.132.178)  10.965 ms
16.013 ms  17.955 ms
 6  ae-72-72.csw2.Washington1.Level3.net (4.69.134.150)  13.026 ms
15.972 ms  17.020 ms
 7  ae-21-79.car1.Washington1.Level3.net (4.68.17.67)  8.967 ms  8.983
ms  8.988 ms
 8  4.79.228.2 (4.79.228.2)  8.990 ms  9.040 ms  8.971 ms
 9  so-0-0-0.pat1.dax.yahoo.com (216.115.101.145)  65.955 ms  54.982
ms  55.074 ms
10  so-1-0-0.pat1.pao.yahoo.com (216.115.101.132)  98.964 ms  99.129
ms  98.824 ms
11  ge-0-1-0-p300.pat1.sjc.yahoo.com (216.115.106.145)  98.989 ms
99.016 ms  98.952 ms
12  g-0-0-0-p160.msr1.sp1.yahoo.com (216.115.107.57)  100.006 ms
13  ge-1-45.bas-b2.sp1.yahoo.com (209.131.32.49)  98.981 ms
14  freebsd.org (69.147.83.40)  99.978 ms  99.007 ms  99.975 ms
```

Sockstat

The sockstat(1) command is a useful utility that displays the list of open sockets. Using sockstat, you can find out which processes are listening and on what sockets, or see a list of currently connected sockets.

You may see a list of currently listening sockets and the process behind each socket using the -l option:

```
# sockstat -l
```

USER	COMMAND	PID	FD	PROTO	LOCAL ADDRESS	FOREIGN ADDRESS
mysql	mysqld	35726	10	tcp4	*:3306	*:*
mysql	mysqld	35726	12	stream	/tmp/mysql.sock	
www	httpd	93848	20	tcp4	*:80	*:*
www	httpd	93838	20	tcp4	*:80	*:*
root	httpd	93837	20	tcp4	*:80	*:*
cvsup	cvsupd	95113	3	tcp4	*:5999	*:*
root	sshd	627	3	tcp6	*:22	*:*
root	sshd	627	4	tcp4	*:22	*:*
root	syslogd	520	4	dgram	/var/run/log	
root	syslogd	520	5	dgram	/var/run/logpriv	
root	syslogd	520	6	udp6	*:514	*:*
root	syslogd	520	7	udp4	*:514	*:*
root	devd	461	4	stream	/var/run/devd.pipe	

In the above example, the **httpd** process that is running as user **www** with **PID 93848**, is listening on the TCP port 80 and is bound to all available interfaces (note the "***:80**").

You can also use the `sockstat(1)` utility to see a list of currently connected sockets as well:

```
# sockstat -c

    USER        COMMAND     PID     FD   PROTO   LOCAL ADDRESS    FOREIGN ADDRESS
    farrokhi    sshd        41221   3    tcp4    10.0.11.2:22     172.16.31.9:1175
    farrokhi    sshd        41221   4    stream      ->              ??
    root        sshd        41219   3    tcp4    10.0.11.2:22     172.16.31.9:1175
    root        sshd        41219   5    stream      ->              ??
    cvsup       cvsupd      95113   6    dgram       ->              ??
    root        login       686     3    dgram       ->              ??
    root        cron        646     5    dgram       ->              ??
```

netstat

The `netstat(1)` utility is another all-in-one utility that displays various sorts of network related information. Using various `netstat` parameters, you can see the statistics of the network subsystem. The following table contains a list of `netstat` parameters and describes what they would display:

Parameter	Description
No Parameters	Displays list of active network sockets per protocol
-i	Network interface statistics
-s	Protocol statistics
-si	Protocol statistics per interface
-m	Memory buffers (mbuf(9)) statistics
-B	bpf(4) interface statistics
-r	Displays routing table contents
-rs	Routing statistics

Combination of different `netstat` parameters can be used to display very useful information that would come in handy, while troubleshooting network. One example is that, you can see the statistics of a specific the network interface from different perspectives as shown in the following command:

```
# netstat -i -I bge1

    Name  Mtu Network        Address             Ipkts           Ierrs
    Opkts         Oerrs  Coll
```

```
bge1  1500 <Link#2>       00:16:35:80:ac:52 19972917 52791  22219879
0        0
bge1  1500 81.91.129.64/ devbox                    19755146      -
22207004     -           -
```

This example shows the statistics for the `bge1` network interface. There are two lines of statistics, one for the layer2 protocol (Ethernet in this example) information and another for layer3 protocol (IP in this example).

The first (after the header) indicates the interface name, current MTU size, Network information (which is not available in layer2), address (which is MAC address in layer2), number of Input Packets, number of Input Errors , Number of output packets, Number of output errors and finally the number of detected collisions on the interface. The next line displays the same information (if applicable) for layer3. The information that is useful for troubleshooting is the number of packets, and more importantly, the number of errors that might be caused due to faulty hardware.

ARP

FreeBSD maintains a layer2-to-layer3 address mapping database called ARP table. ARP is thoroughly explained in RFC 826. The `arp(8)` utility is used to manipulate the system's ARP table.

While the system automatically takes care of updating and refreshing the ARP database, the systems administrator can manipulate (add or remove) the ARP database entries, when needed. The `arp(8)` utility is used to display the contents of the system's ARP table:

```
# arp -an

  ? (172.21.0.13)    at 00:10:db:58:4d:49 on bge1 [ethernet]
  ? (172.21.0.1)     at 00:11:0a:9c:fe:c5 on bge1 [ethernet]
  ? (192.168.2.133) at 00:02:b3:8c:9f:c2 on bge1 [ethernet]
```

If you want to remove a specific ARP entry from the table, you may use the `arp -d` command:

```
# arp -d 172.21.0.1

  172.21.0.1 (172.21.0.1) deleted
```

You can also use the `arp -d -a` command to clean up the ARP table by removing all existing entries.

There may be cases where you need to disable the ARP discovery on your network (for example. to prevent ARP poisoning attack) and you should manually update the ARP database. In this case, you can use the `arp -s` command to add static ARP entries to ARP table. The following is an example of adding a static entry to the ARP table:

```
# arp -s 172.21.0.50 00:04:aa:bb:cc:dd
```

The static entries are marked with the **permanent** tag, which means the entries will not be expired and automatically removed. To verify the result, you should check the ARP database:

```
# arp -an

   ? (172.21.0.13)    at 00:10:db:58:4d:49 on bge1 [ethernet]
   ? (172.21.0.1)     at 00:11:0a:9c:fe:c5 on bge1 [ethernet]
   ? (172.21.0.50)    at 00:04:aa:bb:cc:dd on bge1 permanent [ethernet]
```

A static ARP entry can also be "published", which means that the host will act as an ARP server and answer ARP queries for the address you specify, even if the address does not belong to the host. Basically, this is the ARP proxy behavior and the host can selectively perform as an ARP proxy for specific addresses:

```
# arp -s 172.21.0.50 00:04:aa:bb:cc:dd pub
```

> The `arp(8)` utility can be used to selectively respond to ARP requests for published ARP entries. However, if you want your host to act as an ARP Proxy for all addresses, you should set the `net.link.ether.inet.proxyall` sysctl variable to one.

Tcpdump

The `tcpdump(1)` utility is an advanced network troubleshooting tool that is integrated into the FreeBSD's base system. It uses the `libpcap` library to listen on a specific network interface and sniffs for all packets that are passing through the network interface. If the network interface is in promiscuous mode, the `tcpdump` will receive any traffic that is passing from the network adapter, regardless of its source or the destination address.

The output of `tcpdump` can be simply printed on stdout (in different levels of verbosity) in real-time or can be saved in a file for later analysis.

There are several tools available to analyse the `pcap` dump files. The most popular application is Wireshark (formerly Ethereal) that is available in ports tree at `/usr/ports/net/wireshark`.

A sample `tcpdump` output on STDOUT taking 10 packets (note `-c 10`) from `bge1` interface (note `-i bge1`) would look like the following:

```
# tcpdump -i bge1 -c 10 -n

    tcpdump: verbose output suppressed, use -v or -vv for full protocol
    decode
    listening on bge1, link-type EN10MB (Ethernet), capture size 96 bytes
    22:02:51.906888 IP 10.0.21.3.22 > 172.16.214.125.2423: P
    975531592:975531788(196) ack 959264752 win 256
    22:02:52.145987 IP 172.16.214.125.2423 > 10.0.21.3.22: . ack
    4294967140 win 8572
    22:02:52.421072 IP 172.16.214.125.2423 > 10.0.21.3.22: . ack
    4294967244 win 8468
    22:02:52.536168 STP 802.1d, Config, Flags [none], bridge-id
    8034.00:0e:83:ba:78:00.8026, length 43
    22:02:52.557813 IP 172.16.214.125.2423 > 10.0.21.3.22: . ack 196 win
    8760
    22:02:52.906661 IP 10.0.21.3.22 > 172.16.214.125.2423: P 196:344(148)
    ack 1 win 256
    22:02:52.906703 IP 10.0.21.3.22 > 172.16.214.125.2423: P 344:668(324)
    ack 1 win 256
    22:02:52.906731 IP 10.0.21.3.22 > 172.16.214.125.2423: P 668:800(132)
    ack 1 win 256
    22:02:53.633585 IP 172.16.214.125.2423 > 10.0.21.3.22: . ack 668 win
    8288
    22:02:53.636802 IP 172.16.214.125.2423 > 10.0.21.3.22: P 1:53(52) ack
    668 win 8288
    10 packets captured
    12 packets received by filter
    0 packets dropped by kernel
```

In the above example, a very short network conversation is shown, that contains some SSH and STP (802.1d) traffic. From the above conversation, the system administrator can figure out a SSH session between **10.0.21.3** (the host that capture was taken from) and **172.16.214.125** (a host that is connected to server via SSH) is ongoing. There is also a network switch that is talking STP on the port that is connected to the host.

Note that when you are running the `tcpdump` on an interface, it puts the network interface into promiscuous mode (explained earlier in this chapter) in order to receive all traffic passing from the interface. This will show all packets that are received by your network hardware, regardless of the source and destination hardware. This would be more interesting if you are connected to a network hub (so you will see packets for all connected nodes) or to a network tap (or an SPAN switch port). If this is not what you want, and you only want to sniff the traffic that is actually for your host, you can disable this mode by using the `tcpdump`'s -p options.

You can filter out the packet capture by using expressions you specify on the command line. For example, to see last 5 UDP packets, you may use the following command:

```
# tcpdump -i bge1 -c 5 -n udp
```

Or to capture traffic that is going to or coming from network `172.21.3.0/24`, you may use:

```
# tcpdump -i bge1 net 172.21.3.0/24
```

 The expression can match any rule from layer2 packets to layer4 packets. It is also capable of capturing and decoding complex protocols such as MPLS and IPv6 protocol set. For more information, please refer to `tcpdump(1)` man pages.

Using `tcpdump` you can set up a stealth network capture device that is passively capturing network traffic. In order to achieve this, you should put your interface in monitor mode. Hence your sniffing network interface does not transmit any packets and only diverts packets to `bpf(4)` packet filter, so there will be no trace (no packets with your source IP or MAC address) from your system on the wire.

 Before enabling the monitor mode on the interface that you want to sniff, make sure this is not the interface that you have connected to your box via SSH. Otherwise, you will lock yourself out of your box.

It would be wise to have a host with multiple NICs, so one NIC would be dedicated for traffic sniffing and the other for typical network connection, on which you can SSH or run a web interface.

The `tcpdump` utility can fully decode packets in real-time. If you use the `-vvvv` options (that gives the most verbosity-level) as well as `-s0` (that captures whole packet payload off the wire), you will have the complete packet decoded on STDOUT.

For example, the following command tells `tcpdump` to take one STP packet off the wire (on `bge1` interface) and completely decode it:

```
# tcpdump -i bge1 -c1 -n -s0 -vvvv stp

    tcpdump: listening on bge1, link-type EN10MB (Ethernet), capture size
    65535 bytes
    23:10:07.513554 STP 802.1d, Config, Flags [none], bridge-id
    8034.00:0e:83:ba:78:00.8026, length 43
            message-age 0.00s, max-age 20.00s, hello-time 2.00s,
    forwarding-delay 15.00s
            root-id 8034.00:0e:83:ba:78:00, root-pathcost 0
    1 packets captured
    3 packets received by filter
    0 packets dropped by kernel
```

As mentioned earlier, `tcpdump` can be used to capture traffic to a file in the `pcap` format.

 Pcap is a standard packet capture API that is used by many applications to capture packets from network interfaces. In fact, `tcpdump` uses libpcap as its packet capture facilities. Pcap is supported by various open-source and commercial packet analysis applications. Hence, the output of `tcpdump` can also be analysed by many different graphical packet analyzers such as the open-source Wireshark (`http://www.wireshark.org`) or commercial applications such as WildPacket's OmniPeek (`http://www.wildpackets.com`).

Since it is not always possible to analyse traffic in a real-time manner, especially when a high amount of traffic is passing through the interface, you may want to save the captured packets and analyse them with different criteria sometime later. It is possible to capture traffic based on the expression defined in the command line and save it to a `pcap` file for further analysis. Here is an example of such a setup:

```
# tcpdump -c 1000 -w sample1.pcap -s0 -i bge1

    tcpdump: listening on bge1, link-type EN10MB (Ethernet), capture size
    65535 bytes
    1000 packets captured
    1025 packets received by filter
    0 packets dropped by kernel
```

This will capture 1000 packets (note `-c 1000`) from the `bge1` interface (note `-i bge1`) and save the capture to a `pcap` file called `sample1.pcap`. This file can be read later by `tcpdump`'s `-r` option and information extracted using expressions, or can be processed using Wireshark. The following screenshot shows Wireshark in action:

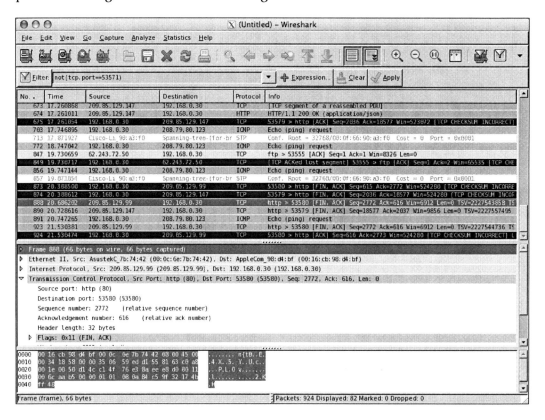

The `tcpdump` utility is also capable of decrypting IPSEC ESP packets if the ESP secret key is known. This is possible using `tcpdump`'s `-E` option:

```
# tcpdump -E des3:b1dd0bfffee -n -i bge1

    tcpdump: verbose output suppressed, use -v or -vv for full protocol
    decode
    listening on bge1, link-type EN10MB (Ethernet), capture size 96 bytes
    09:42:26.855518 esp 11.11.11.11 > 9.9.9.9 spi 0x00000305 seq 426 len
    92 [|esp] [tos 0x1 (C)]
    09:42:26.876694 esp 9.9.9.9 > 11.11.11.11 spi 0x00000305 seq 942078
    len 92 [|esp] [tos 0x21 (C)]
    09:42:27.860240 esp 11.11.11.11 > 9.9.9.9 spi 0x00000305 seq 427 len
    92 [|esp] [tos 0x21 (C)]
    09:42:27.880190 esp 9.9.9.9 > 11.11.11.11 spi 0x00000305 seq 942079
    len 92 [|esp] [tos 0x21 (C)]
```

Summary

FreeBSD has most of the network configuration and test utilities already installed with the base system. The `ifconfig(8)` utility that was explained earlier in this chapter is the all-in-one tool used to configure network interfaces with different layer3 protocols. While most of the features were explained in this chapter, there are also some major parts of the interface configuration. This will be covered in the next chapters, which include Bridging, IPv6, and Point-to-Point interfaces including tunnels and PPP.

The base system also includes almost any tool that you would need to troubleshoot your network connectivity, ranging from the classic `ping` and `traceroute` to more modern and complex `tcpdump` utilities. All these are supposed to help the system administrator in configuring the FreeBSD's network connectivity.

8

Network Configuration— Tunneling

When talking about tunneling, different definitions come to people's minds. Basically, tunneling is transmitting data that is encapsulated into a pipe, over a public network (for example, the Internet).

However, there are different methods to tunnel data over a public network for different approaches. For example, when security is a concern, tunnel protocols with cryptography are more favorable. But when performance has higher priority, protocols with lower packet overheads will be chosen.

FreeBSD 7 has a built-in support for a number of important tunneling protocols, although there are also many third-party applications in FreeBSD packages that support more tunneling protocols.

A list of supported tunneling protocols is shown in the following table:

Tunneling protocol	Description
GRE	RFC 1701 and 1702—Generic Routing Encapsulation
IPSEC	RFC 4301—Cryptographically-based security for IPv4 and IPv6
NOS	Cisco compatible IP-in-IP tunneling—also known as KA9Q
GIF	Generic tunnel interface from WIDE project to tunnel IPv[46] over IPv[46]

This chapter introduces the manipulation of tunnel interfaces in the FreeBSD 7 operating system.

In this chapter, we will look into the following:

- GRE
- IPSEC

Generic Routing Encapsulation (GRE) protocol

GRE creates a virtual end-to-end network link between network nodes (that is routers), over a public network.

GRE can be used to create simple VPN networks for customers that are connected to a service provider network, or between edge routers in a service provider environment, to exchange routing table updates. As this simple GRE interface does not support encryption, you may want to reconsider using GRE, if security is a priority.

FreeBSD 7 natively supports creating and manipulating standard GRE tunnels.

 GRE support should be available in the FreeBSD's kernel. If you have not compiled GRE support into kernel, the GRE kernel module will be dynamically loaded into memory upon first usage.

Creating `gre(4)` interface in a simple way using `ifconfig(8)` utility is shown here:

```
# ifconfig gre0 create
```

Note that if you do not specify the device node number, `ifconfig` takes the first available number and returns the new interface name, after creating the interface as follows:

```
# ifconfig gre create

  gre1
```

You can also remove unnecessary `gre(4)` interface using `ifconfig`'s `destroy` option:

```
# ifconfig gre1 destroy
```

Now that you have created a GRE interface, you should configure both sides of the GRE interface (on both hosts). This is basically done using the `ifconfig` utility.

Consider the following scenario in the figure to establish a GRE tunnel between Host A and Host B:

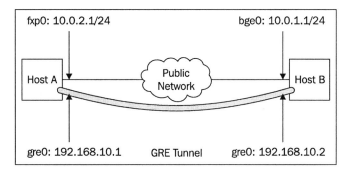

To configure Host A, you should first create a `gre0` interface and then specify both ends of the link on the interface.

```
# ifconfig gre0 create
# ifconfig gre0 192.168.10.1 192.168.10.2 netmask 255.255.255.0
# ifconfig gre0 tunnel 10.0.2.1 10.0.1.1
```

On Host B, you should do the same; but remember not to swap the source or destination addresses:

```
# ifconfig gre0 create
# ifconfig gre0 192.168.10.2 192.168.10.1 netmask 255.255.255.0
# ifconfig gre0 tunnel 10.0.1.1 10.0.2.1
```

The first line in the above procedure, a virtual tunnel interface (`gre0`) is created. The second line configures the tunnel IP address on `gre0` interface and also specifies the tunnel IP address of the other endpoint (connected tunnel interface). And finally the third line establishes the tunnel between two hosts. This time, you need the real IP addresses on your physical interfaces.

Now you can verify the tunnel setup on Host A:

```
# ifconfig gre0

   gre0: flags=9051<UP,POINTOPOINT,RUNNING,LINK0,MULTICAST> metric
0 mtu 1476
           tunnel inet 10.0.2.1 --> 10.0.1.1
           inet 192.168.10.1 --> 192.168.10.2 netmask 0xffffff00
```

The MTU size will be automatically calculated and configured on interface (in this case, 1476 byte) to compensate the GRE protocol overhead.

Now that the tunnel interface seems to be up, you should verify the tunnel connectivity using the `ping` command by pinging the tunnel IP address of Host B from Host A and vice versa:

```
# ping -c3 192.168.10.2

    PING 192.168.10.2 (192.168.10.2): 56 data bytes
    64 bytes from 192.168.10.2: icmp_seq=0 ttl=128 time=0.359 ms
    64 bytes from 192.168.10.2: icmp_seq=1 ttl=128 time=2.512 ms
    64 bytes from 192.168.10.2: icmp_seq=2 ttl=128 time=0.196 ms

    --- 192.168.10.2 ping statistics ---
    3 packets transmitted, 3 packets received, 0.0% packet loss
    round-trip min/avg/max/stddev = 0.196/1.022/2.512/1.055 ms
```

It would be pretty straightforward to set up the GRE tunnel between two hosts so that both support the GRE tunneling protocol. This is also possible using a Cisco or Juniper Router to peer with a FreeBSD host using the GRE tunnel.

So far we did the entire configuration manually, which is good for testing the tunnel setup in the lab. In order to make the changes permanent, you need to add appropriate configuration to the `/etc/rc.conf` configuration file. Tunnel configuration for Host A in the `/etc/rc.conf` file looks like the following code:

```
    cloned_interfaces="gre0"
    ifconfig_gre0="inet inet 192.168.10.1 192.168.10.2 netmask
    255.255.255.0 tunnel 10.0.2.1 10.0.1.1"
```

Note that you can specify multiple GRE interfaces using the `cloned_interfaces` variable, separated by spaces. On the second line, you can see that, we have merged the whole interface configuration in one line, which is also possible when you set up using the command line.

IPSEC

FreeBSD's IPSec stack is based on IPSec implementation from the KAME project (see `http://www.kame.net`). The IPSec feature is not available in stock `GENERIC` kernel and a new customized kernel should be built with the following options added to the kernel configuration file:

```
    options         IPSEC
    options         IPSEC_ESP
```

Once you reboot your host with the customized kernel, the IPSec protocol is available for implementation.

FreeBSD's IPSec implementation supports both Authenticated Header (AH) and Encapsulated Security Payload (ESP) protocols, which can be used either together, or separately.

The AH protocol protects the packets to be modified on their way to their destination, by cryptographically hashing the IP header. Consequently, when a packet is modified by an attacker in a man-in-the-middle scenario, this will be easily detected and discarded by the receiving host. AH does not encrypt the actual packet payload and is not protected against sniffing and wiretapping.

On the other hand, ESP offers a method to encrypt the packet payload using symmetric algorithms, including 3des and blowfish. When ESP encryption is in effect, sniffing traffic does not reveal the actual contents of the packets.

There is no conflict between ESP and AH, and they can be used together. Consequently, the packet content can be encrypted while the header is also hashed to prevent modification of packet on the wire.

Operating Modes

IPSec can operate in two modes—**Tunnel mode** and **Transport mode**.

In the Tunnel mode, the packet will be completely encrypted and encapsulated into another IP packet before being sent to the destination host. In fact, the packets are actually being tunneled over another IP packet. This mode is suitable to get connected to another host over an untrusted public network (for example, the Internet). This mode is mostly referred to as **IPSec Tunneling** or **IPSec VPN**.

The Transport mode offers another method of communication without modifying the routing (the source and destination address in IP packet header are not modified). Instead it encrypts the packet payload or hashes the header to ensure that the packet does not get modified in the path between source and destination. This mode is more suitable for host-to-host communications.

Transport mode does not basically work behind a NAT router. Since NAT needs to modify layer3 or layer4 addressing, this cannot be done when the packet is encrypted. Nevertheless, there are some NAT-T (NAT Traversal) methods available as per RFC 3715. However, the Tunnel mode is safe to be used with NAT.

Tunnel Mode

There are a few steps involved in creating an IPSec tunnel between two hosts. Now, suppose you have two networks in two different places that are connected to the Internet and you now want to interconnect both sites using the IPSec tunnel.

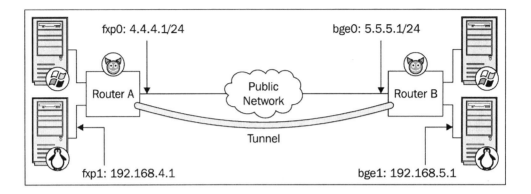

The first step is to create a simple tunnel between the two sites.

The gif(4) virtual interface offers basic IP over IP tunneling which is compatible with both the IPv4 and IPv6 protocol stacks. A gif(4) interface can be deployed like a gre(4) interface, as described earlier in this chapter.

For example, on Router A, you may use this setup:

```
# ifconfig gif0 create
# ifconfig gif0 tunnel 4.4.4.1 5.5.5.1
# ifconfig gif0 192.168.4.1 192.168.5.1 netmask 255.255.255.0
```

On the Router B, you should deploy the same configuration, but the source and destination IP addresses should be swapped:

```
# ifconfig gif0 create
# ifconfig gif0 tunnel 5.5.5.1 4.4.4.1
# ifconfig gif0 192.168.5.1 192.168.4.1 netmask 255.255.255.0
```

The tunneling with the gif(4) interface without encryption should be up and running. You may verify this by using the ping utility and test the reach ability of the IP address on gif interface of the opposite site:

```
# ping -o 192.168.5.1

   PING 192.168.5.1 (192.168.5.1): 56 data bytes
   64 bytes from 192.168.5.1: icmp_seq=0 ttl=64 time=7.200 ms
```

```
--- 192.168.5.1 ping statistics ---
1 packets transmitted, 1 packets received, 0.0% packet loss
round-trip min/avg/max/stddev = 7.200/7.200/7.200/0.000 ms
```

Once the tunnel is up and running, you should add static routes (unless you are already running a dynamic routing protocol) to route each network's traffic towards the tunnel interface. For example, to reach the network behind Router B from Network A, you must add the following `route` command to Router A:

```
# route add 192.168.5.0/24 192.168.5.1

    add net 192.168.5.0: gateway 192.168.5.1
```

You can verify the routing table updates using the `route get` command as follows:

```
# route get 192.168.5.0/24

      route to: 192.168.5.0
   destination: 192.168.5.0
          mask: 255.255.255.0
       gateway: 192.168.5.1
     interface: gif0
         flags: <UP,GATEWAY,DONE,STATIC>
 recvpipe  sendpipe  ssthresh  rtt,msec   rttvar  hopcount     mtu
 expire
       0         0         0         0        0         0     1280        0
```

Now the first part of the VPN setup is ready. The next step is to apply an encryption on the packets that are going through the tunnel interface.

There are different components involved in setting up the encryption. They are as follows:

- The `setkey(8)` utility is the kernel's "Security Policy" manipulation utility.
- An IPSec key management utility such as the `ipsec-tools` or `racoon2`.

Since you do not want to encrypt any outgoing packet or decrypt any incoming traffic, you need to specify which packets should be encrypted or decrypted. Kernel keeps a Security Policy Database (SPD) which holds the security policies you specify using the `setkey(8)` utility. This is where you can actually specify which traffic you want to encrypt.

On the other hand, the system needs an IPSec key management utility to manage the Security Association (SA) between two IPSec endpoints. SA is the mechanism for hosts to agree on encryption methods. To achieve this, you should run an Internet Key Exchange (IKE) daemon. IKE daemon takes care of key management as well as SAs between hosts.

The `racoon2` utility (available online at `http://www.racoon2.wide.ad.jp/`) is an advanced IKE daemon that supports IKEv1 (defined in RFC 2407, 2408, 2409, and 4109), IKEv2 (defined in RFC 4306), and Kerberized Internet Negotiation of Keys (KINK, defined in RFC 4430) key exchange protocols. It can be installed from ports collection and is located at `/usr/ports/security/racoon2`.

However, there is another IKE daemon that does not support IKEv2 and newer protocols, but is very easy to set up and configure, which is called `ipsec-tools` (`/usr/ports/security/ipsec-tools`). The `ipsec-tools` utility, which is basically a fork from the original `racoon` project, offers basic key exchange using IKEv1 protocols and shares the same configuration syntax with the original `racoon` daemon.

In order to configure the `racoon` daemon, you should first set up `ipsec-tools` and create appropriate configuration files as follows:

```
# cd /usr/ports/security/ipsec-tools && make install clean
```

Once the software is installed, you should create a configuration file based on the installed sample configuration files:

```
# mkdir /usr/local/etc/racoon
```

```
# cp /usr/local/share/examples/ipsec-tools/racoon.conf.sample /usr/local/etc/racoon/racoon.conf
```

Now you should edit the configuration file to fit your specific requirements. A sample `racoon.conf` file looks like the following code:

```
path pre_shared_key "/usr/local/etc/racoon/psk.txt" ;
remote anonymous
{
   exchange_mode aggressive;
   lifetime time 24 hour ;
   proposal
   {
      encryption_algorithm 3des;
      hash_algorithm sha1;
      authentication_method pre_shared_key ;
      dh_group 2 ;
   }
}

sainfo anonymous
{
   pfs_group 2;
   lifetime time 12 hour ;
```

```
        encryption_algorithm 3des, cast128, blowfish 448, des, rijndael ;
        authentication_algorithm hmac_sha1, hmac_md5 ;
        compression_algorithm deflate ;
    }
```

This is actually a generic configuration for `racoon` that should simply work for any source and destination address (note `remote anonymous` tag). You may want to modify the configuration to fit your needs. However, when changing IKE setup, make sure you are applying change on both hosts. A comprehensive guide to `racoon` configuration can be found online at `http://ipsec-tools.sourceforge.net/`.

To enable `racoon` daemon to launch at system start-up, make sure you add the following line to the `/etc/rc.conf` file:

```
    racoon_enable="yes"
```

To manually start `racoon`, run the appropriate rc script as follows:

```
# /usr/local/etc/rc.d/racoon start

    Starting racoon.
```

The `racoon` daemon will take care of setting up SA between two endpoints based on the security policies (SP) you specify, using the `setkey(8)` utility.

The policies should be added to the `setkey` configuration file which is usually located in the `/etc/ipsec.conf` file.

In order to encrypt the tunneled traffic between two hosts, you may create a `setkey` configuration file that contains the following lines:

```
    flush;
    spdflush;
    spdadd 0.0.0.0/0 0.0.0.0/0 ipencap -P out ipsec esp/transport//
    require;
    spdadd 0.0.0.0/0 0.0.0.0/0 ipencap -P in ipsec esp/transport//require;
```

The first two lines of the file actually flush SAD and SPD entries from the kernel's SPD. The third line specifies encryption policy for the outgoing traffic (note `-P out` flag), that has a protocol number four in their layer3 header (note `ipencap` which is actually IP encapsulated in IP packets on GIF interface), from source `0.0.0.0/0` (any) to `0.0.0.0/0` (any). As the encapsulation type is ESP, the packet payload is encrypted. And the last line specifies decryption for the incoming packets.

The `ipsec.conf` file should be configured on both hosts, considering that the outgoing policy on each host should match the incoming policy on the other host and vice versa.

Once the policies are configured, you may enable automatic IPSec setup from the `/etc/rc.conf` file by adding the following lines:

```
ipsec_enable="YES"
ipsec_file="/etc/ipsec.conf"
```

Note that you do not have to specify the second line, as it points to `/etc/ipsec.conf`, by default. It is only needed if you have chosen a different name for your `setkey` configuration file.

You should manually load security policies by running the following `ipsec` rc script:

```
# /etc/rc.d/ipsec start

    Installing ipsec manual keys/policies.
```

You are almost done. You should check the following three steps to make sure everything is in place:

1. Check the status if `gif` tunnel is using the `ifconfig` utility.
2. Check whether `racoon` daemon is running and is listening on udp 500, using the `sockstat -14` command.
3. Check whether the `setkey` policies that you defined are actually installed using the `setkey -DP` command.

If appropriate policies are installed, the output of the `setkey -DP` command should look like the following command line:

```
# setkey -DP

    0.0.0.0/0[any] 0.0.0.0/0[any] ip4
            in ipsec
            esp/transport//require
            created: Jun 23 23:41:41 2007   lastused: Jun 23 23:41:41 2007
            lifetime: 0(s) validtime: 0(s)
            spid=16435 seq=1 pid=1534
            refcnt=1
    0.0.0.0/0[any] 0.0.0.0/0[any] ip4
            out ipsec
            esp/transport//require
            created: Jun 23 23:41:41 2007   lastused: Jun 23 23:41:41 2007
            lifetime: 0(s) validtime: 0(s)
            spid=16434 seq=0 pid=1534
            refcnt=1
```

At this point, there is no SA established between two hosts, as there has been no traffic between the hosts, so far. This can be verified using the `setkey -D` command as follows:

```
# setkey -D

   No SAD entries.
```

Once you `ping` the other side of the tunnel, the IKE daemons should exchange encryption keys and establish SA:

```
# ping -oq 10.10.6.1

   PING 10.10.6.1 (10.10.6.1): 56 data bytes

   --- 10.10.6.1 ping statistics ---
   1 packets transmitted, 1 packets received, 0.0% packet loss
   round-trip min/avg/max/stddev = 87.537/87.537/87.537/0.000 ms
```

Now that the host is reachable, it means the SA is established and the keys are installed.

```
# setkey -D

   192.168.0.5 192.168.0.6
          esp mode=transport spi=85769720(0x051cbdf8)
   reqid=0(0x00000000)
          E: 3des-cbc   26715dcd c77affd3 39165b39 073637a1 ee8b979d
   eebd8368
          A: hmac-sha1   6eb62659 5058e91e e36b19ab abec245c 76bd67bd
          seq=0x00000007 replay=4 flags=0x00000000 state=mature
          created: Jun 23 23:50:09 2007   current: Jun 23 23:51:49 2007
          diff: 100(s)     hard: 43200(s)   soft: 34560(s)
          last: Jun 23 23:51:10 2007       hard: 0(s)       soft: 0(s)
          current: 952(bytes)      hard: 0(bytes)   soft: 0(bytes)
          allocated: 7     hard: 0 soft: 0
          sadb_seq=1 pid=1554 refcnt=2
   192.168.0.6 192.168.0.5
          esp mode=transport spi=61669162(0x03acff2a)
   reqid=0(0x00000000)
          E: 3des-cbc   99792546 3c0e0a2c 9cde2a3b be503817 4efc7422
   573d7014
          A: hmac-sha1   f3da6e46 10bec5b7 0e21f167 2387136e 656da322
          seq=0x00000006 replay=4 flags=0x00000000 state=mature
          created: Jun 23 23:50:09 2007   current: Jun 23 23:51:49 2007
          diff: 100(s)     hard: 43200(s)   soft: 34560(s)
          last: Jun 23 23:51:10 2007       hard: 0(s)       soft: 0(s)
          current: 624(bytes)      hard: 0(bytes)   soft: 0(bytes)
          allocated: 6     hard: 0 soft: 0
          sadb_seq=0 pid=1554 refcnt=1
```

To make sure that the traffic is actually being encrypted, it is a good idea to run `tcpdump(1)` on one host, send ICMP packets from the other host (`ping`), and see the incoming packets. If the traffic is being encrypted, you should see ESP packets in `tcpdump` output on the other end.

Summary

Tunnels are different scenarios when you may want to set up a tunnel between two hosts on a network. For example, tunneling is used to exchange routing updates between edge routers, or to create a site-to-site VPN over a public network.

Before choosing a tunneling method, you should decide whether the encryption is important or not.

If data encryption is not a concern while setting up GRE or GIF tunnels, using FreeBSD is quite straightforward. GRE is an established protocol that is also supported by different vendors. So if you are establishing a tunnel between a FreeBSD gateway and a Cisco or Juniper router, you can simply go with GRE.

If security is a concern, you can use the industry standard IPSec protocol between your FreeBSD gateway with other FreeBSD gateways or gateways from different vendors.

Setting up an IPSec is also very straightforward, especially when setting up the site-to-site IPSec tunnels. However this may get more complex depending on your network architecture and specific needs.

Network Configuration—PPP

9

Point-to-Point Protocol (PPP) is a layer2 protocol used to encapsulate layer3 traffic (that is IP) over a point-to-point physical medium, such as an asynchronous serial interface. PPP was introduced in 1989 based on HDLC protocol and was extended subsequently, based on the need to support more protocols and extensions. The latest standard (RFC 1661) was updated in 1994. Numerous extensions have become available for the protocol since then, including authentication, compression, and control protocols as well as some vendor-specific extensions.

FreeBSD 7 supports PPP protocol in the base system (which means no third-party software should be installed for normal usage).

There are two implementations of PPP stack in FreeBSD which are known as **User PPP** and **Kernel PPP**.

As the names suggest, the User PPP does not engage kernel in the process of inbound and outbound traffic encapsulation. It uses an external process and a generic tunnel driver for PPP encapsulation. This implies lower performance as compared to Kernel PPP, which uses codes in kernel for PPP encapsulation, but offers more features and flexibility over Kernel PPP.

Another difference between these two implementations is that User PPP uses tun(4) device, while Kernel PPP uses the ppp(4) interface between lower layers and the network.

There are also two special (and important) implementations of PPP protocol that are supported in FreeBSD—**PPPoE** and **PPPoA**.

PPP over Ethernet (PPPoE, defined in RFC 2516) is a special version of PPP protocols that encapsulates PPP frames inside Ethernet frames. It is mostly used on broadband access networks (for example ADSL and Wireless) to provide a method to authenticate and authorize users.

PPP over ATM (PPPoA, RFC 2364) offers encapsulating PPP frames on ATM AAL5 frames. This protocol is used on some ATM-based broadband access services, such as ADSL.

In this chapter we will look into the following:

- Setting up PPP client
- Setting up PPP server
- Setting up PPPoE client
- Setting up PPPoE server

Setting up PPP Client

There are two methods to set up a PPP client on a FreeBSD host: either by using User PPP or by using Kernel PPP.

Using ppp(8) and a configuration file that is typically located at /etc/ppp directory, you can set up a PPP connection over a serial line or other media types that are supported.

There are also a few examples for different PPP scenarios located at /usr/share/examples/ppp that can be taken as a reference when trying to set up complex PPP configurations.

To set up a PPP session using the ppp(8) daemon, you need to create a new entry in the /etc/ppp/ppp.conf file. A typical PPP configuration file looks like the following:

```
default:
 set log Phase Chat LCP IPCP CCP tun command
 ident user-ppp VERSION (built COMPILATIONDATE)
 set device /dev/cuad1
 set speed 115200
 set dial "ABORT BUSY ABORT NO\\sCARRIER TIMEOUT 5 \
          \"\" AT OK-AT-OK ATE1Q0 OK \\dATDT\\T TIMEOUT 40 CONNECT"
 set timeout 180
 enable dns
myisp:
 set phone 333 456 7890
 set authname USERNAME
 set authkey PASSWORD
 set ifaddr 10.0.0.1/0 10.0.0.2/0 255.255.255.0 0.0.0.0
 add default HISADDR
```

There are various tags in the configuration file that are identified with a trailing ":" character. Each of these tags specifies an entry in the configuration file. The above example has two tags—default and myisp.

The ppp(8) utility always reads the default tag upon start up, so the global default settings should be placed under this tag.

As you noticed, there are a few dial-up related settings under this tag which specify different logging options, serial port device (in this case /dev/cuad1, which is equivalent to COM2), serial line communication speed, and finally the dialing string.

 The first serial port (COM1) is identified as /dev/cuad0 and COM2 is identified as /dev/cuad2.

These settings would be working fine on a simple dial-up scenario in which you should specify your modem port, based on your hardware configuration.

Note that these configurations are specified under the default tag, which is used for any specific connection that you may want to use. If, for any reason, you want to use a specific serial port or dial string in different connection entries, you should move these lines under the appropriate tags.

As mentioned earlier, each connection is defined under its own entry that is identified by a name. In the previous example, myisp tag contains specific configuration for an ISP, such as the dialing number, username, password, default gateway setting, and static interface IP address, if applicable. This is a simple scenario that you may use to connect to another host using a dial-up modem.

There are seven different ways in which you can use ppp(8) to establish a PPP connection, each specified by a command line option. The option name and its description are listed in the following table:

Option	Description
-auto	The Dial-on-demand mode. The ppp(8) utility goes to background and establishes connection upon detecting outgoing traffic on the tun interface.
-background	Establishes the connection and then goes to into the background, once the connection is up.
-foreground	Establishes the connection and stays in the foreground.
-direct	Uses STDIN and STDOUT instead of network interface. This method is useful while running PPP over TCP/UDP for tunneling.

Option	Description
-dedicated	PPP assumes the link is always connected and that there is no need to establish the physical link. This mode is mostly used for PPPoE/PPPoA.
-ddial	Dial-on-demand mode (just like -auto) with auto redialing, when the line is dropped.
-interactive	Enters the interactive prompt mode, where the user can manually control the PPP connection establishment.

To establish a PPP connection to myisp in the previous example, you may run ppp(8) as follows:

```
# ppp -ddial myisp

    Loading /lib/libalias_cuseeme.so
    Loading /lib/libalias_ftp.so
    Loading /lib/libalias_irc.so
    Loading /lib/libalias_nbt.so
    Loading /lib/libalias_pptp.so
    Loading /lib/libalias_skinny.so
    Loading /lib/libalias_smedia.so
    Working in ddial mode
    Using interface: tun0
```

This runs the user PPP daemon in the background (note -ddial option), and establishes a PPP connection as configured under myisp tag in the /etc/ppp/ppp. conf file. It also tries to re-establish the connection if it drops.

PPP also has built-in support for Network Address Translation (NAT) without involving third-party applications. This can be achieved by using the -nat option in the command line.

For example, to enable NAT in the previous example, you may use the following command:

```
# ppp -ddial -nat myisp
```

By enabling the NAT function, PPP will masquerade all packets with private IP addresses (as per RFC 1918) as the source address.

A typical scenario of using NAT is to set up a LAN interface with private IP addresses (for example 172.16.10.0/24) and use it as the default gateway of your network. So when clients with the source IP address within the 172.16.10.0/24 network send their packets towards Internet using their gateway, PPP daemon will automatically pick up and translate the traffic using its established PPP interface. So you do not need to set up NAT using the traditional natd and ipfw combination.

Since ppp(8) runs in the background (except in the foreground and interactive modes), you have no information about what is actually happening, unless you take a look at the ppp log file that is located at /var/log/ppp.log. This is especially useful while troubleshooting link failures.

To run user PPP on system boot-up, in the previous example, you should add the following lines to your /etc/rc.conf file:

```
ppp_enable="YES"
ppp_profiles="myisp"
ppp_mode="ddial"
ppp_nat="YES"
```

Setting up PPP Server

In this mode, ppp(8) can be used to accept incoming PPP connections on stdin or stdout.

There are several steps involved in setting up a PPP dial-in server. These are listed here:

1. Create a ppplogin script.
2. Configure the /etc/gettytab file.
3. Configure serial device.
4. Configure the /etc/ppp/ppp.conf file.
5. Add users to the /etc/ppp/ppp.secret file.

The first step is to create a typical ppplogin file in the /etc/ppp directory. This file is a simple shell script file that runs upon receiving an incoming call. The file should contain the following lines:

```
#!/bin/sh

    exec /usr/sbin/ppp -direct incoming
```

The **incoming** parameter used here will be configured, later on, in the PPP configuration file as a configuration tag.

You should also adjust the permissions on this file so that the PPP program has necessary access to this file by running the following commands:

```
# chgrp network ppplogin
# chmod 0650 ppplogin
```

The next step is to modify the `/etc/gettytab` file, telling it to run the `ppplogin` script in case you detect a point-to-point connection on the line. The `default` clause should be modified to look like this:

```
default:\
        :cb:ce:ck:lc:fd#1000:im=\r\n%s/%m (%h)  (%t)\r\n\r\n:sp#1200:\
        :if=/etc/issue:\
        :pp=/etc/ppp/ppplogin:
```

Now you should make your system accept incoming dial-in requests on the serial ports. This should be done by modifying the `/etc/ttys` file. This file contains a few lines defining the serial port behavior. The following is the default configuration that you will see in `/etc/ttys`:

```
# Serial terminals

# The 'dialup' keyword identifies dialin lines to login, fingerd etc.

    ttyd0    "/usr/libexec/getty std.9600"    dialup  off secure
    ttyd1    "/usr/libexec/getty std.9600"    dialup  off secure
    ttyd2    "/usr/libexec/getty std.9600"    dialup  off secure
    ttyd3    "/usr/libexec/getty std.9600"    dialup  off secure
```

There are four lines, each of which belongs to a serial port. In FreeBSD, `ttyd0` is equal to the first serial port (COM1), `ttyd1` to the second serial port (COM2), and so on. Depending on which port you have connected the modems to, you should enable serial ports by modifying relevant lines of configuration. For example, if you have connected two modems to `ttyd0` and `ttyd1`, your configuration file should be modified to look like this:

```
    ttyd0    "/usr/libexec/getty std.115200"   dialup   on secure
    ttyd1    "/usr/libexec/getty std.115200"   dialup   on secure
```

 You may also want to change the serial connection speed. The default is set to 9600 baud, which is not enough in most cases. It is recommended to set it to the maximum (115200). If you are experiencing any problems with the maximum speed, it would be a good idea to reduce the connection speed to 57600 baud which would be sufficient for a 56kbps connection.

Once you finish editing the `/etc/ttys` file, you should reload the tty configuration:

```
# init q
```

This command will reload the tty configuration information from the `/etc/ttys` file, and from this moment, the incoming calls to your modems should be answered.

The next step is to modify the PPP server configuration parameters, so the clients can establish a PPP connection after they establish the serial line connection (using modem). This is done by adding an `incoming` tag to the PPP configuration file located at `/etc/ppp/ppp.conf`:

```
incoming:
    enable pap
    allow users *
    enable dns
set ifaddr 10.1.1.2 10.1.1.5 255.255.255.248
```

This is the typical PPP configuration that authenticates users using the Password Authentication Protocol (PAP) against the `/etc/ppp/ppp.secret` file. This also allows all authenticated users to log in (hence the `allow users *` statement). There may be cases where you want to authenticate only some specific users that you have defined in the `ppp.secret` file, using this profile. In such cases you should change this line to the following:

```
allow user john
```

This will allow only user **john** to login using PPP protocol.

The `enable dns` statement tells PPP to return system's DNS server addresses to the client, if requested.

And the last line, which is the most important line, configures the IP address pool that will be used to assign IP address to users. In our example, an IP address between `10.1.1.2` and `10.1.1.5` with subnet mask `255.255.255.248` will be assigned to the user.

 Do not forget to enable IP routing on your server, if you want to route traffic between your PPP client interfaces and the LAN interface.

There is one last note—when you want to change the default gateway of your client, you should also add the following line to the `incoming` tag:

```
add default HISADDR
```

This will set the address of the client's default gateway to the IP address of the PPP link.

Now that you finished tweaking the ppp.conf file, there is one more step that you should take, to make things work, and that is setting up the users database.

As we have configured `PPP` daemon, it reads the usernames and passwords from the `/etc/ppp/ppp.secret` file. The format of this file is pretty straightforward and the passwords are kept in a cleartext format. A typical `ppp.secret` file looks like this:

```
john      MyPa$$word
babak     3ecRe+
```

 The first parameter in each line specifies the username, and right after that, separated with a space or tab, is the password.

Setting up PPPoE Client

There may be certain circumstances when you have to run PPP over a packet-switched network (for example Ethernet), instead of a circuit-switched network (for example PSTN), as in the case of broadband access services such asADSL.

Basically, service providers need to authenticate or authorize users, and also calculate their usage statistics for billing or other uses. PPPoE is very suitable for this scenario, as there is an Ethernet network extended from your workstation to the service provider edge, using broadband access technologies. In a PPPoE scenario, you are like a dial-up user from a service provider's point of view except the fact that you are using a broadband connection instead of serial connection.

The provider will terminate PPP connection on a Broadband Remote Access Server (BRAS) platform to perform the per-user Authentication, Authorization and Accounting (AAA) as well as routing traffic towards external networks.

From a user's point of view, PPPoE seems like a normal PPP connection, except when you do not have to actually dial a destination number. The PPPoE client discovers PPPoE server by broadcasting PPPoE Active Discovery Initiation (PADI) message over available (or specified) Ethernet links.

Setting up a PPPoE client session in FreeBSD 7 is almost as simple as initiating a dial-up connection. A sample `/etc/ppp/ppp.conf` file for PPPoE looks like the following code:

```
default:
  set log Phase tun command
  enable dns
yourprovider:
  set device PPPoE:fxp0
  set authname YOURUSERNAME
  set authkey YOURPASSWORD
  set dial
  set login
  add default HISADDR
```

The above code is a generic configuration for a PPPoE client connection. You just need to set up the correct network interface name that is connected to your modem (in this case, `fxp0`), and the login information.

Some providers require a `service name` tag to be transmitted, in addition to your login information. In this case, if the service tag is `yourtag`, you should modify the `set device` line to look like following code:

```
set device PPPoE:fxp0:yourtag
```

Setting up PPPoE Server

Now that you are on the side of the service provider, you may want to set up a basic PPPoE BRAS for your broadband customers. The logic behind setting up a PPPoE server is pretty much the same for the PPP server over the serial line, unless there is no serial line involved in this process, and Ethernet media is used instead.

Since the incoming PPPoE requests come over Ethernet media, a special daemon called `pppoed(8)` handles these requests. The `pppoed(8)` daemon listens for the PPPoE discovery requests and launches `ppp(8)` to handle the PPP protocol upon receiving an incoming request.

In order to run a PPPoE server, you should customize your kernel and add necessary `NETGRAPH` modules to the kernel. At least the following three lines should be added to your kernel configuration:

```
options NETGRAPH
options NETGRAPH_PPPOE
options NETGRAPH_SOCKET
```

Once you have successfully built your kernel and rebooted your host with the new kernel, you can set up `pppoed(8)` to accept the connection. To enable `pppoed`, the following line should be added to the `/etc/rc.conf` file:

```
pppoed_enable="YES"
pppoed_interface="bge0"
pppoed_provider="*"
pppoed_flags="-P /var/run/pppoed.pid -a "server1" -l "pppoe-in" "
```

This configuration will enable `pppoed` to automatically start upon system boot up. It will listen on `bge0` Ethernet interface for the incoming PPPoE requests. As the `pppoe_provider` variable is set to "*", `pppoed` does not care about the `provider` name that is sent in the PPPoE request.

There may be certain cases when you are running multiple PPPoE servers, each for a specific group of clients, and each group is distinguished using a `provider name` tag. This can be set in the PPPoE client settings. Your PPPoE server then picks only the incoming requests whose `provider name` tag matches with the one you specified in your configuration.

And finally the last line in your configuration specifies some parameters such as the `PID` file location (using `-P` parameter), and the name of the PPPoE server that is returned to the clients (in this case `server1` using the `-a` parameter), and finally the relevant tag name in the `ppp.conf` configuration file is specified using the `-1` parameter (in this example, `pppoe-in` tag is used). You can change this information to reflect your setup.

Final step is to modify the `ppp.conf` configuration file and then create a `ppp.secret` file as the user database.

In our example, we specified the `pppoe-in` tag in the PPP configuration file to be used (hence the `-1` parameter). So your `ppp.conf` file looks like this:

```
pppoe-in:
    enable pap
    enable chap
    allow mode direct
    enable proxy
    disable ipv6cp
    set mru 1492
    set mtu 1492
    set ifaddr 10.0.0.1 10.0.0.100-10.0.0.199
    set speed sync
    set timeout 0
    enable lqr
    accept dns
    allow users *
```

There are some magical parameters in this configuration file, which if missed will lead to major issues with your PPPoE server deployment. Two of the most important parameters to be configured correctly would be MTU and Maximum Receive Unit (MRU). The default frame size (and therefore the MTU and MRU) of a typical Ethernet frame is 1500 bytes. PPPoE introduces 8 bytes of protocol overhead in addition to Ethernet frames. This is where you should reduce the MTU and MRU size in order to compensate the overhead. The specified MTU and MRU size is in fact 1500 – 8 =1492.

If you are experiencing weird behavior on your established PPPoE connections, such as problems with HTTP or FTP not working, (although ICMP packets are flowing very well) they can be attributed to MTU or MRU problems that cause packets to fragment. In such cases, you should check the MTU size on both the client and server and ensure that the correct MTU or MRU is being used.

Another important parameter is "proxy", which is in fact the Proxy ARP feature. By enabling this feature, your PPPoE server acts as the ARP proxy server for the clients and responds to ARP requests on behalf of the connected clients, whenever necessary.

You may also have noted that we are assigning the IP addresses from 10.0.0.100 to 10.0.0.199 to the users, and use 10.0.0.1 as the virtual IP address of the gateway from the client's perspective.

The only thing remaining is setting up the ppp.secret file, as in the example you have seen in the section on dial-in server.

Once all the necessary configuration is in place, you should now either reboot your server or manually start pppoed daemon by running the following command, and test connectivity from your clients:

```
# /etc/rc.d/pppoed start
```

Summary

Establishing a PPP connection under FreeBSD 7 is more or less similar to establishing other forms of tunnels, unless there is a daemon (or the kernel module) that takes care of encapsulation and hence, there is no need to perform manual ifconfig configuration.

While using user PPP (the stand-alone PPP process), almost all the configuration is done through the /etc/ppp/ppp.conf file. Once you have configured one or more connection entries under ppp.conf, you can use the ppp(8) utility to control the establishment of the PPP tunnel.

10
Network Configuration— Routing and Bridging

Your FreeBSD host can be used as a router. In fact, some vendors such as Juniper Networks use FreeBSD as the base operating system for their high-end routers. Since a router is an important and vital node in every network, using FreeBSD as a router is a good choice. It is already stable and supports many cutting edge standards and protocols, out of the box.

In this chapter, you will get familiar with basic IP forwarding in FreeBSD, as well as `routed` and `route6d` daemons, the built-in routing daemons that support RIPv1, RIPv2, RIPng (for IPv6) and RDISC.

There are plenty of IP routing related software that you can find in FreeBSD's ports system. Two of them — OpenOSPFD and OpenBGPD — are covered in this chapter. As their name suggests, they both support a major routing protocol that almost every network incorporates — OSPF and BGP.

Other routing software include Zebra, Quagga, and XORP, which are not covered in this chapter. But they are worth looking into, as they might fit into your network infrastructure.

Using these tools, you can turn your FreeBSD 7 host into a routing powerhouse.

In this chapter, we will look into the following:

- Basic routing–IP forwarding
- Running OSPF — OpenOSPFD
- Running BGP — OpenBGPD
- Bridging
- Proxy ARP.

Basic Routing—IP Forwarding

The default behavior of a FreeBSD host is only to pick up packets that are destined for the same host. In case there are multiple network interfaces installed on the host, the system does not forward traffic between interfaces by default.

This behavior is changed by enabling IP forwarding using the `sysctl(8)` utility:

```
# sysctl net.inet.ip.forwarding=1
# sysctl net.inet6.ip6.forwarding=1
```

The above commands will enable forwarding for IPv4 and IPv6 respectively.

To make these changes permanent, you can also add the following lines to the `/etc/rc.conf` file:

```
gateway_enable="YES"
ipv6_gateway_enable="YES"
```

By enabling IP Forwarding (routing) between interfaces, the system will pick up all the packets that have the layer2 destination, (MAC) address of the same host, and will forward it to an appropriate network interface, according to the system's routing table.

Once the forwarding is enabled, the forwarding behavior can be controlled by modifying the routing table. This is done using three methods of routing:

- **Automatic**: The system updates routing tables automatically. For example, a route for each "directly connected" network (taken from IP Address and Subnet mask of each interface) will be added to the routing table.
- **Manual**: You can update the routing table using the `route(8)` utility.
- **Dynamic**: A dynamic routing daemon (e.g. RIP, OSPF, etc) learns routes from peers over the network and updates local routing table accordingly.

The current status and content of the routing table is displayed using either `route(8)` or `netstat(1)` utilities.

In the IPv4 routing table, the following command line displays its status and content:

```
# netstat -rn -finet

Routing tables

Internet:
Destination      Gateway         Flags    Refs     Use      Netif    Expire
default      192.168.129.65      UGS       1     2162458    bge1
```

```
192.168.129.64       ff:ff:ff:ff:ff:ff    UHLWb   1      2      bge1    =>
192.168.129.64/26        link#2           UC      0      0      bge1
192.168.129.65       00:10:db:58:4d:49    UHLW    2    192400   bge1    1025
192.168.129.95       00:16:35:80:ac:52    UHLW    1     87134   lo0
192.168.129.127      ff:ff:ff:ff:ff:ff    UHLWb   1      2      bge1
127.0.0.1                127.0.0.1        UH      0     69621   lo0
```

And to display the current status of the IPv6 routing table use the following command line:

```
# netstat -rn -finet6

    Routing tables

    Internet6:
    Destination                  Gateway            Flags      Netif Expire
    default                      gif0               ULS        gif0
    ::1                          ::1                UHL        lo0
    2001:618:400::515b:815f      link#4             UHL        lo0
    fe80::%lo0/64                fe80::1%lo0         U         lo0
    fe80::1%lo0                  link#3             UHL        lo0
    ff01:3::/32                  fe80::1%lo0         UC        lo0
    ff01:4::/32                  link#4             UC        gif0
    ff02::%lo0/32                fe80::1%lo0         UC        lo0
    ff02::%gif0/32               link#4             UC        gif0
```

Each routing entry has four important fields—Destination, Gateway, Flags, and Netif.

Kernel will route the traffic destined for "Destination" to "Gateway" via "Netif".

Flags are special bits associated to each route. A table of valid flags and a description for each, is listed in the following table:

Flag	Description
1	Protocol specific routing flag #1
2	Protocol specific routing flag #2
3	Protocol specific routing flag #3
B	Just discard pkts (during updates)
b	Broadcast address
C	Generate new routes on use
c	Protocol-specified generates new routes on use
D	Dynamic route (created by redirect)
G	Gateway

Flag	Description
H	Host entry (represents network entry if flag is not present)
L	Valid protocol to link address translation
M	Modified dynamically (by redirect)
R	Host or network unreachable
S	Static route (manual entry)
U	Usable
W	Generated from cloning
X	External daemon translates proto to link address

Static Routing

You can manipulate the routing table manually using the route(8) utility. Using this utility, you can add static routes, modify an existing routing entry, remove a route, display routing table information and monitor the routing table changes.

To add a static routing entry to a routing table, you should use the route add command, as given in the following example:

```
# route add 172.21.30.0/24 10.1.1.5

   add net 172.21.30.0: gateway 10.1.1.5
```

The above command adds an entry to the routing table that makes the system route packets for destination 172.21.30.0/24 subnet to 10.1.1.5.

 The next-hop (in the above example: 10.1.1.5) should be on the same subnet with your FreeBSD router. In fact, the next-hop cannot be multiple hops away from your host, and the MAC address for this host should be discoverable using ARP. Otherwise, the route cannot install the entry in the routing table.

To add a default gateway to your routing table, you can add either 0.0.0.0/0 subnet or use the default keyword:

```
# route add default 10.1.1.2
```

This will add 10.1.1.2 as the default gateway to the routing table.

You can `add` a route to the routing table, only if it does not already exist in the table. In case you want to modify an existing route, you should use the `route change` command as shown:

```
# route change 172.21.30.0/24 10.1.1.5

    change net 172.21.30.0: gateway 10.1.1.5
```

This will update the routing table with a new gateway address (that is next-hop) for network `172.21.30.0`, which in this example is `10.1.1.5`.

And to remove an existing route from the routing table, you may use the `route delete` command as shown here:

```
# route delete 172.21.30.0/24

    delete net 172.21.30.0
```

The `add`, `change`, and `delete` commands are three basic commands that you need to maintain a routing table. However, you will also need to see the current routing table status for a specific route or for all existing routes.

To view the routing table entries, you may use the `route get` command:

```
# route get 172.21.30.0/24

      route to: 172.21.30.0
   destination: 172.21.30.0
          mask: 255.255.255.0
       gateway: 10.1.1.5
     interface: bge1
         flags: <UP,GATEWAY,DONE,STATIC>
   recvpipe  sendpipe  ssthresh  rtt,msec   rttvar  hopcount      mtu
   expire
          0         0         0         0        0         0     1500
          0
```

This will show you the routing table entry for a specific route (in this example, `172.21.30.0/24`). For example, this subnet is routed to `10.1.1.5` via the `bge1` network interface.

You can also use `netstat -r` to see the status of all routing entries in the routing table.

To clean up the routing table, the `route flush` command is used. This will remove all the existing routing table entries.

If you are connected to a FreeBSD host via a network (For example SSH) and you are not on the same subnet as the host, you may lose network connectivity upon using the `route flush` command, as the `default gateway` will also be removed from the routing table. Make sure you are not locking yourself out of the host and not making the host lose its network connectivity.

To make the static routes permanent, and to add them to the routing table when system starts up, you should add the appropriate entries to the /etc/rc.conf file. The following is a sample that adds two static routes to the routing table:

```
static_routes="sample1 sample2"
route_sample1="172.21.30.0/24 10.1.1.5"
route_sample2="192.168.0.0/16 10.1.1.6"
```

Alternatively, in an IPv6 environment:

```
ipv6_static_routes="sample3"
ipv6_route_sample3="2a01:3c8::/64 –interface gif0"
```

In the first example, two static routes are added (loaded from route_sample1 and route_sample2 variables). You may have multiple route_XXXX variables in /etc/rc.conf, but only those that are specified in the static_routes variables are picked.

In the second example, the same static routing for IPv6 addresses is shown. The IPv6 routing will be discussed later, in Chapter 12.

To manually load the routes from /etc/rc.conf without rebooting the system, use the following command:

 # /etc/rc.d/routing static

Manipulating the FreeBSD's routing table manually, using the route(8) utility, is quite straightforward. However, it is highly recommended that you consult the relevant man pages as well as FreeBSD handbook, for more information about this utility.

routed and route6d

FreeBSD has two built-in dynamic routing daemons that support RIP protocol family:

- routed(8): It supports RIPv1 (RFC1058), RIPv2 (RFC2453) and RDISC (RFC1256).
- route6d(8): It supports RIPng or RIP6 (RFC2080).

These daemons update the kernel's routing table based on the routes they learn from the updates they receive from other routing daemons over the network.

In fact, the routing daemon keeps its own routing table, which may contain different destinations for a subnet. But it installs only the best route for each destination, calculated using the distance vector algorithm.

 You may not want to use RIPv1 in your network, because it is not a classless protocol and hence does not respect the subnet mask, and assumes the obsolete concept of "classes" instead of subnets. New generations of the protocol (that is RIPv2) have solved this issue by transmitting subnet masks in routing update messages. Due to this fact, RIPv1 is not covered in this chapter. However, the routed(8) manual pages contain useful information, in case you are interested in running RIPv1, using routed on your network.

To enable the routing daemon, you should modify your /etc/rc.conf file:

```
router_enable="YES"
ipv6_router_enable="YES"
```

The above lines enable routed and route6d respectively. You can also manually run the routing daemons by running the following rc scripts:

```
# /etc/rc.d/routed start
# /etc/rc.d/route6d start
```

Once the routed daemon is launched, it looks for all available (up and running) interfaces, creates appropriate routing entries in the kernel's routing table and removes all non-static routes from it. After that, the routing daemon starts sending routing updates to all active interfaces, every thirty seconds.

When only one active interface is present (or when -q parameter is passed to routed), it does not transmit any routing information on the interface, and only listens for incoming routing advertisements.

Running OSPF—OpenOSPFD

OpenOSPFD is an open-source implementation of the IETF standard Open Shortest-Path First (OSPF) protocol, a widely used link-state IGP protocol. OSPF protocol uses Dijkstra's algorithm to find the shortest path between two hosts.

Unlike many other protocols, OSPF does not rely on TCP or UDP to talk to other routers. Instead, it encapsulates its messages directly on top of the IP (protocol 89).

OpenOSPFD can be installed using FreeBSD's ports system from the `/usr/ports/net/openospfd` directory.

OpenOSPFD runs as a daemon on your FreeBSD host and talks to other OSPF talking routers on your network, calculates the best path for each destination and installs the best route in FIB (that is, the kernel's routing table).

The following figure shows a typical OSPF network:

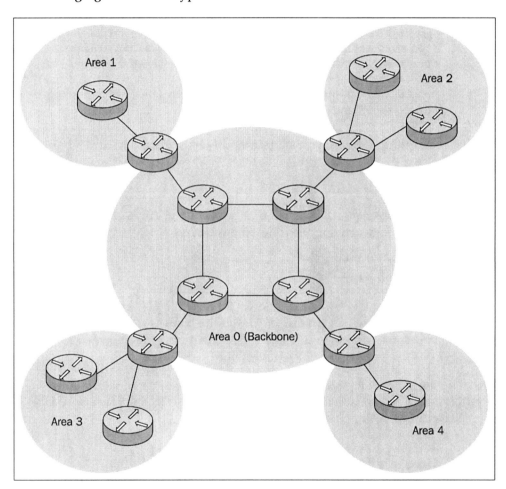

This is actually what a typical `/usr/local/etc/ospfd.conf` file looks like:

```
redistribute static
router-id 10.0.0.1

area 0.0.0.0
{
```

```
    interface fxp0
    {
        auth-key "tHeKeY"
        auth-type simple
    }
    interface fxp1
    {
        hello-interval 5
    }
    interface bge0
    {
        passive
    }
}
```

This sample configuration shows a router, which has three network interfaces. The router-id for this router is manually set to 10.0.0.1. If it is not set, the OpenOSPFD will take the lowest IP address assigned to your interfaces to be the router-id. This router also redistributes (announces) the routes for the directly connected networks over OSPF, to other routers (note the redistribute statement).

Each of the three interfaces is configured differently. The first interface, fxp0, is configured with the OSPF authentication. The fxp1 interface has no authentication but is configured to transmit hello packets every five seconds instead of the default, ten seconds, for faster convergence at the cost of more network overhead. And the last interface, bge0, is set to passive mode in which, the OSPF hello packets are not transmitted over this interface, and the network connected to this interface is advertised as a stub network over the OSPF protocol.

When you have configured your OpenOSPFD preferences, you should start the daemon by enabling the appropriate variable in the /etc/rc.conf file, first:

```
    openospfd_enable="YES"
```

And then run the rc script, manually:

 # /usr/local/etc/rc.d/openospfd start

Once the daemon is started, you can control the behavior of OSPF daemon using the ospfctl(8) utility.

Running BGP—OpenBGPD

Border Gateway Protocol version 4(BGP4) is one of the most important protocols in the today's Internet that glues networks together. Internet is a complex set of interconnected networks, each called an **Autonomous System**. An Autonomous System (AS) is a network that is controlled by an administrative entity, such as an ISP. Each AS has at least one unique AS number that is assigned by the Regional Internet Registry (RIR) as well as a few network prefixes.

BGP Protocol (RFC 4271) is used to exchange routing information between ASs. It uses permanents TCP connections (typically on port 179) to send routing updates to the directly connected peers. Each BGP router makes routing decisions based on its own view of the network, and installs appropriate routes in the routing table.

OpenBGPD is a secure and open-source implementation for BGP4 protocol which comes from OpenBSD project. It is available in ports system under `/usr/ports/net/openbgpd`.

Before running OpenBGPD, you should have the following information:

- AS number
- Network prefixes

Once you have installed the software, you should create a configuration file to specify your environment, such as your AS number, peers, which routes should be advertised to each peer, and which routes should be permitted to be imported (that is route filters).

A sample network representing the `bgpd.conf` example is shown in the following figure:

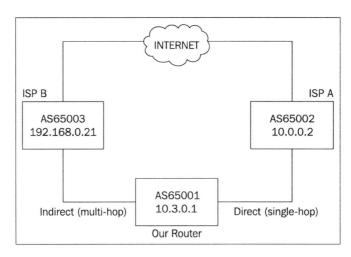

A sample `bgpd.conf` file looks like the following command lines:

```
# BGP Configuration

   AS 65001
   router-id 10.3.0.1

# Address of networks we advertise to peers

   network 10.3.0.0/23
   network 172.17.8.0/21

# Peering with ISP A with TCP MD5 signatures enabled

   neighbor 10.0.0.2 {
    remote-as 65002
    descr "ISP A"
    tcp md5sig password changethis
   }

# Peering with ISP B that is not directly connected

   neighbor 192.168.0.21 {
    remote-as 65003
    descr "ISP B"
    multihop 5
   }
```

We have assumed our AS number to be 65001 (That is a valid AS number for private use, as AS numbers 64512 to 65535 are reserved by IANA for this reason), and set the router-id to `10.3.0.1`.

If nothing is specified, `router-id` is automatically set to the highest IP address that is assigned to your host interfaces. While setting the `router-id` manually, make sure that the IP address is already assigned to an interface on your host.

In the above example there are also two lines that specify the networks that we want to advertise to our peers. There are two networks in this example: `10.3.0.0/23` and `172.17.8.0/21`

These networks have literally originated from AS65001, and are advertised to our peers. They may in turn advertise the routes they learned from our router to their peers (depending on their policy).

There are two neighbors in this example, each with its unique AS number and policies—ISP A and ISP B. ISP A, with IP `10.0.0.2` on its BGP speaking router, requires TCP MD5 security for peering. Whereas ISP B is not directly connected to our router and is a few hops away.

OpenBGPD supports TCP MD5 signatures (RFC2385) that are required for some peers to avoid session spoofing.

In order to use this feature, your network stack should provide this feature. You need to reconfigure your system kernel to enable TCP MD5 Signatures capabilities.

The following lines should be added to your kernel configuration file before the kernel is compiled:

```
device      crypto
options     IPSEC
options     TCP_SIGNATURE
```

BGP protocol assumes that the peering routers are connected directly, and there are no multiple hops (layer3 network nodes) between the routers. However, this assumption is not always correct, and in certain cases the BGP speaking routers may be multiple hops away from each other. This can be achieved by enabling EBGP multi-hop on this peer. The keyword `multihop` defines how many hops (the maximum) away from the hosts (in this case, 5), these peers are.

Please see the `bgpd.conf(5)` manual pages for a complete set of configuration options.

The following line should be added to `/etc/rc.conf` to enable an automatic start-up of bgpd:

```
openbgpd_enable="YES"
```

You can also start the openBGP daemon manually, by running its rc script:

```
# /usr/local/etc/rc.d/openbgpd start
```

Once the daemon is running, you can control its behavior using the `bgpctl(8)` utility. This utility provides a few commands that are used to display the current status of bgpd as well as to modify the parameters on the fly.

The five main commands of `bgpctl` include:

- **reload**: This command forces the daemon to reload the configuration file.
- **show**: This command displays various information about the daemon.
- **fib**: This command manipulates fib (Forwarding Information Base), which is actually the kernel's routing table.
- **neighbor**: This command manipulates per-neighbor peering.
- **network**: This command manipulates advertised network prefixes.

The term Forwarding Information Base (FIB) points to the kernel's routing table, while the term Routing Information Base (RIB) actually means routing daemon's internal routing table.

The most used feature of `bgpctl` is the `show` command that displays information about the current status of peers as shown here:

```
# bgpctl show

   Neighbor    AS     MsgRcvd  MsgSent  OutQ   Up/Down    State/PrefixRcvd
   ISP B     65003   38700    141      0      01:09:02           182394
   ISP A     65002   38620    137      0      01:08:41           182322
```

You can also manipulate sessions with peering routers using the `bgpctl neighbor` command. For example, you may use the following syntax to temporarily disable peering with a specific peer:

```
# bgpctl neighbor 10.0.0.2 down
```

To enable the same peer, you can use the same command, this time with the `up` command:

```
# bgpctl neighbor 10.0.0.2 up
```

There may be certain times when you want to clear a session (force a reset on the connection). This is achievable by using the `neighbor clear` file:

```
# bgpctl neighbor 10.0.0.2 clear
```

You can also dynamically add a `network` prefix to your advertised networks on the fly, using `bgpctl`:

```
# bgpctl network add 10.10.32.0/20
```

And to remove the network, you can use the `network delete` command.

Bridging

Using the `ifconfig(8)` utility, which we've discussed in Chapter 7, and the multiple network interfaces installed on your host, you can create a network **bridge**.

Network bridges are used to separate different segments of a network in layer2 of the OSI model (for example Ethernet). Unlike routers, a bridge makes forwarding decisions based on the layer2 (MAC) addresses. In fact, a typical bridge does not understand higher levels of the OSI model. A good example of a network bridge is, layer2 network switches. You can consider your bridge a layer2 switch if it had fewer ports.

To create a bridge, your host should have at least two network cards installed.

Creating a bridge is very straightforward as shown here:

```
# ifconfig bridge0 create
```

This will automatically load appropriate bridging modules into the memory, if not compiled in the kernel, and create a virtual bridge interface. Once the interface is created, you can add several interfaces into the bridge group, again, using the `ifconfig` utility as follows:

```
# ifconfig bridge0 addm fxp0
# ifconfig bridge0 addm fxp1
```

To verify bridge interface configuration and interface membership, `ifconfig` is used:

```
# ifconfig bridge0

    bridge0: flags=8802<BROADCAST,SIMPLEX,MULTICAST> metric 0 mtu 1500
            ether e2:72:9e:1e:de:5b
            id 00:00:00:00:00:00 priority 32768 hellotime 2 fwddelay 15
            maxage 20 holdcnt 6 proto rstp maxaddr 100 timeout 1200
            root id 00:00:00:00:00:00 priority 0 ifcost 0 port 0
            member: fxp0 flags=143<LEARNING,DISCOVER,AUTOEDGE,AUTOPTP>
            member: fxp1 flags=143<LEARNING,DISCOVER,AUTOEDGE,AUTOPTP>
```

 You can assign an IP address to the bridge interface for remote management reasons. However, it is not advisable to assign IP addresses to bridge members.

You can add as many interfaces as you like to a bridge group. However, only interfaces with the same MTU size can be assigned to the same group.

To remove an interface from a bridge group, you may use `deletem` instead of `addm` parameter.

Each bridge keeps a table of addresses. It learns from each interface, in order to make the right forwarding decision. You can display the contents of this table using the `addr` command. This is shown in the following command:

```
# ifconfig bridge0 addr

    00:0b:5f:af:ca:00 fxp1 1073 flags=0<>
    03:00:00:00:00:0d  0 flags=46<STICKY>
    00:00:00:1d:02:00 ?? 0 flags=0<>
    00:00:00:00:00:00  0 flags=0<>
    00:00:00:00:00:00  828729186 flags=0<>
```

```
67:65:31:00:00:00   1 flags=62<STICKY>
00:00:00:62:67:65   3159772 flags=1<STATIC>
59:80:00:01:00:00   2516844544 flags=10<>
00:04:96:10:5b:90 fxp1 1173 flags=0<>
04:00:00:00:00:04   0 flags=17<STATIC,STICKY>
00:00:00:a6:04:00 ?? 0 flags=0<>
```

As you can see in the `ifconfig` output, Bridge-member interfaces have different flags, each having its own meaning, which is given in the following table:

Flag	Ifconfig switch	Description
DISCOVER	`discover`	Interface forwards packets to all interfaces for unknown destinations.
LEARNING	`learn`	Learns host addresses from incoming packet headers.
STICKY	`sticky`	Does not expire address entries and keeps them in tact.
SPAN	`span`	Puts interface into monitor mode. The interface transmits a copy of all bridge packets. Used for sniffing on bridge interfaces.
STP	`stp`	Enables 802.1d Spanning Tree protocol to prevent loops.
EDGE	`edge`	Edge ports are connected directly to hosts and hence, cannot create loops. Interface starts forwarding packets as soon as it is up.
AUTOEDGE	`autoedge`	Automatically detects `edge` status.
PTP	`ptp`	Point-to-point link that starts forwarding immediately. This is used for connection to other switches that support RSTP protocol.
AUTOPTP	`autoptp`	Automatically detects `ptp` mode.

Filtering Bridges

A bridge is used as a firewall in situations where you do not want to segment your network. Since a typical firewall is also a router (a layer3 node), you actually need to place it as your network gateway. In such case, you will have to justify your subnets. But when a firewall acts as a layer2 host (a bridge), there is no need to reconfigure your network and the firewall can be deployed ad-hoc.

To enable IPFW to filter traffic between bridged interfaces, you should enable the appropriate `sysctl` variable:

```
# sysctl net.link.ether.bridge.ipfw=1
```

More detail about firewalling functionality in FreeBSD 7 is covered in Chapter 12. Here, basically we learn how to configure an `ipfw`-based firewall as a bridge.

To configure a filtering bridge, you need to enable the native firewall functionality of FreeBSD (that is `ipfw`) in kernel. However, your bridge should pass all ARP traffic between interfaces. You should instruct your firewall to pass ARP traffic using one of these scenarios:

- To pass all traffic by default by adding `options IPFIREWALL_DEFAULT_TO_ACCPET` in the kernel configuration file and then block all inappropriate traffic.

- Block all traffic by default, except the ARP traffic, using a simple rule like this— `ipfw add pass mac-type arp layer2`.

Using this trick, your firewall seems almost transparent. Now you can define appropriate rules to filter out or pass traffic based on your security policies.

Proxy ARP

When a host wants to transmit a packet to another host on the same subnet, it will look up for the Ethernet address of the destination host in the local MAC address mapping (ARP) table. If a mapping entry does not exist, the host broadcasts an ARP discovery request. All the hosts on the same subnet pick up the request from the wire, and the host in question will answer the request.

In normal circumstances, only the host that has the requested address on its interface will answer with an ARP reply packet. But there may be cases where hosts on the same subnet are not on the same physical network, and typically, a layer3 host (for example router) is in between. A good example for this could be the dial-in or VPN gateways.

In this situation, the hosts behind the router do not see the ARP requests, and the requests fail. The router should answer the ARP requests on behalf of these hosts. This is called Proxy ARP.

 Proxy ARP should not be confused with bridging, as the host in between is actually a router (layer3 host) instead of a bridge (layer2 host).

This can be achieved by manually adding static ARP entries, for each individual host, to the ARP proxying router:

```
# arp -s 10.0.21.14 00:11:de:ad:be:ef pub
```

The keyword `pub` tells ARP that the host should act as an ARP server for the specified host, even though the address is not assigned to the host. This way, you should manually add all hosts to the ARP table on the ARP proxy server.

You can also tell the kernel to automatically act as an ARP server, whenever appropriate. This can be achieved by tweaking the `sysctl` variables:

```
# sysctl net.link.ether.inet.proxyall=1
```

Or by adding the following variable to the `/etc/rc.conf` file, which makes this behavior permanent:

```
arpproxy_all="YES"
```

Summary

FreeBSD 7 offers a stable platform to act as router or bridge in a network. Built-in tools plus a few software, which you can install from ports collection, will help you set up a reliable network router that supports all the important protocols that you need in a modern network. All major routing protocols including RIPv2, OSPF, and BGP are supported using the `routed`, `openbgpd`, and `openospfd` utilities. There is also an excellent routing toolkit called Quagga in the ports tree that supports these protocols, and also offers a CLI interface and a Juniper Networks JUNOS like configuration syntax. Using some advanced network interface cards (those which support hardware offloading), you can set up a high throughput routing platform for your network.

11

Network Configuration—IPv6

Today, everyone knows that the internet is running out of IP addresses. In fact, the current infrastructure of the internet is running over legacy IP (aka IPv4) protocol that was not designed for such wide-spread and complicated use (for example, IPv4 was not designed to run in a refrigerator).

The original design of Internet Protocol (IPv4) is not efficient for today's networks. And even worse, we are running out of IPv4 addresses in a few years!

Several methods were introduced to reduce the usage of IP addresses in the internet including:

- **Classless Interdomain Routing (CIDR)**: This introduced the death of classful addressing (for example Class A, B, C) by a new subnetting method which is not limited, unlike the classful method.
- **Network Address Translation (NAT)**: Using NAT you do not need to use public IP addresses on your internal hosts.

Using CIDR subnets and NAT only helped IPv4 to live a few years longer, but was not the ultimate cure to the problem. Besides the addressing issues, there were other problems with IPv4 which could not be easily solved. These issues include the following:

- The size of internet routing tables was growing rapidly and this forced backbone providers to upgrade their networking gears.
- The IPv4 was very inefficient for high throughput links and did not support QoS by nature.

Back in the early 90s, IETF had started a workgroup to solve the deficiencies of the IP protocol. In 1995, the IETF published the initial drafts of IPv6 as the next generation IP. Since then, the protocol has matured enormously and been implemented in many operating systems.

FreeBSD uses the IPv6 code from the KAME project. The KAME project (see www.kame.net) has been inactive since 2005, and FreeBSD developers have eversince maintained the IPv6 protocol stack.

In this chapter, we will look into the following:

- IPv6 facts
- Using IPv6
- Routing IPv6
- RIP6
- Multicast routing
- Tunnelling

IPv6 Facts

If you are not familiar with IPv6, here is a very quick look at the difference between IPv4 and IPv6. (For a more detailed insight into IPv6 and its configuration in various operating systems, it is recommended that you read *Running IPv6* book by Iljitsch van Beijnum).

Fact One—Addressing

Addressing in IPv6 is quite different from legacy IPv4 addresses. IPv6 uses 128-bit address space unlike the 32-bit addressing system in IPv4. A typical IPv6 address would look like — 2002:a00:1:5353:20a:95ff:fef5:246e

Fact Two—Address Types

There are 4 types of addresses in IPv6:

- **Unicast**: A typical IPv6 address you use on a host.
- **Multicast**: Addresses that start with ff:: are equivalent to IPv4 multicast.
- **Anycast**: A typical IPv6 address that is used on a router.
- **Reserved**: Includes loopback, link-local, site-local, and so on.

Fact Three—ARP

There is no ARP! MAC to IP mapping is no longer needed as MAC addresses are embedded into IPv6 addresses. Instead, ND is born. ND is used to auto-configure addresses on hosts, duplicated detection, and so on.

Fact Four—Interface Configuration

If you are new to IPv6, you will be shocked to see an IPv6 address, telling yourself that you are in trouble assigning addresses to interfaces or remembering the addresses. However, it is not all that hard. In most cases, you can have your host autoconfigure IPv6 address on its interfaces. Typically, you should set this up only on your network gateway (router) manually.

Using IPv6

Running FreeBSD 7, the kernel is already IPv6 enabled. However, you should manually enable IPv6 in the UserLand, by adding the following line to the /etc/rc.conf configuration file:

```
ipv6_enable="YES"
```

And manually start the appropriate rc script (or reboot the system) for the changes to take effect:

```
# /etc/rc.d/network_ipv6 start
```

This will enable IPv6 on all interfaces that are IPv6 capable. This behavior is changed by modifying the following variable in the /etc/rc.conf file:

```
ipv6_network_interfaces="fxp0 bge0"
```

This will enable IPv6 support on specified interfaces. The default value for this variable is auto.

Once you enable IPv6, interfaces will discover the IPv6 enabled routers on the network and build their own IPv6 addresses based on the network prefix they receive from the router.

Configuring Interfaces

In a typical scenario, IPv6 network stack will automatically look for an IPv6 enabled router on the same network for each interface and try to automatically configure the IPv6 address on the interface.

The following is an example of an automatically configured interface:

```
# ifconfig ed0

ed0: flags=8843<UP,BROADCAST,RUNNING,SIMPLEX,MULTICAST> metric
0 mtu 1500
        ether 00:1c:42:8d:5d:bf
```

```
inet6 fe80::21c:42ff:fe8d:5dbf%ed0 prefixlen 64 scopeid 0x1
inet 192.168.0.225 netmask 0xffffff00 broadcast 192.168.0.255
inet6 2a01:3c8::21c:42ff:fe8d:5dbf prefixlen 64 autoconf
media: Ethernet autoselect (10baseT/UTP)
```

Beside the IPv4 address, there are two IPv6 addresses on the interface. One address begins with `fe80::` and identified with the `scopeid 0x1` tag, which is called a **link-local address**. Another address begins with `2a01:3c8::`, which is the unicast address of this interface.

The unicast address prefix is obtained from the IPv6 router on the network. The whole address is created using the 64 bits Extended Unique Identifier (EUI-64) algorithm, which consists of the hosts MAC address with some minor modifications.

The link-local address (that is from the reserved address pool) always starts with `fe80::` and is used for local network usage. This can be compared with RFC1819 private addresses that are suitable for local use. The network stack will automatically assign a link-local address to each IPv6 enabled interface, regardless whether an IPv6 router is discovered on the network. This means that in a scenario of a home network or a lab network, you do not need to run an IPv6 router or have a valid IPv6 prefix in order to establish an IPv6 network. All the hosts will be automatically provisioned with a link-local address, so they can exchange IPv6 traffic.

The network discovery protocol (NDP) helps the host find the router on the network and then create a unicast address for the interface. NDP is known as the equivalent to ARP protocol in IPv6. The `ndp(8)` utility is used to control the behavior of this protocol:

```
# ndp -a
```

```
Neighbor                      Linklayer Address  Netif   Expire      S Flags
2a01:3c8::                    0:16:cb:98:d4:bf    ed0     20s           R R
2a01:3c8::21c:42ff:fe8d:5dbf  0:1c:42:8d:5d:bf    ed0 permanent         R
fe80::216:cbff:fe98:d4bf%ed0  0:16:cb:98:d4:bf    ed0  23h58m48s      S R
fe80::21c:42ff:fe8d:5dbf%ed0  0:1c:42:8d:5d:bf    ed0    permanent      R
fe80::1%lo0                   (incomplete)        lo0    permanent      R
```

The above example shows the discovered IPv6 hosts. The `ed0` interface is connected to an IPv6 enabled network and receives a valid prefix via a router (the first entry of the list). The second entry is the unicast address of the `ed0`. The third and the fourth entries are link-local address for the router and our host. And the last entry belongs to the local host.

As you have seen so far, there are some special (reserved) IPv6 addresses. The following table shows a list of reserved addresses:

Address	Name	Description
::	Unspecified	Equivalent to 0.0.0.0 in IPv4
::1	Loopback address	Equivalent to 127.0.0.1 in IPv4
fe80::	Link-local	
fec0::	Site-local	
ff00::	Multicast	

In case you want to configure the static IPv6 address on an interface, it can be done as in a typical IPv4 scenario:

```
# ifconfig vr0 inet6 2a01:3c8::21c:42ff:dead:beef prefixlen 64
```

This will manually configure an IP address on the specified interface. Note the `prefixlen` keyword that is equivalent to subnet mask in IPv4.

Routing IPv6

Similar to IPv4, your host does not automatically forward IPv6 traffic between interfaces, by default. In order to enable packet forwarding between the two IPv6 enabled interfaces, you should modify the `net.inet6.ip6.forwarding` sysctl variable:

```
# sysctl net.inet6.ip6.forwarding=1
```

This can also be achieved by adding the following variable to the `/etc/rc.conf` file:

```
    ipv6_gateway_enable="YES"
```

After enabling IPv6 forwarding in the `/etc/rc.conf` file, you should reboot your system or run relevant rc script:

```
# /etc/rc.d/network_ipv6 restart
```

The `rtadvd(8)` daemon is another component that you may want to enable on a IPv6 router. As mentioned earlier, the hosts automatically configure the IPv6 addresses on their interface, based on the advertisements they receive from the IPv6 enabled routers on the same subnet. These advertisements are called **Router Advertisement (RA) packets**. The `rtadvd(8)` daemon sends router advertisements on the specified network interfaces, helping hosts to automatically configure IPv6 address on their interfaces. This is done based on the IPv6 prefix it advertises, as well as identifying itself as the gateway for the network.

To enable `rtadvd(8)`, add the following lines to `/etc/rc.conf` (ensuring that your host is also configured to forward IPv6 traffic):

```
rtadvd_enable="YES"
rtadvd_interfaces="bge0"
```

 Make sure that you only enable transmission of RA packets on interfaces that you need to do. This can be done using the `rtadvd_interfaces` variable.

Now you should create a configuration file for the `rtadvd(8)` daemon. This file controls the behavior of the `rtadvd(8)` daemon. The `rtadvd` daemon reads `/etc/rtadvd.conf` upon start up, to find out how it should send RA packets. A sample `rtadvd.conf` file looks like the following:

```
bge0:\
    :addr="3ca1:511:ffff:4000::":prefixlen#64:
```

This tells `rtadvd` daemon to advertise itself as a router for subnet `3ca1:511:ffff:4000::/64`.

Please see the `rtadvd.conf(5)` manual pages for more information about various options that you can use in this configuration file.

 It would be a good idea to use the `tcpdump(1)` utility to see how the RA packets are being sent.

Please note that in this case your machine is configured as a *router* and not a *host*, which has a special meaning in IPv6. In IPv6 terminology, a *host* is a machine that sends **Router Solicitation** messages or listens for *RA* packets to figure out its IPv6 address configuration as well as its gateway. On the other hand, a *router* is a machine that sends RA packets and is able to forward packets to the correct destination.

RIP6

FreeBSD 7 has built-in routing daemons that support RIPv1 and RIPv2 for IPv4 and RIPng or RIP6 (RFC 2080) for IPv6. The routing daemon that supports RIP6 is `routed6d(8)`.

The `route6d(8)` daemon is almost equivalent to its IPv4 counterpart and can be enabled by setting the following variable in the `/etc/rc.conf` file:

```
ipv6_router_enable="YES"
```

Multicast Routing

The ability to route multicast traffic in FreeBSD 7 is available using third-party software that can be used from ports collection. The `net/mcast-tools` port allows Protocol Independent Multicast Sparse-Mode (PIM-SM Version 2), PIM-Source-Specific Multicast (SSM using PIM-SM), and Protocol Independent Multicast Dense-Mode (PIM-DM Version 2) routing.

Once installed, the functionality is enabled by adding this line to `/etc/rc.conf`:

```
mroute6d_enable="YES"
```

This will automatically enable the `pim6dd(8)` (dense mode) daemon. If you are planning to use `pim6sd(8)` (sparse mode), you should also add the following line to `/etc/rc.conf`:

```
mroute6d_program="/usr/local/sbin/pim6sd"
```

Tunneling

There are certain cases where you want to set up a tunnel to transport IPv6 traffic over your existing IPv4 network. This can be a site-to-site VPN between two IPv6 enabled networks, or getting IPv6 connectivity to an IPv6 service provider. There are different methods by which you can set up such tunnels. The most popular methods are `gif(4)`, `faith(4)`, and `stf(4)`.

GIF Tunneling

There are chances that you do not have native IPv6 connectivity to the internet. In that case, you can still set up a non-native (tunneled) IPv6 connection to the internet.

There are several services that offer tunneling to IPv6 networks, such as `www.sixxs.net`. The only thing you should do is to sign up for such a service and set up a tunnel internet according to their instructions.

This is mostly done by encapsulating IPv6 traffic over a `gif(4)` tunnel that is established over IPv4 to the other end. In most cases, setting up such connectivity is pretty straightforward.

A sample tunnel setup would look like this:

```
# ifconfig gif0 create
# ifconfig gif0 tunnel x.x.x.x y.y.y.y
# ifconfig gif0 inet6 2001:470:1F03:26c::2 2001:470:1F03:26c::1
prefixlen 128
# route -n add -inet6 default 2001:470:1F03:26c::1
# ifconfig gif0 up
```

In the above example, a `gif` interface is created and established between `x.x.x.x` (your IPv4 address) and `y.y.y.y` (your tunnel broker's IPv4 address). Then you should assign IPv6 addresses to the tunnel. In this case, `2001:470:1F03:26c::2` is assigned to your side of the tunnel and `2001:470:1F03:26c::1` to the other side of the tunnel. The latter is used as your IPv6 gateway as well.

The tricky part is setting up a default gateway for all IPv6 traffic to the other side of the tunnel, which is done using the `route` command (note the `-inet6` flag).

Once you have finished setting up the tunnel, you may want to test your connectivity by pinging the other side of the tunnel using the `ping6(8)` utility.

Summary

FreeBSD has had IPv6 support in the base operating system since its early versions. This support has become more mature in recent releases. Since we covered basic configuration for IPv6 in this chapter, you may want to do more complex things that are not covered here. There are a few useful and up-to-date resources that you can find on the net—one of them being the FreeBSD handbook section on IPv6 and *IPv6 internals* in the developer's handbook. It is also recommended that you read *Running IPv6* book, which contains detailed explanations of deploying the IPv6 network, with examples involving various operating systems, including the FreeBSD.

12
Network Configuration— Firewalls

According to FreeBSD's CVS commits history, FreeBSD has had built-in firewall capability since 1994. Obviously, the built-in firewall has improved a lot to meet today's needs. There are two main firewall technologies available in FreeBSD 7—IPFW and PF, each of which offers almost similar functionalities, but with different rule-set syntax.

IPFW is a FreeBSD firewall utility which has been in the source tree since 1994. It offers basic firewall capabilities such as stateless and stateful packet inspection, as well as DUMMYNET pipes, ALTQ for traffic shaping, and DIVERT sockets.

PF is a new firewall utility ported from the OpenBSD project, back in 2003. PF is a full-featured firewall utility with optional QoS support using ALTQ framework.

This chapter will explain the basic and intermediate setup and configuration of both IPFW and PF. IPFW and PF are both in active development and more features will be added later. There are plenty of valuable resources, on both these powerful firewall programs, available on the internet.

In this chapter, we will look into the following:

- Packet filtering with IPFW
- Packet filtering with PF
- Network address translation.

Packet Filtering with IPFW

IPFW (IPFIREWALL) is the oldest firewall package in FreeBSD. However, it has evolved since its initial import in 1994, although it is still widely used on FreeBSD installations. It is also natively available on Apple Mac OS X (which is itself based on FreeBSD code).

 IPFW is a complicated firewall package. We will discuss the basics of its functionalities in this chapter. It is highly recommended that you read `ipfw(8)` manual pages for detailed information about this firewall package.

IPFW is not statically linked into the system's default GENERIC kernel, but will be automatically loaded if IPFW is enabled in the `rc.conf` configuration file.

To enable IPFW, you should add the following line to the `/etc/rc.conf` file:

```
firewall_enable="YES"
```

Upon system boot up process, the system will automatically load the `ipfw.ko` module and dynamically link it to the kernel.

 The default policy for IPFW is to deny all IP traffic. Be careful while enabling IPFW from a remote network session (for example SSH) or on a production server, as it may completely lock you out of the box and block all outgoing and incoming network traffic.

You may also prefer to re-build a customized kernel with built-in IPFW module for better performance and more control. To do so, you will need to create a customized kernel configuration file and add the following line to it (for more information on how to build a customized kernel, please refer to Chapter 2):

```
options          IPFIREWALL
```

This will statically link IPFIREWALL module into the kernel. Statically linking the IPFIREWALL module offers better performance as compared to the dynamically loaded module.

IPFW blocks all traffic by default. To change this behavior, you should also add the following line to your kernel configuration file:

```
options          IPFIREWALL_DEFAULT_TO_ACCEPT
```

As the name suggests, this will change the default behavior to accepting all traffic instead of blocking it.

There are also a few more options that you can add to the kernel configuration file that affects the `ipfw` behavior. This includes enabling the `syslogd(8)` logging feature:

```
options         IPFIREWALL_VERBOSE
options         IPFIREWALL_VERBOSE_LIMIT
```

This can also be done by adding the following line to the `/etc/rc.conf` file:

```
firewall_logging="YES"
```

Once you have finished enabling the firewall, either by rebuilding the kernel or by loading the kernel module dynamically, you should create your own firewall **ruleset**. The ruleset is then saved to any custom configuration file and loaded by `ipfw` during boot time (or manually).

> Obviously, you should have a clear plan on which packets you are going to permit or block. You are advised not to start writing firewall rules without having a well thought-out firewall plan. Otherwise you may create a big mess rather than securing your network or host.

Basic Configuration

The good news is that `ipfw(8)` has a very clear and readable rule syntax. A simple `ipfw(8)` rule looks like the following:

```
# add 100 permit ip from 192.168.1.0/24 to any
```

The first keyword in the above example is a command that tells `ipfw` that you are actually "adding" a new rule, and the rule number you selected is `100`, which is optional. If you do not specify a rule number, `ipfw` will choose the first free number (starting from 100) and increments the number by 100 for further rules (for example 200, 300 and so on). This is very useful, when you want to actually "insert" a firewall rule in a specific location into an existing ruleset (we will come back to this, later in this chapter).

> IPFW evaluates the rules sorted by the rule number. A packet is tested against first rule in the list and action will be taken once packet matches with a rule in the list. Once matched, no further check will be performed on the packet, and the specified action (for example permit, deny, forward, and so on) will be taken before IPFW proceeds to the next packet.

The very last rule in a ruleset is either a DENY ALL (default behavior), or a PERMIT ALL rule. In normal mode, if a packet does not match with any of the rules, it will be matched with the last rule in the ruleset. Depending on your configuration, the packet may be permitted (or be allowed) to pass.

The next keyword in the rule (in this case `permit`) is the "action" that you want to perform on the matching packet. If you want to actually permit the packet, you should choose either `allow`, or `accept`, or `pass`, or `permit` keyword. Use the one you are more comfortable with, as they are all the same. If you want to drop the matching packet, you should use either the `drop` or `deny` keyword. We will discuss more keywords later in this chapter.

After the "action", the actual packet-matching pattern is placed. In this case—`permit ip from 192.168.1.0/24 to any`—we are trying to match all IP traffic coming from subnet `192.168.1.0/24` to `any` host on the network.

In this case, only IP headers are looked into, hence we should use the `ip` keyword. IPFW can look into layer2 (for MAC addresses), layer3 (for IPv4 and IPv6 addresses), and layer4 (for TCP/UDP port numbers) to match the packet.

After the `from` keyword, the source address should be specified. This can be done by specifying the subnet, or host information (since we are looking into layer3 header) using a very flexible syntax. You can use a CIDR notation (like we did in this example) or use traditional subnet mask style (for example `192.168.1.0:255.255.2 55.0`, note the colon character between the address and the mask).

There are also a few special keywords that are used instead of the actual address, like the keyword `any` that we used after the `to` keyword, to specify the destination address.

The keyword, `any`, matches any IP address, while the `me` keyword matches IP addresses that are configured on any of the interfaces of our host.

To add this sample rule to *active* firewall configuration from command line, the following syntax is used:

```
# ipfw add 100 permit ip from 192.168.1.0/24 to any
```

You can then verify the change by using the `ipfw show` command:

```
# ipfw show
   00100     0        0 allow ip from 192.168.1.0/24 to any
   65535  8465   888556 deny ip from any to any
```

The `ipfw show` command shows the current "static" ruleset, and does not show any dynamically created rules, by default. The static ruleset is the ruleset that you have created. On the other hand, IPFW also adds "dynamic" rules to your ruleset, which we will discuss later in this chapter.

As you may have noticed, the last line of the `ipfw show` command output is the default firewall action. In any case, if the packet going through the firewall rules does not match any of the rules, this rule is applied to the packet. In this case, the default behavior of the firewall is to "deny" any packet that did not match any rule in the ruleset. This rule is always the last rule (number 65535), and cannot be manually modified.

Another note about the `ipfw show` command is that it shows the number of packets matched with each rule, (second column) and the traffic volume in bytes (third column), which is very useful while troubleshooting your firewall configuration.

To change the default firewall behavior, you should reconfigure your kernel by adding the `IPFIREWALL_DEFAULT_TO_ACCEPT` option, or by simply adding another rule right before the last statement:

```
# ipfw add 65000 allow ip from any to any
```

 Though it is not recommended to have a default permit rule in your firewall configuration, this is needed in some configurations.

Ruleset Templates

Now that you know the basic configuration syntax for `ipfw`, you can create a simple firewall ruleset for your host. Your FreeBSD 7 system also includes several configuration templates defined in the `/etc/rc.firewall` configuration file that are quite useful in some scenarios.

You can use one of the following five templates (or create your own customized ruleset):

Ruleset name	Description
open	Simply permits all IP traffic from any interface.
closed	Disallows all traffic except on the loopback interface.
client	Protects the host with some basic firewall rules and prevents all incoming connections, as this host is a client(tweak the /etc/rc.firewall file to set up your network information).
simple	Considers your host to be a router with two interfaces, and installs some basic firewall rules to prevent IP spoofing and also blocks inappropriate traffic such as RFC 1918 and other reserved addresses on the outside interface. Also permits HTTP, DNS and SMTP traffic from the outside world to the host. (tweak /etc/rc.firewall for appropriate network setup)..
workstation	Typical workstation setup where a connection from the host to the outside world is allowed and a few types of incoming traffic (such as icmp) are permitted. This template can be customized by setting up appropriate variables in the /etc/rc.conf file.

Using any of the above templates is achieved by adding appropriate variables in /etc/rc.conf. For example, in order to use the open template, you should add the firewall_type variable to the /etc/rc.conf file:

```
firewall_enable="YES"
firewall_type="open"
```

This will load and apply the open profile from /etc/rc.firewall.

Customized Rulesets

In case you want to create your own ruleset, disregarding the default system firewall templates, you should create a configuration file containing your ruleset. After this, load it from rc.conf by specifying the ruleset filename, instead of the template name. For example, if you have created a configuration file called /etc/myrules.conf, you should add the following line to /etc/rc.conf:

```
firewall_type="/etc/myrules.conf"
```

This will load your firewall ruleset when the /etc/rc.d/ipfw script is called (either manually or during system startup).

The file should contain one or more lines each containing a single IPFW rule, just like the command line syntax.

It is always a good idea to clear all existing firewall rules by specifying the `flush` command in the first line of the configuration file.

A sample ruleset file looks like the following code:

```
flush
add check-state
add allow tcp from me to any setup keep-state
add allow tcp from 192.168.1.0/24 to me keep-state
add allow ip from 10.1.1.0/24 to me
add allow ip from any to any
```

The above example shows a typical ruleset file that is loaded from the command line or from `rc.conf`, upon system startup, as mentioned earlier.

This sample also illustrates a **stateful ruleset**. A stateful ruleset is a set that contains one or more `keep-state` keywords. Once a packet matches a rule with a `keep-state` keyword, a "dynamic rule" with the exact information about the matched packet, and a limited lifetime, is created automatically. This will let the firewall pass the traffic for this specific traffic flow, without checking further rules in the ruleset.

To make this happen, you should add a `check-state` rule before any other stateful statement (the first line in your ruleset would be a good idea; but you can relocate it to any place of your choice depending on your firewall configuration).

Once a `check-state` is seen in a firewall ruleset, the packet will be checked against all dynamic rules.

To see a list of existing dynamic rules, you should use `-d` in conjunction with the `ipfw show` command as shown here:

```
# ipfw -d show

    00010    0       0 check-state
    00020  9562    4123 allow tcp from me to any setup keep-state
    00030   718    9965 allow tcp from 192.168.1.0/24 to me keep-state
    00040   618    6565 allow ip from 10.1.1.0/24 to me
    00100  1671    2734 allow ip from any to any
    65535   465    4556 deny ip from any to any
    ## Dynamic rules (4):
    00020  1024   53913 (242s) STATE tcp 192.168.1.2 63142 <->
    210.21.10.239 443
    00020    0     734 (239s) STATE tcp 192.168.1.2 49313 <-> 209.216.195.2 80
    00020 12032 495902 (177s) STATE tcp 192.168.1.2 56770 <-> 72.14.215.99
    80
    00020 10752 571074 (287s) STATE tcp 192.168.1.2 55407 <-> 84.241.58.34
    443
```

Dynamic rules have a limited lifetime. The default lifetime for a dynamic rule is 300 seconds, and this can be changed using variables under the `net.inet.ip.fw` sysctl subtree.

Logging

There may be times when you have to have a deeper look into your firewall rules, and get more details on what is being matched by a rule. This is possible using the IPFW's built-in logging facility. Logging can be enabled for each rule in a firewall ruleset as follows:

```
# add 200 allow log tcp from 192.168.0.0/24 to any
```

The above rule tells `ipfw` to log every matching packet with this rule (hence the `log` keyword right after the action keyword, in this case `allow`) into the `LOG_SECURITY` facility of `syslogd(8)`.

 In order to enable logging feature in IPFW, you should either add the `IPFIREWALL_VERBOSE` option to kernel or set the `net.inet.ip.fw.verbose` sysctl variable to 1.

Once a packet is matched with a firewall rule with the `log` keyword, a message will be logged to syslog. In a normal system configuration, you can find these messages in the `/var/log/security` file as shown here:

```
# tail /var/log/security

    Oct  9 19:43:33 home kernel: ipfw: 60 Accept TCP 192.168.0.5:22
    192.168.0.222:52195 out via fxp0
    Oct  9 19:43:33 home kernel: ipfw: 60 Accept TCP 192.168.0.5:22
    192.168.0.222:52195 out via fxp0
    Oct  9 19:43:33 home kernel: ipfw: 60 Accept TCP 192.168.0.222:52195
    192.168.0.5:22 in via fxp0
    Oct  9 19:43:33 home kernel: ipfw: 60 Accept TCP 192.168.0.222:52195
    192.168.0.5:22 in via fxp0
    Oct  9 19:43:33 home kernel: ipfw: 60 Accept TCP 192.168.0.5:22
    192.168.0.222:52195 out via fxp0
    Oct  9 19:43:33 home kernel: ipfw: 60 Accept TCP 192.168.0.5:22
    192.168.0.222:52195 out via fxp0
    Oct  9 19:43:33 home kernel: ipfw: 60 Accept TCP 192.168.0.222:52195
    192.168.0.5:22 in via fxp0
    Oct  9 19:43:34 home kernel: ipfw: 60 Accept TCP 192.168.0.5:22
    192.168.0.222:52195 out via fxp0
    Oct  9 19:43:34 home kernel: ipfw: 60 Accept TCP 192.168.0.5:22
    192.168.0.222:52195 out via fxp0
```

```
Oct  9 19:43:34 home kernel: ipfw: 60 Accept TCP 192.168.0.222:52195
192.168.0.5:22 in via fxp0
```

In the above example you can see the SSH traffic (TCP port 22) between `192.168.0.222` and `192.168.0.5` being transmitted and received on the `fxp0` interface. The log entry includes the date and time, as well as the direction of the packet.

Network Address Translation (NAT)

IPFW has built-in support for NAT function that can be enabled using the `nat` keyword.

IPFW's NAT support would be available, only if kernel is configured with following options:

```
options        IPFIREWALL_NAT
options        LIBALIAS
```

To add a NAT rule, a firewall rule for matching traffic should be added:

```
add nat 100 ip from any to any
```

This will create a new NAT instance (in this case the instance number is 100) that matches all IP traffic. Then you should add another rule that contains more detailed configuration about this NAT instance:

```
nat 100 config ip 81.20.55.1 deny_in unreg_only
```

This configuration statement indicates the NAT behavior. In this case, the matched packets will be translated to the IP address `81.20.55.1` (which is obviously already configured on an interface). There are also two other options used in this sample. The `deny_in` keyword indicates that all incoming connections are denied. And the other keyword, `unreg_only`, tells IPFW that only packets coming from unregistered IP address space (RFC1719) should be translated (which is what we use NAT for in most cases).

The following is a list of acceptable keywords in NAT configuration with a short description:

Keyword	Description
ip	Indicates the IP address that should be used for aliasing. An IP address should be specified after this keyword.
if	Indicates an Interface to be used for aliasing, instead of an IP address. An interface name should be used after this keyword.

Keyword	Description
log	Enables syslog logging for the NAT instance.
deny_in	Denies all incoming connections.
same_port	Does not translate port numbers but keeps the same port number on the alias IP address.
unreg_only	Performs translation only on RFC 1719 (unregistered) addresses.
reset	Resets NAT translation table, when the IP address on the interface changes.
reverse	Reverses NAT (swap inside and outside).
proxy_only	Does not actually translate packets. Is used for transparent proxying.

Traffic Shaping

Basically, IPFW supports traffic shaping, with dummynet(4) pipes and queues , using WFQ2+ algorithm. In fact, IPFW is the user interface to dummynet(4) traffic shaper framework. In order to shape (or limit) traffic flow, the flow should be passed from two objects—a pipe and a queue.

A pipe is basically a virtual path that emulates a connection with a specified bandwidth, propagation delay, and packet loss pattern. On the other hand, a queue is actually a buffer object to enforce the WFQ2+ queuing strategy on the traffic.

Using IPFW's traffic shaping facilities, you can define pipes with specific bandwidth, packet-loss rate, propagation delay, and assign a queue with specific size to the pipe.

For example, here we can create two pipes, each of them with different behavior:

```
pipe 1 config bw 512kbps delay 10 plr 0.01
pipe 2 config bw 256kbps delay 10
```

This will simply configure the first pipe to limit matching traffic to 512kbps with 10ms propagation delay, and one percent packet-loss. It also configures the second pipe to limit matching traffic to 256kbps, with 10 milliseconds propagation delay, and no packet-loss rate configured.

Pipes are ineffective unless they are assigned to policies. So here we've assigned them with traffic-matching policies:

```
add pipe 1 ip from any to any in  via xl0
add pipe 2 ip from any to any out via xl0
```

This will assign rules to pipes. The first pipe matches *all incoming IP traffic on interface xl0,* and the second pipe matches *all outgoing IP traffic on interface xl0.*

The pipe configuration can be verified later using the `ipfw pipe show` command:

```
# ipfw pipe show
   00001: 512.000 Kbit/s  10 ms   50 sl.plr 0.010000 0 queues (1 buckets)
   droptail
   00002: 256.000 Kbit/s  = 10 ms  50 sl. 0 queues (1 buckets) droptail
```

Possible configuration parameters for pipes are listed in the following table:

Parameter	Description
bw	Indicates bandwidth limit in kbps, mbps, or their equivalents, to given network device name.
delay	Indicates propagation delay in milliseconds.
plr	(Packet Loss Rate) A floating-point number between 0 and 1 that causes packets to be randomly dropped, simulating an unstable network link.
queue	Specifies the size of each pipe's queue. A queue holds packets before forwarding them. If a queue has no space left for more packets, it starts dropping packets.

Packet Filtering with PF

Compared to IPFW, that has been in FreeBSD for a long time, PF is a newcomer. It was imported from the OpenBSD project, in 2003 as a third-party software and found its way to the base system in 2004. Since then, PF has been a very popular and a powerful firewall package that many FreeBSD users prefer to use.

PF is not statically linked to the GENERIC kernel, and should be enabled either by loading the kernel module dynamically, or by statically linking it into a customized kernel.

In order to create a new kernel with PF support, you should add at least one line to your kernel configuration file, recompile it, and install the new kernel:

```
device          pf
```

You should then enable PF in the `rc.conf` file by adding the following line:

```
pf_enable-="YES"
```

 PF kernel module will be automatically loaded if it is not statically compiled into the kernel. You can choose to use either the in-kernel or the dynamic module.

By default, PF reads its configuration from the `/etc/pf.conf` file. So make sure that the file exists before you can make PF start automatically on system startup.

PF Configuration Syntax

Compared to the IPFW, PF has a complex syntax. However, with greater complexity comes greater flexibility. Creating a PF configuration file is very similar to writing shell scripts. This is because, PF takes advantage of Macros, Tables, and many other advanced features that we will learn in this chapter.

 PF has many configuration options and advanced features that we will not cover in this chapter. It is recommended that you read the official PF FAQ at http://www.openbsd.org/faq/pf for more up-to-date and in-depth information about PF.

We will create a typical PF configuration sample in this chapter and discuss the anatomy and syntax of the configuration file:

```
# Macros

    ext_if="fxp0"
    int_if="bge0"
    internal_net="192.168.10.0/24"
    external_addr="192.168.1.1"

# Tables

    table <trusted> { 192.168.32.0/19, !192.168.35.0/24, 192.168.0.0/24,
    192.168.1.18 }

# Options

    set loginterface $ext_if
    set block-policy drop

# Scrub

    scrub in all

# Queueing

    altq on $ext_if bandwidth 8Mb cbq queue { other, datacenter, sales }
    queue other bandwidth 5% cbq(default)
    queue sales       bandwidth 15%
    queue datacenter bandwidth 80%

# Translation

    nat on $ext_if from $internal_net to any -> ($ext_if)
    rdr on $ext_if proto tcp from any to $external_addr/32 port 1234 ->
    10.1.1.1 port 5678
```

```
# Filtering

    pass out all
    block in log all

    pass   in   quick on $ext_if proto tcp from any to $ext_if port 22
    pass   out on $ext_if proto { tcp, udp } all

    pass in on $ext_if proto { tcp, udp } from any to <truested> port 80

    pass out on $ext_if from 192.168.0.0/24 to any queue datacenter
    pass out on $ext_if from 192.168.1.0/24 to any queue sales
```

A typical PF configuration file consists of several sections, which are listed here:

1. Macros
2. Tables
3. Options
4. Scrub
5. Queuing
6. Translation
7. Filter Rules

Note that you should keep the same order of sections (if that section exists at all) within your configuration file.

Macros

A Macro is actually a variable that you would use several times in your configuration file. The macros are meant to simplify the task of administration. A typical example of using macro is for interface names and frequently used IP addresses and port numbers as you saw in the above example. A macro is referenced later in the configuration with a leading "$" character. There is also the concept of "list" in the configuration, which is a list of items enclosed in "{" and "}" brackets. The list is then expanded into separate items when PF interprets the configuration files. You can use the lists to simplify the configuration file and make it more compact. In the example above, the line that contains a "list" is shown in the following code:

```
    pass   out on $ext_if proto { tcp, udp } all
```

The above code is expanded into the following codes:

```
    pass   out on $ext_if proto tcp all
    pass   out on $ext_if proto udp all
```

The keyword `all` is the short version of `from any to any`. In the above example, the rule will ultimately translate to the following code:

```
pass   out on fxp0 proto tcp from any to any
pass   out on fxp0 proto udp from any to any
```

Tables

A Table is a list of IP addresses. You can also keep the list of IP addresses in Macros. However, the main difference between tables and Marcos is the speed of lookup in tables. You can keep a large number of IP addresses in a table with very low overhead and very fast lookup. A table can be marked `persistent`, which means, it will not be removed from memory if it is empty.

As you see in the sample configuration, a table name is always enclosed within "<" and ">" signs.

Options

There are a number of global options that PF uses internally. These options start with the `set` keyword and have global effects on PF behavior. As you saw in our sample configuration file, we have used two options. also in our example, we are using two options:

```
set loginterface $ext_if
set block-policy drop
```

The first option enables statistics logging on the `$ext_if` interface which is in fact the `fxp0` interface while the second option defines the default behavior of the `block` keyword. Using this option, we can specify whether the "block" action should simply "drop" a packet or return a message to the sender (such as ICMP unreachable message or TCP RST) which indicates that the packet has not reached its ultimate destination.

Scrub

Scrub or Normalization is an important feature of PF. Scrubbing means receiving a full packet, reassembling it, if it's fragmented, and checking it for any abnormal patterns. This process will help identify and then drop abnormal packets (for example orphan fragments). The single rule under the `scrub` section in our configuration sample indicates that all incoming packets on any interface should be passed through a scrub sanity check.

Queuing

This section contains necessary rules for managing traffic using the ALTQ framework.

Translation

The NAT (**nat**, **binat**) as well as redirection and port forwarding rules (**rdr**) are placed in this section. NAT is discussed later in this chapter.

Filter Rules

This is the most important part of the configuration file where most of the actual packet-filtering rules reside. All the lines starting with `block` and `pass` actions are placed under this section.

There are a number of things that you should remember while dealing with PF configuration. First of all, remember that unlike IPFW, in which the first matching rule wins, in PF, the last matching rule wins. This means that the packet is evaluated against rules and it would match different rules within the ruleset. But the last match is always taken into account, and the action specified by the last match is enforced. However, the `quick` keyword is an exception to the rule. When a packet matches a rule with a `quick` keyword, no more rules are evaluated and an action is enforced immediately.

Unlike the IPFW, that had an explicit `deny` or `pass` rule at the end of our ruleset, here we have the explicit rule at the beginning of the ruleset.

Each filter rule has an action and criteria that if a packet matches with the criteria, it will be processed with associated action:

```
pass  in  quick on $ext_if proto tcp from any to $ext_if port 22
```

This line from our configuration sample has a `pass` action for any packet that matches its criteria. The criteria states that the action should be enforced on packets coming inside (hence the `in` keyword) from outside, on the interface `fxp0` (extracted from `$ext_if` variable).Their layer4 protocol is TCP, layer4 destination is port 22, and their layer3 destination is the address that we have on `fxp0` interface. Once this criteria is met, the action is immediately enforced; hence the `quick` keyword. In case, there is no `quick` keyword in the rule, the packet is evaluated against all remaining rules until it reaches the end of ruleset.

Controlling PF

The `pfctl(8)` utility is the universal control utility for the PF firewall. It is used to communicate with PF driver to send commands or query for information.

You can disable PF filtering engine by running `pfctl -d` and enabling it by using the `pfctl -e` commands. This is useful when you want to temporarily disable your firewall.

You can also see the current PF configuration and statistics using the
`pfctl` command:

```
# pfctl -s rules

    No ALTQ support in kernel
    ALTQ related functions disabled
    scrub in all fragment reassemble
    pass out all flags S/SA keep state
    pass in log all flags S/SA keep state
    pass in quick on msk0 inet6 proto tcp from any to fe80::215:f2ff:
    fe6f:5468 port = ssh flags S/SA keep state
    pass out on msk0 proto tcp all flags S/SA keep state
    pass out on msk0 proto udp all keep state
    pass in on msk0 proto tcp from any to <truested> port = http flags S/
    SA keep state
    pass in on msk0 proto udp from any to <truested> port = http keep
    state
    pass out on msk0 inet from 192.168.0.0/24 to any flags S/SA keep state
    queue datacenter
    pass out on msk0 inet from 192.168.1.0/24 to any flags S/SA keep state
    queue sales
```

Using `-s` parameter, PF displays various information about the PF configuration.
The following table shows a list of keywords that are used in combination with
the `-s` flag:

Keyword	Description
nat	Displays NAT rules
queue	Displays Queue rules
rules	Displays filter rules
Anchors	Displays anchors
state	Displays contents of state table
Sources	Displays contents of source tracking table
info	Displays statistics for active rules
labels	Displays detailed per-rule statistics
timeouts	Displays time-out settings
memory	Displays memory limits
Tables	Displays list of currently loaded tables
osfp	Displays list of OS fingerprints database
Interfaces	Displays list of interfaces. Also displays verbose per-interface statistics when used with "-vv" parameter
all	Displays all above information except for interfaces and osfp

Network Address Translation using PF and IPFW

Different methods of NAT can be implemented using both PF and IPFW in FreeBSD. Several combinations are listed here:

- IPFW in conjunction with `natd(8)`
- IPFW and in-kernel NAT (libalias)
- built-in PF NAT

Prior to FreeBSD 7, there was no built-in support for NAT in IPFW. This is where `natd(8)` kicks in. IPFW can be used to `divert` raw traffic to `natd(8)` daemon, which is a network address translation daemon. IPFW cannot divert packets, unless necessary kernel options are enabled:

```
options          IPDIVERT
```

Adding this line to your kernel configuration enables your kernel to be able to divert raw IP packets to an external daemon, using the IPFW's `divert` rule:

```
# ipfw add divert natd ip from any to any via fxp0
```

Using this rule, `ipfw` redirects all `ip` traffic that is passing from the `fxp0` interface to `natd` daemon. The `natd` daemon then decides whether the packet should be translated or not, and then re-injects the packet into the network stack after processing.

The configuration for `natd` daemon is pretty straightforward. The daemon should be enabled from the `/etc/rc.conf` configuration file, as usual:

```
natd_enable="YES"
```

This basically enableas `natd(8)` daemon to start automatically, upon system boot. However, you should also tell `natd`, which interface is your public or WAN interface, so that `natd` uses the addresses on that interface for translation. This can be done using variables in the `/etc/rc.conf` file:

```
natd_interface="bge0"
natd_flags="-u -l"
```

This is a typical scenario where we have enabled `natd` and configured it to translate traffic to the address that is configured on interface `bge0`. There are also two important options we have configured along with `natd`. The first parameter, `-u`, tells `natd` to translate only the traffic, whose source address is an "unregistered" or basically RFC1918 (private) addresses. This is very useful in a typical NAT scenario, where you want to translate all traffic from private addresses to a public address. The other parameter we used is `-l` that logs some statistics to the `/var/log/alias.log` file.

As of FreeBSD 7, you can enable in-kernel NAT by adding appropriate options to the kernel configuration:

```
options         LIBALIAS
options         IPFIREWALL_NAT
```

Of course you also need to add other IPFW options to your kernel configuration to enable IPFW. By enabling this option, `ipfw` will be able to perform network address translation, without any help from external daemons such as `natd`. Now you can directly use ipfw's `nat` rule to perform any type of address translation.

Typical examples of `ipfw nat` rule look like the following commands:

```
# ipfw add nat 50 ip from any to any via fxp0
# ipfw nat 50 config if bge0 log unreg_only
```

This is equivalent to the previous example where we used `natd`. We added a `nat` rule that is applied on all `ip` traffic that is passing from interface `fxp0`. On the next line, we configured that `nat` is to translate all traffic from private addresses (hence `unreg_only` parameter) to the IP address that is configured on `bge0` (the `if bge0` parameter), and also `log` the statistics.

For more information about various options of `ipfw`'s built-in NAT functionality, it is recommended that you read `ipfw(8)` manual pages.

As noted earlier, `pf` can also be used for network address translation. PF has built-in address translation capability by design and there is no need for any external daemon or any special kernel configuration to enable PF NAT.

You should add only the necessary NAT configuration to your PF configuration file at `/etc/pf.conf`, under "translation" section. A typical PF NAT clause looks like the following code:

```
nat on fxp0 from 192.168.0.0/16 to any -> (bge0)
```

This rule simply does the same as in our previous scenario. Any traffic from a private address that we have specified manually will be translated to an `ip` address on the `bge0` interface. Please note the `bge0` in parentheses means that PF will detect and take care of IP address changes on `bge0` interface for translation.

Summary

FreeBSD's IPFW and PF firewalls let you turn your host into a complicated firewall with many features that are available on commercial grade firewall appliances. All you need to do is to get familiar with different configuration options of the firewall software of your choice, and start writing your firewall rules.

IPFW is the legacy firewall package having many features, and ease of configuration while PF is a newer firewall package with more features and better flexibility.

As a systems or network administration, having at least basic knowledge about any of these two firewall packages and their features, is a must.

13
Network Services—Internet Servers

FreeBSD is the operating system of choice for many enterprises as well as individuals, especially for running various types of internet services. In fact, many major service/content providers use FreeBSD as a reliable platform for their mission-critical applications.

A typical FreeBSD installation can be easily turned into an internet server with minimum effort. For example, you can set up a secure and reliable web server in a few minutes, thanks to FreeBSD's easy-to-use, yet powerful, package management system.

Whatever you might need to turn your system into, a powerful internet server is already available in the base system installation or in the ports/packages system.

In this chapter, we will quickly go through some important internet services and the way you can set them up on your FreeBSD system. These include the following:

- inetd daemon
- SSH
- NTP
- DNS
- FTP
- Mail
- Web
- Proxy

inetd Daemon

The internet "super-server" or `inetd` is a wrapper around various smaller network services. The `inetd(8)` utility listens to specified TCP or UDP ports. Once a connection for each port is detected, it will launch an appropriate daemon and handover the connection to that daemon. Once the connection is closed, the daemon is also closed.

This will be very useful for the smaller services, such as tftp, finger, and ftp, as they may not have a lot of requests, and consequently don't have to be loaded as a separate daemon. So, they can listen in the background for new requests. Instead, `inetd(8)` will play this role for these services and listen to as many ports, as specified. Rather than running multiple services, only one service (`inetd` daemon) will be loaded.

The `inetd` configuration file is located at `/etc/inetd.conf`, and it can be enabled by adding the following line to the `/etc/rc.conf` file:

```
inetd_enable=YES
```

The default configuration of `inetd` does not listen for any incoming connection. The configuration file contains sample configuration lines for popular services, but is commented out. Hence, you should uncomment any line, depending on the service you want to enable, and restart the `inetd` daemon.

For example, to enable FTP service on your host using `inetd`, you should uncomment the appropriate line (remove the # mark from the beginning of the line) in the `/etc/inetd.conf` file:

```
ftp     stream tcp   nowait root   /usr/libexec/ftpd      ftpd -l
```

You may have noticed that there are two lines for most of the services listed in the `inetd` configuration file. Each line specified in the `inetd` configuration file should listen to TCP (IPv4) or TCP6 (IPv6), if it is supported by the service, so that you can specify each service over IPv4 or IPv6, separately.

In the previous example, we enabled FTP service over TCP/IPv4. In order to reload the `inetd` configuration (if running), the following command should be issued:

```
# /etc/rc.d/inetd reload
```

You can verify the `inetd` services using the `sockstat(1)` utility as follows:

```
# sockstat -l | grep inetd
    root     inetd     797   5  tcp4   *:21              *:*
```

This shows that `inetd` is listening to TCP4 port 21 (which is FTP service).

In case you want to add a service to `inetd` that is not listed in the default configuration file, you can take any of the lines as a sample and modify it to suit your own daemon.

The first parameter in each line (in this case, **ftp**) is the service name. The service name is then looked up from the `/etc/services` file, to find out the actual port number that should be listened to. In this example, the second parameter, **stream,** specifies the socket type. A socket type can be one of `stream`, `dgram`, `raw`, `rdm`, or `seqpacket`. A typical service running on TCP uses `stream`, while UDP socket type is `dgram`. The third parameter in this example is protocol **tcp**. For UDP services, this parameter should be changed to `udp`.

 It is advisable to use `tcp4`, `udp4`, `tcp6`, `udp6`, `tcp46`, or `udp46` instead of `tcp` or `udp`, to specify whether a service should work on IPv4 or IPv6 (or both) protocol stacks.

The fourth parameter in each line (in this example, **nowait**) specifies whether `inetd` should wait for the server to exit before listening for new requests. Generally, services running on TCP protocol should use `nowait` and UDP should use the `wait` option.

As TCP is a connection-oriented protocol, `inetd` accepts the new connection request and passes the connection to the daemon. Once a new connection request is received, `inetd` launches a new instance of the daemon, and passes the connection to the daemon.

Unlike TCP, the UDP is connection-less and therefore the `wait` option is used.

The fifth parameter on the line (**root** in this example) is actually the user whom daemon will launch, with its privilege. You may have noticed that almost all sample services in the `inetd.conf` file will run with root privilege, which is not a good practice in the production environment.

 It is proposed that each daemon to run with a specific user having limited privilege (for example, only have permission on required files and directories), so that in case of any security breach, the scope of the damage will be limited to that specific service and related files and directories.

Finally the last parameter on the configuration line is the full path to the daemon program including the command line parameters (if applicable).

To have a quick look at a custom `inetd` service, the following example shows that `inetd` should listen to a port 69 UDP (`tftp` service), which is a `dgram` socket using root user privileges to run the `tftpd` binary at `/usr/libexec/tftpd` with appropriate parameters:

```
tftp    dgram   udp     wait    root    /usr/libexec/tftpd        tftpd
-l -s /tftpboot
```

tcpd

The `inetd` daemon does not give all the necessary controls over the service, such as an access list to control the access to each service, or log incoming connection attempts. The `tcpd(8)` utility introduces a method to control remote access to the daemons that are launched from `inetd`.

In fact, `tcpd(8)` is a wrapper that wraps around the daemon and checks incoming requests against access lists, and logs the connection attempt before actually passing the connection to the daemon. This is achieved by modifying appropriate lines in the `inetd.conf` file. The following example shows FTP daemon wrapped in a `tcpd` wrapper:

```
ftp     stream  tcp     nowait  root    /usr/libexec/tcpd       ftpd -l
```

Once an incoming request arrives for FTP service, `tcpd` will be invoked first. The `tcpd` wrapper looks in the `/etc/hosts.allow` file for a set of access rules. It will then reject or accept the request, based on the access list.

In this example, we modify the `hosts.allow` file to limit `ftp` access to specific subnets in our network. The default FTP related section in the `hosts.allow` file looks like the following code:

```
# Provide a small amount of protection for ftpd
ftpd : localhost : allow
#ftpd : .nice.guy.example.com : allow
#ftpd : .evil.cracker.example.com : deny
ftpd : ALL : allow
```

Note that the comments lines start with a # sign. The second line indicates that all connections to the `ftpd` daemon from the `localhost` should be allowed. The last line also allows access from any host (`ALL` keyword) to the `ftp` service.

Once a match is found, `tcpd` will not look for more rules in the file. So if you want to add a limiting rule to `ftp` section, it should be added before the explicit `allow` rule at the end of the section.

Now, to add a rule to limit FTP access to `192.168.50.0/27` subnet, the following line should be added:

```
ftpd : 192.168.50.0/27 : allow
```

You may want to comment out the other lines that permit the access to `ftpd`.

Looking at the `hosts.allow` file, you will find a few other examples for other services such as sendmail, fingerd, ypserv (NIS), etc. You may want to add your own service restrictions to the file, based on the `inetd.conf` definition.

You should also note that there are some lines starting with the `ALL` keyword that would be applied on any service. For example, the default `hosts.allow` file contains the following default line at the beginning of the file:

```
ALL : ALL : allow
```

This will permit connections from any source to any service. Once you add a customized rule to the file, you should comment out this line. Leaving this line uncommented on top of the file makes your further rules ineffective, as the `tcpd` matches this rule at the beginning of the file, and does not process further rules.

SSH

SSH service is used to manage your host securely over the network. However, SSH does more than just a secure shell protocol. It can be used to transfer files securely or tunnel (and encrypt) network traffic between two hosts using tunneling techniques.

FreeBSD 7 uses SSH tools and libraries that are based on OpenSSH 4.5. Most of the FreeBSD hosts are running the `sshd(8)` daemon. The daemon accepts incoming connection on port 22 TCP, authenticates the user against system's user database (the default behavior), and lets user in, if authentication succeeds (and user has a valid shell and `home` directory).

If `sshd` daemon is not enabled on the host, it can be enabled by adding the following line to the `/etc/rc.conf` file:

```
sshd_enable="YES"
```

The daemon can also be started manually by invoking the following command:

```
# /etc/rc.d/sshd start
```

Once the server is started, you can remotely log into the server using the ssh command:

```
# ssh joe@192.168.0.5
```

This will start a secure shell to host 192.168.0.5 using the username "joe".

 The ssh command will use your current system login name if the username is not specified.

Once you have authenticated with the destination host, basically using a password, you will get a shell prompt on an encrypted tunnel to the server.

This is the very basic usage of the ssh command. However, SSH offers many more features than just a simple shell connection.

Running a Command Remotely

If you want only to run a command on a remote host, and you do not need a fully functional shell, you can run that command using a single the ssh command.

```
# ssh 192.168.0.5 ps ax
```

The above example establishes a secure shell connection to host 192.168.0.5 and runs the command ps ax (that shows a list of currently running processes for all users) and then closes the secure shell connection to the server and returns to your local host's prompt.

There is no login information specified in the command prompt. In this case, SSH assumes that you want to use the username that you are currently logged on to your system with it. It also asks for a password, once the connection is established.

SSH Keys

Asking for a password during login is the default behavior of SSH. However, there are various authentication models than can be used in stead of passwords.

A widely used method is using the SSH keys, instead of a password. Using keys has some advantages over using password. Using keys is more secure as no one can look over your shoulder to find out what you are typing as a password, or run a brute-force attack on the SSH server to find out your password (if your account is not configured to using a password for login).

Another major advantage is that you do not have to enter your password every time you want to log into a remote server. So if you are using SSH frequently, you do not have to enter the password every time you log into a host.

To create a SSH public/private key pair on a FreeBSD host, the `ssh-keygen(1)` utility should be used as follows:

```
$ ssh-keygen
    Generating public/private rsa key pair.
    Enter file in which to save the key (/home/babak/.ssh/id_rsa):
    Created directory '/home/babak/.ssh'.
    Enter passphrase (empty for no passphrase):
    Enter same passphrase again:
    Your identification has been saved in /home/babak/.ssh/id_rsa.
    Your public key has been saved in /home/babak/.ssh/id_rsa.pub.
    The key fingerprint is:
    cc:73:cd:6f:9e:72:da:cd:54:ab:2f:f1:56:7c:b5:b2 babak@myhost
```

In the above example, simply running the `ssh-keygen` command starts creating a fresh pair of SSH public and private keys using the RSA encryption algorithm. Once the key is generated, it asks where it should save the private key file. The default file name is `id_rsa` and it is saved under the `.ssh` directory, in your `home` directory. You can change it if you want to save it under a different name or path. Otherwise, pressing enter will take the defaults.

You also have the choice to protect your key using a password, which is a very wise thing to do. If your keys are not protected, anyone can use these keys to log into your hosts without any restriction. Protecting keys with a password will reduce the risk of abusing the keys in case of key theft. The `ssh-keygen` utility asks whether you want to protect the private key through a password. You can enter a password (a strong password is suggested) or simply hit enter to bypass password protection.

Then it saves the public key under the same path that you've chosen, in the default name `id_rsa.pub`. It also shows your unique key fingerprint, which in this case is a 128-bit hexadecimal string.

You can verify the result by seeing your keys under the `.ssh` directory as follows:

```
$ ls -l .ssh/
    total 4
    -rw-------  1 babak   babak   1679 Nov  7 21:15 id_rsa
    -rw-r--r--  1 babak   babak    412 Nov  7 21:15 id_rsa.pub
```

The private key, `id_rsa`, has a default permission of 0600, which means that only the owner of the key can read or modify the key file. However, the public key, `id_rsa.pub`, is readable by all other users. In fact, you should safeguard your private keys, though you can freely distribute the public keys to be used on the other hosts.

In case you have lost your private key, or the key is stolen, you should remove all public keys that you have installed on your hosts, and replace it with your new public keys. Otherwise, the intruders can log into your system using the private key.

Losing your private key is just as if the intruder knows your password. So you should change your passwords (in this case, replacing or removing the related public key) on all the hosts where you have used the password (or public key).

Now that you have created your first set of keys, you should install the public key on the hosts that you want to log into. This can be achieved by transferring the public key to the destination host and adding it to the `authorized_keys` file.

```
# scp .ssh/id_rsa.pub 192.168.0.5:.ssh/
```

This will simply transfer the public key file to the destination host under the `.ssh` directory. However, this time you will be authenticated using password. Once the public key is transferred, you should add the key to the list of authorized keys that can log in to the account. This would be as simple as logging into the remote host and adding the file to the `authorized_keys` file under the `.ssh` directory.

```
# cd .ssh
# cat id_rsa.pub >> authorized_keys
```

Every time you start SSH for a secure shell connection, the SSH client looks for SSH private keys under the `.ssh` directory as well as the SSH key agent (This will be discussed later in this chapter). If a key is found, the SSH client tries to authenticate the session using the key. In case of success, you will log into the remote host. Otherwise SSH keeps trying other authentication methods, for example, a password.

If your key is protected using a password, you will be asked the password, once the key is loaded. If you are using SSH with keys frequently, it can be annoying to enter the same password every time you run the SSH client. The `ssh-agent(1)` utility will help in solving this issue by loading the keys into the memory, for future use.

SSH Authentication Agent

If you are a frequent SSH user (like every other system administrator), you will find `ssh-agent(1)` very useful. The main goal of `ssh-agent` is to load one or more private keys into the memory, so that the SSH client can use the keys from the agent. If the keys are password protected, you will be asked the password, once the key is loaded to the memory.

There may also be cases where you use multiple pairs of keys for authentication on different hosts. The ssh-agent utility will let you load multiple keys, and try using all keys while authenticating with a remote host.

 Since multiple users on a host may have their own ssh-agent process loaded, you may have multiple ssh-agent processes running on the same host. SSH client uses environment variables to figure out which ssh-agent it should use.

The ssh-agent utility does not set the appropriate environment variables upon start up by default, instead writes the variables on stdout. However, you can update environment variables using the eval command:

```
# eval `ssh-agent`

  Agent pid 82485
```

Now that the agent will run with PID 82485 (so that you can kill the agent when not needed) and the environment variables are set, the SSH client can communicate with the agent. The next step is to add one or more keys to the keychain, using ssh-add(1).

When you first run the ssh-add command, it looks for private keys in the default location (.ssh directory) and loads them into the memory, as shown here:

```
# ssh-add

  Identity added: /home/babak/.ssh/id_rsa (/home/babak/.ssh/id_rsa)
```

You can also add more keys to the keychain (if they are not installed in the default location) by specifying a private key file name as a parameter for the ssh-add command.

The operation can then be verified by listing the loaded keys, as shown here:

```
# ssh-add -l

  2048 cc:73:cd:6f:9e:72:da:cd:54:ab:2f:f1:56:7c:b5:b2 /home/babak/.ssh/
  id_rsa (RSA)
```

From now on, the SSH client uses keys from ssh-agent to authenticate with the remote hosts, as the first option.

SSH Tunneling or Port Forwarding

A SSH port forwarding tunnel can basically be considered an encrypted VPN connection that can be used to transfer data over a public network. The benefit of SSH tunneling is the ease of setup, and the lack of the need for a separate daemon. Hence, you can use your default SSH configuration to establish a secure tunnel to your server, or the network behind your server. Using SSH tunneling, you can transmit almost any protocol that uses TCP as transmission protocol over an encrypted SSH tunnel.

A SSH tunnel can be established in two modes — **Dynamic forwarding** and **Static forwarding**.

Dynamic forwarding is, in fact, turning your host into a SOCKS 4/5 proxy server and forwarding all network traffic from the proxy server to the destination host over a secure tunnel. This can be used to connect to a remote network through a firewall, like a VPN client into a private network.

The following example shows an example of SSH connection to a remote host with dynamic port forwarding:

```
# ssh -D 4567 -l babak 172.16.25.1
```

This example establishes an SSH connection to the host 172.16.25.1 with username "babak". It also listens on TCP port 4567 on localhost, and acts as a SOCKS proxy server and forwards traffic to the destination host over the secure connection.

Now you should configure your application (for example web browser) to use your SOCKS proxy on the localhost port 4567. Please note that you can use any other unused port number on your host for the proxy server to listen on.

This method can also be used to get through restrictive firewalls and access public internet without restrictions, by tunneling traffic over a secure SSH tunnel to an external host that runs the SSH server.

Static port forwarding offers much simpler methods compared to dynamic port forwarding for simple scenarios in which you want to forward traffic to one specific application on another host. An example is forwarding traffic from your host to your remote SMTP server, over a secure SSH tunnel.

In this example, SSH listens to the port 4425 on local host and forwards any connection on this port to host the mail.example.org port TCP 25 via secure SSH tunnel that is established to remote SSH server on 172.16.25.1 as shown here:

```
# ssh -L 4425:mail.example.org:25 172.16.25.1
```

Using this method, the SMTP traffic will be forwarded from your host to your remote shell server securely. However, the connection from the shell server to the ultimate destination (SMTP server on `mail.example.org` in this example) may not be secure.

NTP

Keeping time in sync, has more importance than people realize. For example a server that sends event logs to another server, using `syslog` protocol, should be in sync with each other. Otherwise, the log time will differ from the time,when the event actually happened. Alternatively a caching web proxy will not remove the expired cached objects correctly, as it relies on the server's date and time while looking for the `expire` field in the http header.

The solution for having server times in sync (beside correcting date and time manually) is the Network Time Protocol (NTP, as per RFC 1305).

Before trying to synchronize your clock using NTP protocol, make sure you have set the correct time zone. To modify the current time zone, use `tzsetup(8)`.

Syncing

Synchronizing system time to an ntp server can be done manually using the `ntpdate(8)` utility. The `ntpdate(8)` needs an ntp server name to synchronize with:

```
# ntpdate pool.ntp.org

    Looking for host pool.ntp.org and service ntp
    host found : ferret.eicat.ca
     9 Nov 00:15:41 ntpdate[72515]: step time server 66.96.30.91 offset
    138.608584 sec
```

There are plenty of public NTP servers available (see: `www.ntp.org`). However, it is suggested that you use `pool.ntp.org`, as it actually balances the load between a large pools of NTP servers.

You can also have the system run `ntpdate` automatically during boot up process, by adding the following variable to the `rc.conf` file:

```
ntpdate_enable="YES"
```

However, your server may get out of sync because you are unlikely to reboot your servers frequently. The ntpd(8) utility does this by running as a daemon in the background and keeping time synchronized with the servers that you have specified. The ntpd daemon also acts as the NTP server that can be used as a clock reference for your local hosts.

NTP Server

Running ntpd(8) can be very useful for keeping local time in sync, as well as serving as an accurate clock for other hosts in your network. Configuring ntpd is as easy as setting up the configuration file located at /etc/ntp.conf and starting the ntp daemon (which is already included in the base system).

A default ntp.conf file does not come with the default installation and it should be created from scratch. The configuration should consist of the definitions for one or more servers, as well as a drift file address, as shown here:

```
server pool.ntp.org prefer
server ntp0.nl.uu.net
server clock.isc.org
driftfile /var/db/ntp.drift
```

The configuration, above, has introduced three servers (to make sure you always have accurate time), and marked the first server as prefer. The drift file is the file that ntpd keeps the calculated drift value in. So it knows the drift value across server restarts.

The server can then be enabled by adding the following line to the rc.conf file:

```
ntpd_enable="YES"
```

 It may take a few minutes before your ntp server shows accurate time. This can be verified by querying the server using the ntpq(8) utility.

To view the current status of the ntpd (running on the same server), you may use ntpq(8):

```
# ntpq -c rv
    status=06d4 leap_none, sync_ntp, 13 events, event_peer/strat_chg,
    version="ntpd 4.2.0-a Mon Jul 16 09:19:35 BST 2007 (1)",
    processor="i386", system="FreeBSD/7.0-STABLE", leap=00, stratum=2,
    precision=-19, rootdelay=343.773, rootdispersion=290.834, peer=55622,
    refid=192.43.244.18,
    reftime=cade029c.cad8daf3  Fri, Nov  9 2007  1:18:12.792, poll=10,
    clock=cade0320.d6d74a76  Fri, Nov  9 2007  1:20:24.839, state=4,
    offset=51.066, frequency=25.407, jitter=16.671, stability=0.738
```

Once the host is synchronized, the stratum value shows a real value (below 15) that is actually the number of ntp servers between you and the accurate clock (atomic, gps, or other type of radio clocks). In this case, the stratum 2 means that our uplink ntp host, which is a stratum 1 device, is directly connected to an accurate reference clock. If the ntpd is out of sync, you will see stratum 16. Please see ntpq(8) manual page for more information on querying from an ntp server.

DNS

Domain Name System (DNS) defined by RFC 1035 (and many other RFCs that introduce enhancements and extensions), is one of the protocols that is gluing the whole internet together, and makes life easier by mapping names to hard-to-remember IP addresses. Despite looking simple, DNS has evolved since its invention back in 1983, and is getting more and more complex every day.

Today's DNS servers are even able to map telephone numbers using the ENUM extension (RFC 3401 through 3404). As the DNS protocols evolves, the DNS related software are also getting more and more complicated, facing more performance and security challenges.

BIND software

FreeBSD 7 bundles ISC's BIND version 9.4.1 with the base system. BIND (or named(8) which is the actual daemon name) offers various modes of operations.

There are also older versions of BIND still being used (8.x and 4.x). But the 9.4 series offers the latest performance and security enhancements as well as support for IPv6 and DNSSEC.

If you are interested in running older versions or modified versions of BIND, you can install them using ports system under the /usr/ports/dns directory.

Operating Modes

BIND can be used in two modes—Authoritative and Caching forwarder.

Authoritative: In this mode, BIND has the mapping information in the zone files on the disk, and answers queries based on the locally stored zone information.

Caching forwarder: In this mode, BIND does not have any name to address mapping information locally, and it forwards DNS requests to specified upstream DNS servers (or root DNS servers) to find out the answer, and caches the answer after sending the response to the client.

[　💡　While it is possible to run the DNS server in a mixed mode (authoritative and forwarding simultaneously), it is not advisable to do so.　]

Forwarding/Caching DNS Server

This is the case that is used on a LAN or service provider environment to provide users with faster DNS responses and lower upstream network overhead.

To set up a DNS forwarder on FreeBSD 7, first, you need to enable BIND by adding the following variable to the /etc/rc.conf file as shown here:

```
named_enable="YES"
```

And start the server manually, as shown here:

 # /etc/rc.d/named start

Since you have not defined any zone information, the server is running in forwarding mode. By default, the server listens on localhost (127.0.0.1) so that the clients on your network will not be able to communicate with the server. You need to edit the bind configuration file located at /etc/namedb/named.conf to remove this restriction. You can comment out the following line to completely disable this restriction, or modify it based on your network configuration to have the named(8) daemon listen on the IP address you have specified:

```
listen-on        { 127.0.0.1; };
```

Once you have removed or modified the configuration, you should restart the named(8) daemon for changes take effect:

 # /etc/rc.d/named restart

In this mode, the named daemon contacts the ROOT DNS servers (as defined in /etc/namedb/named.root file) and then other DNS servers, recursively, to resolve incoming requests, and caches the results for later reference. This can slow things down although you always get the authoritative and accurate result.

There is another option, whereby you can forward DNS requests to one or more specific upstream DNS servers instead of resolving the DNS information from the root servers. This can be done by specifying `forwarders` under the `options` clause in the `named.conf` configuration files, as shown:

```
forwarders
{
        10.3.25.2;
        10.3.1.10;
};
```

This will tell the `named` daemon to try forwarding the requests to these servers first. If it is unable to get the result from these servers, it will initiate a new query to the root servers. However, you can also disable this second part (asking root servers) by adding the following line (under the options clause) to the `named.conf` file:

```
forward    only;
```

In this case, if the forwarders you specified are unable to resolve the query, it will fail.

There may be times when you would need to flush the DNS cache, for example, to get rid of some stale data that are cached in the DNS cache. This can be achieved using the `rndc(8)` utility as follows:

```
# rndc flush
```

Authoritative

Running an authoritative DNS server is similar to running forwarder setup, except in that you would have to set up your DNS zone files, and then modify the `named.conf` file to answer the specific domain information for the zone files you have specified.

A typical forward DNS (Hostname to IP address mapping) `named.conf` file looks like this:

```
options
{
   directory "/etc/namedb"; // Working directory
   allow-query-cache { none; }; // Do not allow access to cache
   recursion no; // Do not provide recursive service
};
zone "example.com"
{
   type master;
   file "master/example.com.db";
   allow-transfer
```

```
        {
            192.168.14.2;
            192.168.15.2;
        };
    };
```

This configuration disables recursion. So if the request is not resolved using the local zone files, it will fail. Also a zone definition for the domain, `example.com`, is defined. This server acts as the "master" server for the domain. The zone file is located at `/etc/namedb/master/example.com.db` and the server allows two hosts (as defined under the `allow-transfer` clause) to transfer the whole zone, which in a typical case plays the slave server role.

It is recommended that you store the zone files for the domains that are hosted as master under the `master` subdirectory, and use the `slave` directory if the host acts as slave server for the domain. In this example, the file `example.com.db` contains definitions for the `example.com` domain, and is stored under the `master` directory:

```
$TTL 24h ;

$ORIGIN example.com.;

    @         IN      SOA       ns1.example.com. noc.example.com. (
                                2007102001         ; serial
                                12h                ; refresh
                                15m                ; update retry
                                3w                 ; expiry
                                3h                 ; minimum
                                )
              IN      NS        ns1.example.com.
              IN      NS        ns2.example.com.
              IN      A         192.168.25.1
              IN      MX        10 mail
    ftp                         IN      CNAME     example.com.
    www                         IN      CNAME     example.com.
    mail                        IN      A         192.168.25.10
    ns1               IN      A         192.168.25.1
    ns2               IN      A         192.168.14.2
    portal            IN      A         192.168.25.7
    cvs               IN      A         192.168.25.9
```

This zone file contains basic information about the domain `example.com`, including TTL and other DNS related information, as well as host to IP mapping under this zone.

Monitoring

While setting up a basic DNS server (either caching/forwarding or authoritative) is quite simple, monitoring the performance and health of a DNS server could be somewhat tricky. Luckily, there are some fine tools available in the ports tree under the `/usr/ports/dns` directory. However, we start with some BIND tools that would help.

The BIND's built-in `rndc(8)` is very helpful in extracting status information from a running named process.

```
# rndc status
    number of zones: 3
    debug level: 0
    xfers running: 0
    xfers deferred: 0
    soa queries in progress: 0
    query logging is OFF
    recursive clients: 93/2500
    tcp clients: 0/100
    server is up and running
```

The status shows various counter values, which in turn show a number of in-process queries, which would be helpful in measuring the load of a running server.

The `dnstop(8)` utility is also very useful in monitoring DNS activity in a live environment. `dnstop` can be installed from ports under `/usr/ports/dns/dnstop`. This utility actually captures DNS traffic information from the specified network interface, and shows live statistics of the DNS queries on various parameters, such as source address, destination address, and queried address with different levels of details.

Optimizations

While running a DNS server under load, your server should deal with plenty of small UDP packets, which may sometimes be several hundreds or thousands per second. Your entire setup should be configured in such a way that your server picks up the packet from the NIC, and passes it to upper levels in the network stack, right up to the DNS server. DNS server should also process the packet and return a response back to the lower levels of network stack and finally to your NIC for further transmission over the wire, in the shortest possible time.

This can be achieved by optimizing network stack and DNS server software to minimize the processing delay.

To achieve a better rate of packet pick up from NIC, you should enable POLLING feature on your network interface (please refer to Chapter 6 for more information).

The default configuration for BIND should be sufficient for most deployments. However, there may be cases when you may need to tweak the configuration to get the most out of your name server. This would involve configuring zone-transfer parameters carefully, if you are running an authoritative name server, in addition to tweaking TTL and concurrent queries limitation on forwarding/recursive name servers.

An example setup for a high performance recursive name server is as follows:

```
options
{
        directory        "/etc/namedb";
        pid-file         "/var/run/named/pid";
        dump-file        "/var/dump/named_dump.db";
        statistics-file "/var/stats/named.stats";
        recursion        yes;
        max-ncache-ttl   120;
        max-cache-ttl    7200;
        version          "Geronimo!";
        allow-transfer   {"none";};
        listen-on-v6 { none; };
        notify           no;
        recursive-clients        5000;
        minimal-responses        yes;
        interface-interval       0;
};
```

This is the configuration for a recursive name server than can serve up to a maximum 5000 recursive clients, simultaneously (default in BIND is 1000) and serves only IPv4 clients.

While this forwarding DNS server caches all responses it receives from upstream (including negative responses), you can also tweak the cache aging. This example caches the negative responses for 120 seconds and positive responses for 7200 seconds (2 hours).

ISC BIND is a complicated name server. It is recommended that you read through the documentation of the version you are currently using, or refer to related books for more detailed information about the functionality and performance tuning.

FTP

Since SFTP (from SSH toolset) is meant to be a secure replacement for FTP protocol, FTP protocol is used for different purposes. As FTP does not encrypt or compress data on the fly, it offers superior performance over the SFTP.

Like other core services, FreeBSD has its own ftpd(8) daemon included in the base system. The ftpd daemon can simply be enabled from the inetd daemon, which is suitable for a system with a somewhat low FTP traffic. However, you can run the ftpd in the stand-alone mode, in which the ftpd daemon will run in the background and answers FTP requests.

 If you are setting up a busy FTP server, it is not advisable to run ftpd from inetd, which may reduce performance of the system with many FTP requests, or many simultaneous FTP users.

Adding the following line to the /etc/rc.conf file enables ftpd(8):

```
ftpd_enable="YES"
```

You should then start the ftpd by running the appropriate rc script:

```
# /etc/rc.d/ftpd start
```

Now you are set. The ftpd daemon is listening for incoming connections on TCP port 21, and authenticates users against the system's local passwd scheme, which means that you can log into the FTP server, using your system logins. Users will be directed to their own home directory when they log into the FTP server. Moreover, the same disk access permissions apply to the FTP users. In fact, the ftpd process forks a new ftpd process with the logged in user's permission, and has the same access restriction.

Anonymous FTP Server

An FTP server can also be used as a public file repository for public masses that do not require an individual login access to the system. This is the case where "anonymous ftp access" pops out. An anonymous FTP access lets people download files from the FTP server, or upload to specific directories on the server. Users should log into the FTP user using the username "anonymous" and their email address as the password (which can be ignored).

To enable an anonymous- only FTP access, you should add the following parameter to the rc.conf file:

```
ftpd_flags="-A"
```

And restart the running ftpd daemon.

The next step is to create a special user in the host system, named "ftp". FTP daemon uses this user (actually forks with this user's permission) when an anonymous user logs in. The home directory of this user will also be used as the root directory of the FTP server.

```
# adduser
    Username: ftp
    Full name: Anonymous FTP user
    Uid (Leave empty for default):
    Login group [ftp]:
    Login group is ftp. Invite ftp into other groups? []:
    Login class [default]:
    Shell (sh csh tcsh bash rbash zsh nologin) [sh]: nologin
    Home directory [/home/ftp]:
    Use password-based authentication? [yes]: no
    Lock out the account after creation? [no]:
    Username    : ftp
    Password    : <disabled>
    Full Name   : Anonymous FTP user
    Uid         : 1020
    Class       :
    Groups      : ftp
    Home        : /home/ftp
    Shell       : /usr/sbin/nologin
    Locked      : no
    OK? (yes/no): yes
    adduser: INFO: Successfully added (ftp) to the user database.
    Add another user? (yes/no): no
    Goodbye!
```

The user is now created. There are two important points to be noted here. The first is the shell which is set to nologin so that people cannot gain shell access to the system through this user. The second is the home directory location, which in this example is set to /home/ftp, but you may change this according to your specific system setup.

Now the system has copied some default configuration file into the home directory that you do not need. You should also create a standard directory hierarchy under the FTP home directory, which consists of the etc and pub directories and also an optional incoming directory. The etc subdirectory holds some configuration files, while the pub directory hosts the server content that should be available to anonymous users. The optional incoming directory is a place to which anonymous users have write permission and can upload their files. This directory is used in special cases.

You should also fix the permissions on the directory hierarchy in such a way that anonymous users have read-only access to `etc` and `pub` directory, and write permission on the `incoming` directory.

```
# cd ~ftp
# rm .*
# mkdir etc pub incoming
# chown -R root:wheel /home/ftp
# chmod 755 etc pub
# chown -R nobody incoming
# chmod 5777 incoming
```

And this is finally how the directory structure should look like (note the owners and permissions):

```
# ls -l
   total 6
   drwxr-xr-x  2 root    wheel  512 Nov  9 13:02 etc
   drwsrwxrwt  2 nobody  wheel  512 Nov  9 13:01 incoming
   drwxr-xr-x  2 root    wheel  512 Nov  9 12:38 pub
```

So the anonymous user (actually the "ftp" user that you have created earlier) has read-only access to the `pub` directory (according to file permissions), and also write permission on the `incoming` directory. However, the files written in the incoming directory cannot be removed or modified by anonymous users later on.

 Always make sure that the files have correct permission (owner and mod) under the FTP directory hierarchy to prevent security breaches.

Mail

The Mail Transfer Agent (MTA) is the daemon in charge of transferring electronic mails from one host to another, using the SMTP protocol (RFC 2821 and many other complementary RFCs). Just like other core Internet services, FreeBSD 7 has Sendmail 8.14.1 bundled in the base system. Sendmail is one of the oldest and widely used MTAs and is the default MTA on most of the UNIX based operating systems. Besides sendmail, there are other MTAs available, such as Postfix and Qmail, that have even more advanced features, security and robustness. However the system administrators can choose any MTA that suits their specific applications.

If you are not running a complicated mail server, you may stick with the default sendmail for your daily mail transfer use.

We will also look into Postfix (which is also another widely used and a slightly more advanced MTA), later in this chapter.

Sendmail

Chances are that the default sendmail from the base system is the latest and the most stable sendmail distribution for your current installation. However, the sendmail in the base system is not updated frequently. Hence, if you feel that you may want to use a newer version of the sendmail for any reason, you can find the latest version in the ports under the `/usr/ports/mail/sendmail` directory.

The `sendmail` program can operate in various modes — from a fully loaded MTA that accepts mail from other hosts and routes mails to their destinations, to a minimal configuration that lets local mails be submitted.

To completely enable sendmail, you can use the following lines in the `/etc/rc.conf` file:

```
sendmail_enable="YES"
```

And then start the sendmail by calling its rc script as shown here:

```
# /etc/rc.d/sendmail start
```

This will start the sendmail process that listens on all active network interfaces on TCP port 25, for incoming SMTP requests.

If you do not want to enable sendmail to receive incoming emails over the network, you can modify the `rc.conf` file as shown here:

```
sendmail_enable="NO"
```

Note that this will not actually disable the sendmail. After restarting the process, you will find the sendmail process still running and listening only for SMTP traffic (TCP port 25) on the loopback interface (127.0.0.1). So it will not be able to actually receive emails over the network, and only accepts SMTP connection from the `localhost` on the loopback interface, and routes the local mail to their destination.

If you want to completely disable sendmail, you should modify the `rc.conf` file as shown here:

```
senmail_enable="NONE"
```

Note the NONE keyword, which will completely disable the sendmail process. You should therefore use SMTP servers on the other hosts on the network, if you want to transmit emails.

Once the sendmail process is enabled, it works out of the box in simple scenarios such as routing mails for local users. The sendmail related configuration files are located in the /etc/mail/ subdirectory.

> The sendmail configuration files may seem somewhat bizarre to you, as they are extremely different from the configuration files that you have seen in other parts of the system. This is because the configuration is based on the m4 "macro language processor".

The most important files that you may need to modify in your configuration are aliases, local-host-names, and virtusertable.

The aliases file contains the email address aliases that would be used to redirect emails to the local users. An example of aliases files looks like this:

```
root: babak
postmaster: mail-admins@example.org
bit-bucket: /dev/null
msgs: "| /usr/bin/msgs -s"
```

This example shows the incoming mail messages for specific users being delivered to another local user, remote user, a file, or being piped to a program.

> Once you have modified the aliases file, you should run the newaliases(1) command to update the aliases database.

The sendmail program uses the current hostname to figure out whether the incoming email messages belong to this host, or they should be forwarded to another host (or rejected).

In case the actual hostname is different from the host name that you want to receive mails for, or if you want to receive email for multiple hosts, the hostnames should be specified (one hostname per line) in the /etc/mail/local-host-names file:

```
example.com
mail.example.com
host.example.com
```

This will tell sendmail to receive and deliver emails to local users if the destination address matches any of the listed addresses in this file.

There may also be some cases, where you do not have a system user entry for the email addresses. You can specify virtual email addresses and map them to local system accounts. This can also enable a method called **catchall** that catches all email addresses destined for a specific domain name, and delivers it to the user you have specified:

```
postmaster@example.com          postmaster
root@example.com                root
@example.com                    exampleuser
```

This example shows that emails sent to `postmaster@example.com` and `root@example.com` should be delivered to the equivalent local system users. However, any other emails destined for an address under the `example.com` domain should be delivered to `exampleuser`, which is a local user (or could be an alias too).

Postfix

Postfix is a serious alternative to sendmail, which is widely being used as a full-featured MTA. The major advantages that postfix has over sendmail are modularity (as compared to sendmail's monolithic design) and simplicity (as compared to sendmail's complicated configuration). However, this is a matter of system administrator's choice to use whichever MTA, he or she wishes.

Postfix is not available in the base system. Therefore the latest version should be installed from ports system under `/usr/ports/mail/postfix`.

Once installed, postfix will completely replace the sendmail. It even replaces the sendmail binaries with its own binaries, to maintain compatibility with applications that call sendmail binaries directly by updating the `/etc/mail/mailer.conf` file.

After the postfix is installed, it should be activated by adding appropriate variables in the `rc.conf` configuration file:

```
postfix_enable="YES"
```

And start the postfix by running its rc script:

```
# /usr/local/etc/rc.d/postfix start
```

> **Note:**
> Make sure you have completely disabled sendmail before activating postfix.

Postfix configuration files are located under `/usr/local/etc/postfix`. Unlike sendmail, the postfix configuration files are more readable and have clear inline documentation, so that you can easily tweak the configuration values and start using your MTA. However, for a simple mail routing scenario, postfix will work out of the box.

There are two main configuration files that you will want to have a look into—the `main.cf` file and the `master.cf` file. The `main.cf` file contains main configuration parameters such as queue locations, hostname, and permissions.

At least you may want to modify `myhostname` and `mydomain` variables with your own information, so that postfix is able to receive your incoming emails. You should also set up postfix to know your internal network in order to relay messages correctly. You can do this by restricting the subnets that can transmit outgoing emails.

Another configuration that you may want to look at, is the `master.cf` file that controls the behavior of postfix's master process. Here, you can configure various modules. For example, you can configure a module to enable TLS or interface with other third-party services, such as mailman for running mailing lists.

Web

FreeBSD has proven to be a reliable and high-performance platform for running HTTP service. Millions of websites (Including Yahoo!, NYI, and Pair.com) are relying on FreeBSD to run their web hosting solution (as well as other services of course).

The `httpd` daemon from Apache Project (also known as Apache Web Server) is the de facto standard for hosting websites using HTTP and HTTPS protocols.

Despite the fact that `httpd` is the dominant web server of Internet, there are also other lightweight and robust alternatives that are available to `httpd`. A good example is `lighttpd`, which offers less complexity and more flexibility in some cases.

This section discusses setting up basic web servers using apache `httpd` and `lighttpd` web servers.

Both of the mentioned web servers (among many others) are available in ports tree under the `/usr/ports/www` subdirectory.

Apache

There are various versions of apache web server available under ports tree. The www/apache13 directory contains Apache 1.3 which is the legacy and stable version of apache web server. The newer versions are 2.0 (www/apache20 directory), 2.1 (www/apache21 directory), and 2.2 (www/apache22 directory). Apache 2.0 is the current stable version that introduces many improvements over the previous version as well as a revised and modular configuration system. Newer versions (2.1 and 2.2) are offering cutting-edge features but they are still under development and are not recommended for use in a production environment. If you are deploying apache in a production environment, you may want to choose between Apache 1.3 or Apache 2.0.

 It is actually a matter of taste when it comes to choosing the right version of the apache web server. You are most likely to go for a newer stable version, unless you need an old application, which is not compatible with newer version of web server.

Once you have installed your favorite apache web server from ports, you should enable the daemon in the rc.conf file. Different versions of apache have different variable names. You should find which variable you should set, by running the appropriate rc script. For example:

```
# /usr/local/etc/rc.d/apache2 rcvar
    apache2_enable=NO
```

Then add the appropriate variable to rc.conf as usual:

```
    apache2_enable="YES"
```

Apache stores configuration files under /usr/local/etc/apache. (This may vary slightly in different versions; for example apache 2.0 looks in /usr/local/etc/apache2 and so on.) Moreover, it looks for web pages under /usr/local/www/data. (This would also vary across different apache versions; for example apache 2.2 looks for /usr/local/www/apache22.) Usually, this directory is symlinked to the data-dist directory that contains default web pages. It is suggested that you create your own subdirectory and symlink "data" to your own directory, keeping data-dist intact.

 It is not advisable to use the default data-dist directory, as it may not be preserved across upgrades and your files may be overwritten. It is recommended that you create your own directory and symlink "data" to it.

```
# cd /usr/local/www
# mkdir homepage
```

```
# rm data
```

```
# ln -s homepage data
```

You may want to have a look into the default apache configuration file located under `/usr/local/etc/apache` (or similar name, depending on your installation) to tweak configuration parameters.

Virtual Hosts

Apache can handle name-based virtual hosting, that lets you run multiple sites on the same IP address, but differentiate them based on their hostnames. You should configure your DNS zone files in such a way that they point (for example www host) to the IP address of your web server. You should also configure your apache web server to the server-specified directory as the home page of the specified host.

To enable name-based virtual hosting, you should first modify your `httpd.conf` file and uncomment the following line:

```
NameVirtualHost *:80
```

This will enable the functionality. Now you should add appropriate configuration clauses, for each host, to your configuration file. In this example, we have used Apache 2.0 that supports the external configuration files into `httpd.conf`. Hence, you will not need to modify the `httpd.conf` file for each virtual host. Instead you can create a file, for example, `example.com.conf`, under the `Includes` directory which is under your apache configuration directory. Apache will automatically include all files with a `.conf` extension from the `Includes` directory and append it to the main configuration, during startup. The sample configuration file (for example `/usr/local/etc/apache2/Includes/example.com.conf`) looks like this:

```
<VirtualHost *:80>
    ServerAdmin admin@example.com
    DocumentRoot /usr/local/www/example.com
    ServerName www.example.com
    ServerAlias example.com
    ErrorLog /var/log/example.com-error_log
    CustomLog /var/log/example.com-access_log common
</VirtualHost>
```

As the example configuration suggests, this virtual host configuration will catch all the requests for www.example.org (note the ServerName directive) and also example.com (note the ServerAlias directive, and you can define as many alias names as necessary), from incoming http request headers. Moreover, it serves web pages from /usr/local/www/example.com directory for these requests. The ErrorLog and CustomLog directives specify the error log file and the access log file respectively. The email address specified in front of the ServerAdmin directive will also be shown under the error messages.

Alternative HTTP Servers

While Apache HTTPD server is very popular and widely used, you may want to use other lighter and faster alternatives instead. The reason you may want to choose an alternative to apache web server, is the fact that apache is complex and loaded with different modules and features that would slow things down. Luckily, there are plenty of alternative HTTP servers available via FreeBSD's ports tree that would suite your needs better than the apache web server.

The lighttpd (www/lighttpd under ports directory) server is a lightweight and fast HTTP server. Compared to Apache, it uses much less system resources. The lighttpd server is designed with performance in mind, avoiding Apache's performance bottlenecks and pre-fork model.

It runs as a multi-threaded single process and can serve thousands of sessions simultaneously with minimum processor and memory usage.

Another alternative web server is nginx (available in ports tree as www/nignx). Besides being a high performance and lightweight web server, nignx is also a HTTP and email reverse-proxy server. Just as lighttpd, nignx also serves static content, very fast.

Proxy

A web proxy server is a gateway that receives HTTP requests from the hosts and forwards the request to the destination (perhaps some host on Internet), and relays the answer back to the original requester. HTTP Proxy servers are mostly used as Internet access gateways to bring web access to the users in a campus LAN, while having the ability to control, restrict, and cache the requests.

A very well-known and popular HTTP proxy software is the open-source Squid project. Squid offers high performance web proxy function as well as content caching, in order to improve the web browsing experience. It can also be used to enforce restriction policies, such as time restriction, bandwidth control, and content filtering.

Luckily, Squid is available in FreeBSD ports tree and is ported very well to integrate into the system, and work in conjunction with FreeBSD firewall packages such as `pf` and `ipfw`, where needed.

Squid can be installed from the `/usr/ports/www/squid` port directory, and should be activated in the `rc.conf` file by adding the following variable to the file:

```
squid_enable="YES"
```

Squid requires a little bit of configuration before we actually start its service. First of all you should specify a few things, such as the location of the cache directory (where the cache objects will be stored), its size, and the number of directories. You should also specify a few restriction rules such as the IP address of the clients, in order to restrict web proxy access (unless you want to run a public proxy server).

Squid configuration file can be found under the `/usr/local/etc/squid/` directory called `squid.conf`.

 Squid has a large and complicated configuration file with too many options which you may want to tweak. However, the configuration file is full of samples and explanations on how to use each setting options.

To configure the cache directory, find the `cache_dir` directive and modify it with your desired configuration. The default `cache_dir` directive looks like this:

```
cache_dir ufs /usr/local/squid/cache 100 16 256
```

The `cache_dir` store type specified in the above example is `ufs`, which is the default storage scheme. The other store types are `aufs` and `diskd`. The `aufs` store type is an asynchronous/multi-threaded `ufs` scheme. And `diskd` is the same as `ufs`, except for the fact that it is forked as one or more separate processes, to avoid blocking of the squid process in disk access.

The second parameter is the location of the cache directory. This is where the cached objects are being stored. You may want to use a separate physical disk for this, depending on the load.

The next parameter to consider, after the directory location, is the cache directory. Its maximum size is set to 100 megabytes by this configuration. Make sure you have enough storage, before increasing this number to a bigger value as your cache directory may increase very quickly, and fill up your disk space. Increasing the cache directory size should be done with care. Larger cache disk space does not always mean better performance, as this may have a huge overhead on your disk.

And the 'last' two parameters to consider are the number of first-level and second-level directories that will be created under the cache directory, to hold the cached objects. This configuration creates 16 directories under the cache directory and also creates 256 directories under each of these 16 directories, which will run into a total 4096 directories. Each directory holds 256 files that total up to more than a million files that can be stored according to our configuration.

Now that you have finished configuring disk parameters, you should initialize the cache directory for the first time by running the `squid -z` command. It will take a few seconds to set up the whole cache directory and the necessary database files for the first time.

Now you are set to start the squid for the first time:

```
# /usr/local/etc/rc.d/squid start
```

This will start the squid process. Squid listens on TCP port 3128 for incoming requests so that you can set up your client's web browser's proxy configuration to send their http requests port 3128 of your host.

However, Squid's default policies restrict all requests from other hosts for security reasons. You should set up an access-list in the `squid.conf` file and specify your trusted networks that the Squid should accept requests from. The Squid configuration file already has a fine set of examples on setting up access-lists with different parameters. A simple example of restricting access to a few subnets would look like this:

```
acl our_networks src 192.168.21.0/24 10.1.2.0/23
http_access allow our_networks
http_access deny all
```

This example shows how to restrict HTTP service access to a few subnets, and deny all other requests coming from other source addresses.

Squid can also restrict access based on a few other parameters, such as time-based restrictions, TCP port numbers, and regular expressions in URLs. It can also authenticate users to give different access-levels.

Summary

FreeBSD can be used as a powerful server platform to host any kind of service you need to run an internet server (for example WWW, DNS, FTP, and Mail). Some of the services are already in the base system, while others can be easily installed from ports system. The only thing you need to do is to modify some basic configuration parameters for each service and start the service application. In most cases, the application comes with a default configuration template that mostly fits your basic needs. However, for a high performance and secure setup, you need to spend some time to get more familiar with the configuration of each specific application, and tweak the configuration to suit your environment.

14
Network Services—Local Network Services

While FreeBSD offers a rock solid platform for running network services, it is not only about Internet services. There are also some network services that are designed and being used mostly on the local area networks. Such services include DHCP, NFS, NIS, Printer Sharing, SMB (Windows File Sharing), and so on. There are also a few protocols that a system/network administrator have to deal with frequently, such as TFTP and SNMP.

As you may have guessed already, some parts of the mentioned services are already included in the core FreeBSD system. They do not need to be installed separately, while a few others should be installed from the ports system.

This chapter introduces the mentioned services and a brief introduction of setting up these services in FreeBSD, as well as some tips to getting the most out of them quickly and effectively.

In this chapter, we will look at the following:

- Dynamic host configuration protocol
- Trivial File Transfer Protocol
- Network File System
- Server Message Block/CIFS
- Simple Network Management Protocol
- Printing
- Network Information System (yellow pages).

Dynamic Host Configuration Protocol (DHCP)

In the simplest form, DHCP (as per RFC2131) introduces a method for network devices to obtain network configuration parameters from a centralized server. The obtained information can be the IP address, subnet mask, default router, DNS, or even information required for remote booting.

dhclient

FreeBSD comes with built-in DHCP client called `dhclient(8)`. Once it is executed, it attaches to the specified network interface and goes to daemon mode (runs as a background process). Dhclient then takes care of discovering DHCP server on the specified interface, and receives network configuration information, and applies that to the interface. You can run `dhclient` manually, and bind it to a specific network interface:

```
# dhclient fxp0
```

You can also enable `dhclient(8)` on any interface to run on system start up, by adding a the following line to `/etc/rc.conf`:

```
ifconfig_fxp0="DHCP"
```

ISC DHCPD

FreeBSD does not come with a built-in DHCP server. However, the widely used ISC DHCP server (as well as client and relay) is available from the ports tree, under `/usr/ports/net/isc-dhcp3-server`.

ISC DHCPD (currently at version 3), is the de facto open source DHCP server solution that is available on many platforms, including FreeBSD.

Installing `isc-dhcp3-server` from port installs requires binaries, manual pages, and sample configuration file. A sample configuration file can be found at `/usr/local/etc/dhcpd.conf.sample`. The `dhcpd` daemon looks for its configuration file at `/usr/local/etc/dhcpd.conf`. So, you can simply copy the sample file as the configuration file. Then make your own modifications, before starting the `dhcpd` daemon.

Enabling `isc-dhcpd` is possible by adding the following line to your `/etc/rc.conf` file:

```
dhcpd_enable="YES"
```

This will enable dhcpd to start automatically on system start up, by running the relevant rc script. You can also manually start DHCP server by running its rc script at:

```
# /usr/local/etc/rc.d/isc-dhcpd start
```

This will start the DHCP server that awaits on all active network interfaces for incoming DHCP discovery requests. If your server has multiple network interfaces, there are chances that you may not want dhcpd to be enabled on all interfaces (for example, your WAN uplink interface). This can be achieved by adding the following line to the /etc/rc.conf file:

```
dhcpd_ifaces="fxp0 bge0"
```

This will tell dhcpd to only listen for incoming requests on fxp0 and bge0 interface, and simply ignore all the other active interfaces.

DHCPD Configuration

Now that you have basically installed and enabled ISC DHCPD, you should set up your configuration file carefully, before starting to use your brand new DHCP server. The configuration file contains general information about how your DHCP server should assign IP addresses, and what information it should offer to the clients.

```
ddns-updates off;
ddns-update-style ad-hoc;
option domain-name "example.com";
option domain-name-servers 192.168.0.5, 192.168.0.6;
default-lease-time 600;
max-lease-time 7200;
log-facility local7;

# Our Network
subnet 192.168.0.0 netmask 255.255.255.0
{
        range 192.168.0.30 192.168.0.254;
        option routers 192.168.0.1;
        option subnet-mask 255.255.255.0;
}
```

The above example configuration file assigns dynamic IP addresses to hosts from subnet 192.168.0.0/24. In fact, the server assigns from 192.168.0.30 to 192.168.0.254 (leaving a small subnet of the address space for static allocation). The DHCP server also advertises the 192.168.0.1 as the default gateway for the network and also subnet mask 255.255.255.0 to the clients. In addition, there are two DNS servers and the default domain name (in this case example.com).

According to our configuration, the default lease time for each address is 600 seconds (10 minutes), if the client does not request any specific lease time. The maximum possible lease time we have specified is 7200 seconds (2 hours). You may want to modify these parameters according to your network configuration and resources.

To keep track of assigned IP addresses, DHCP server maintains a lease file at /var/ db/dhcpd/dhcpd.leases. This is where DHCP server writes down the IP addresses assigned to each client, and whether the leases are active or inactive. The file also contains additional information about each client, such as MAC address. This address is used to identify unique hosts, as well as start and end times for leases and also the binding state field. This will be useful for a system administrator to see which systems are online and have active leases (by looking at binding state field) and which hosts are not online. You can also modify this file to remove inactive leases, or easily assign a specific IP address to each client. Removing this file will lead the DHCP server to lose track of its assignment history, and all the leases will be reset.

The following sample shows a dhcpd.leases file that contains two entries, the first entry for an expired (and reserved) address and the second entry for an active (currently assigned) IP address as shown here:

```
# cat /var/db/dhcpd/dhcpd.leases

    lease 192.168.0.220
    {
      starts 0 2008/03/16 17:25:09;
      ends 0 2008/03/16 17:35:09;
      tstp 0 2008/03/16 17:35:09;
      binding state free;
      hardware ethernet 00:18:f3:03:f4:5b;
      uid "\001\000\030\363\003\364[";
    }
    lease 192.168.0.219
    {
      starts 0 2008/03/16 19:22:01;
      ends 0 2008/03/16 19:32:01;
      binding state active;
      next binding state free;
      hardware ethernet 00:a0:d1:3d:00:dd;
      uid "\001\000\240\321=\000\335";
      client-hostname "pixel";
    }
```

Trivial File Transfer Protocol (TFTP)

TFTP (RFC 1350) is a simple and lightweight file transfer protocol, somewhat similar to a slimmed down version of the FTP, without any complexity. TFTP does not need login, does not support changing directories, nor does it show the list of files and directories on the server. When using TFTP, you should know the exact file name you want to receive.

Many network devices use TFTP to download their OS image, or even load/save their configuration on TFTP.

Running TFTP service requires the inetd server to be run. You should first enable TFTP by removing comment from TFTP related line in /etc/inetd.conf. The line should simply look like this:

```
    tftp    dgram   udp     wait    root    /usr/libexec/tftpd
    tftpd -l -s /tftpboot
```

The last parameter on the above line runs tftpd(8) with syslog logging enabled (hence -l parameter) and also sets the root directory to /tftpboot. You may change this to your desired directory. Please note that /tftpboot does not exist on a clean FreeBSD installation and hence should be created.

After configuring the tftpd parameters, you should start/restart the inetd process (for more information on inetd, please refer to Chapter 13).

You can test functionality of your TFTP server using a TFTP client across the network.

FreeBSD also comes with a TFTP client called tftp(1). To test the functionality of your tftpd(8) server using tftp(1) client, you should set up appropriate directories and put some files in your /tftproot directory. Using tftp(1) on the same client you should be able to get (download) the file from TFTP server. Please note that you should remember the filename, since TFTP does not have the ability to see the list of the files on the server.

```
# tftp localhost

    tftp> verbose
    Verbose mode on.
    tftp> get make.conf
    getting from localhost:make.conf to make.conf [netascii]
    Received 853 bytes in 7.0 seconds [975 bits/sec]
    tftp> quit
```

The above example shows a basic TFTP file transfer scenario using FreeBSD's built-in TFTP client. The TFTP client connects to the server on localhost. In this example, I turned on verbose output by entering the verbose command. This will tell the client to show the transfer progress, and more details about the errors, if any. Using the get command, you can download a file from TFTP server. And once the transfer is done, you can leave the client using the quit command.

TFTP can also be used to upload files to a specific server (for example, a network device backing up its configuration or OS image on a TFTP server). However this can be a little tricky as compared to downloading files.

The TFTP server does not basically allow a client to create a file on the server, by default. However, if the file already exists on the server, it will be overwritten. Otherwise, it fails.

If you want to let your clients create files on the server by uploading files to your TFTP servers that do not exist already, you should modify the /etc/inetd.conf file. Then add the -w parameter to the tftpd parameters. This will let the clients upload files to your tftp root directory that does not already exist.

[If you do not want your existing files to be overwritten by TFTP clients, you should make your files read-only, using the chown(8) command (for example, permission 0440 on your files).]

Network File System (NFS)

NFS is the original *nix file sharing protocol. Using NFS, you can share the file system resources (as well as printers) across a network. Hence, other hosts on the network can access the remote storage, just like their local storage.

NFS was developed in 1970 by Sun Microsystems, and has evolved hugely since then. Nowadays NFS is an integrated part of every *nix operating system.

NFS is a client/server protocol, which means a server shares its storage resources and other client(s) can access the shared resources on the server. The clients and servers should be configured separately using FreeBSD's built-in NFS utilities.

Server

NFS server has three main daemons that should be running in order to serve storage resources across the network:

- The nfsd(8) daemon services NFS requests from client machines.

- The `rpcbind(8)` daemon maps Remote Procedure Call (RPC) program numbers to universal addresses and lets NFS clients know which ports the NFS server is using to serve requests.

- The `mountd(8)` daemon processes incoming mount requests.

Enabling the NFS server is as simple as adding appropriate variables to `/etc/rc.conf`, and starting the daemons (or restarting the server):

```
rpcbind_enable="YES"
nfs_server_enable="YES"
```

Running NFS server is the easiest part. Now all you need to do is to specify which resources should be shared (exported), as well as access policies for each export.

This is done using the `/etc/exports` file. The `/etc/exports` file contains information about every resource you want to share, as well as some export options and the hosts you want to permit to have access to each resource.

The above example shows the `/etc/exports` file that specifies three exported directories.

```
/usr/ports/distfiles -network 192.168.11.0 -mask=255.255.255.0
/cdrom   -ro 192.168.0.14
/public -ro -mapall=nobody
```

The first line exports the `/usr/ports/distfiles` directory. The share is only accessible for `192.168.11.0/24` subnet, and is exported with read/write permission (which is available by default).

The second line in the above code, exports the `/cdrom` directory with read-only permission (hence the `-ro` parameter), only for the host `192.168.0.14`.

And the third line exports `/public` directory as read-only for any host, and everyone can access the contents of this export with user access set to `nobody`. The `-mapall=nobody` maps all users to local user `nobody`.

Client

FreeBSD can mount NFS shares using `mount(8)` or `mount_nfs(8)` utility. All you need to do is to prepare the host to be able to mount NFS shares, by enabling NFS client modules:

```
nfs_client_enable="YES"
```

Adding the above variable to the `/etc/rc.conf` file ensures that the current operating environment is prepared to mount NFS shares.

You also need to run the NFS client rc script manually, for the first time:

```
# /etc/rc.d/nfsclient start
```

You can now mount the NFS shares using the mount (8) utility. The following example shows how to mount one of the exports we have done recently:

```
# mount 192.168.0.5:/usr/ports/distfiles /mnt
```

This will mount the export /usr/ports/distfiles from host 192.168.0.5 on the /mnt mount point. You can then verify if the share has been mounted:

```
# mount
    /dev/da0s1a on / (ufs, local)
    devfs on /dev (devfs, local)
    /dev/da0s1e on /tmp (ufs, local, soft-updates)
    /dev/da0s1f on /usr (ufs, local, soft-updates)
    /dev/da0s1d on /var (ufs, local, soft-updates)
    fdescfs on /dev/fd (fdescfs)
    192.168.0.5:/usr/ports/distfiles on /mnt (nfs)
```

You can then unmount the mounted share using the umount (8) command:

```
# umount /mnt
```

Mounting a NFS share manually is quite straightforward. This is useful when you want to mount a share temporarily, any time. But it is highly likely that you may want to have your mounts activated automatically, during system boot. Just as in every other file system you can achieve this by adding necessary mounting information to the /etc/fstab file. However, this might be a little bit tricky. The following example shows mounting the same share we used in the recent example via the /etc/fstab file. To achieve this, the following line should be added to the fstab file:

```
    192.168.0.5:/usr/ports/distfiles    /mnt  nfs  -b    0    0
```

This line in the fstab file will mount the share /usr/ports/distfiles from 192.168.0.5 on /mnt, during system boot up.

> Normally your system will fail to boot if the specified share is not available and therefore cannot be mounted. This is the reason why -b flag is used. This flag tells mount_nfs (8) to fork a background process if it fails to mount the share for any reason, and retry the mount in the background. This will avoid any boot problem if your share is being mounted from the fstab file during the boot-up process.

NFS Locking

Locking files over NFS protocol is not enabled by the default configuration. There may be certain circumstances when you may need to have the file locking feature on your NFS mounts, just as in the local file system. To achieve this, you have to enable `rpc.lockd(8)` and `rpc.statd(8)` on both NFS server and its clients. The `rpc.lockd(8)` daemon in conjunction with `rpc.statd(8)` takes care of file and record locking in an NFS environment.

The following lines should be added to the `/etc/rc.conf` file on NFS server and its clients in order to enable file locking over NFS:

```
rpc_lockd_enable="YES"
rpc_statd_enable="YES"
```

And then start the `rpc.lockd` daemon manually, if you do not want to reboot your host:

```
# /etc/rc.d/lockd start
```

Server Message Block (SMB) or CIFS

In a heterogeneous network, you may have different operating systems running, such as Microsoft Windows, that do not support NFS file sharing natively.

The SMB protocols or Windows File Sharing protocols are Microsoft's file sharing protocols that are mainly used on Windows operating system.

Your FreeBSD host can act as SMB client and server to make the integration into heterogeneous networks, easier.

This means that you can mount SMB shares using `mount_smbfs(8)`, which is a FreeBSD's built-in utility. Your FreeBSD server can also act as a SMB file and print server using popular open-source SAMBA package.

SMB Client

As mentioned earlier, FreeBSD comes with a built-in utility to mount SMB shares. The `mount_smbfs(8)` utility can mount SMB shares to local mount points, and can also be used in the `/etc/fstab` file to mount SMB shares automatically, on system start up.

The typical `mount_smbfs` command looks like this:

```
# mount_smbfs -I 192.168.0.14 //admin@babak-winxp/cygwin /mnt/cygwin
```

This will mount a share called `cygwin` from a host called `babak-winxp` with IP address `192.168.0.14`. The share is mounted with the permission of user `admin` and the password is asked for, during the mount process.

Note that the `-I` parameter takes the actual IP address of the SMB server (in this case `192.168.0.14`). You should also specify the name of the SMB server (for example `babak-winxp`). In case you do not specify the IP address of your server using the `-I` options, the IP address will be looked up from the host name, using NetBIOS name resolver. However, it would be a good idea to use `-I` to speed up the mounting process.

Once you enter this command, the password for the specified user, in this case, `admin`, is asked. If the authentication succeeds, the remote share will be mounted to the node you have specified (`/mnt/cygwin` in this example).

You can also verify whether the share is mounted as you wanted as shown here:

```
# mount

/dev/ad0s1a on / (ufs, local, noatime, soft-updates)
devfs on /dev (devfs, local)
procfs on /proc (procfs, local)
/dev/md0 on /tmp (ufs, local)
//ADMIN@BABAK-WINXP/CYGWIN on /mnt/cygwin (smbfs)
```

The last line of the `mount(8)` output shows that the share has been mounted successfully.

Note that you can also unmount the mounted share like a typical mount point, using the `umount(8)` utility

```
# umount /mnt/cygwin
```

SMB Server

SAMBA is a very popular open-source implementation of the SMB protocol that runs on various operating systems including FreeBSD. Using SAMBA, you can turn your FreeBSD server into a high performance Windows File Sharing server, which can integrate into your hybrid network.

SAMBA is available in FreeBSD's ports collection under `/usr/ports/net/samba3`.

After installing SAMBA via port (or package), just like any other server package you should configure it using the configuration file and enable it in `/etc/rc.conf`:

```
samba_enable="YES"
```

The default configuration file for samba is located at /usr/local/etc/smb.conf. The default configuration file contains the basic configuration including a few sample shared directories and printers. You should modify this file (or create a new one from the scratch) to suit your specific needs.

You need to set up your server name, workgroup name, security-level, and access control rules in your smb.conf file, before actually setting up your shared directories/printers:

```
[global]
    workgroup = MYGROUP
    server string = Samba Server
    security = user
    hosts allow = 192.168.1. 192.168.2. 127.
```

This will set your workgroup name, server name (as it will be seen by other SMB hosts), security-level (which can be chosen from various options such as user, share, server, ads, and domain) as well as the hosts that are allowed to access this server.

There are also further advanced options that can be specified in this configuration file, such as debugging and logging options, Master Browser preference, centralized password server settings, and wins/dns proxy settings. The default configuration file is crafted in a way that it fits in most of the simple deployments. However, all these configuration parameters along with a short description and their default value are present in the sample configuration file, which can be modified to suit your need.

After tweaking general configuration parameters, you should specify your shared resources configuration. Each share has its own configuration block, like the following example:

```
[myshare]
    comment = sample shared directory
    path = /usr/home/babak/mydocs
    valid users = babak jdoe
    public = no
    writeable = yes
    printable = no
```

This example shows a simple shared directory. The share can be accessed on the number using its name (in this example, myshare). We have also specified the actual address of the directories we are going to share over the network. This share would not be available for everyone and users should be authenticated, hence the valid users parameter. Only the users, babak and jdoe, are authorized to access this share. The share is also writable so that users can create and modify the shared files across the network. And as the last parameter, we have also specified that this share is not a printer (which explains the printable parameter).

Authentication

The recent example shows that we can set up shares for specific users that would be authenticated over the network and granted access according to specified access policies.

SAMBA can authenticate users with a local password database, or a password server that you may configure for this reason. The password server can be a Windows Active Directory, Windows NT Domain Controller or even LDAP.

In most simple deployments, administrator chooses the local password database to store user passwords. This local password database can be maintained using the `smbpasswd(8)` utility. Using this utility you can add, delete, enable, disable, and change users' password for the users you configure to access SMB shared over the network.

```
# smbpasswd -a babak

    New SMB password:
    Retype new SMB password:
    startsmbfilepwent_internal: file /usr/local/etc/samba/smbpasswd did
    not exist. File successfully created.
    Added user babak.
```

This will add a new user named `babak` to samba's local password database at `/usr/local/etc/samba/smbpasswd`.

> In the local authentication scheme, the user should also exist in the systems password database (the `/etc/passwd` file) before you can actually add it to SAMBA's password database. Otherwise, it fails to add the user.

Samba Web Administration Tool (SWAT)

SWAT, as the name mentions, is the web administration tool to manage SAMBA configuration such as managing shares, users, and so on.

SWAT makes your life easier, on busy servers in which you have many shares or users to manage. SWAT is also lightweight and fast, and best of all it does not need any third-party web server to run. It has its own web request handler, and can be enabled in a few seconds using the `inetd` daemon. All you need to do is to modify your `/etc/inetd.conf` file and start/restart your `inetd` daemon. The configuration line for swat already exists in the `/etc/inetd.conf` file (the last line of the file) and all you have to do is to un-comment it:

```
    swat    stream  tcp   nowait/400    root   /usr/local/sbin/swat    swat
```

SWAT runs on TCP port 901. So if SWAT is running on a host with IP address 10.1.1.1, you may access SWAT using a web browser on `http://10.1.1.1:901`.

Creating a share using SWAT is shown in the following screenshot:

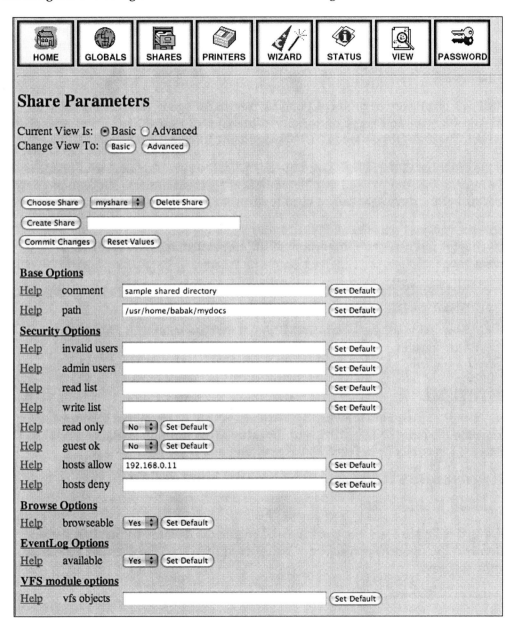

Simple Network Management Protocol (SNMP)

SNMP is a protocol to monitor and control network attached devices. SNMP agents that run on the devices can provide status information about the device upon request, or even send TRAP messages to specific hosts, when an event occurs. SNMP can also be used to manage devices over the network by setting the given parameter on the device.

SNMP is a client/server protocol. A SNMP server (or agent) is a piece of software that runs on hosts and keeps one or more databases of almost live information about the host. These databases are called **Management Information Bases (MIBs)**.

On the other hand, the SNMP client queries SNMP servers/agents for information. This information can be used in a Network Management System (NMS) to monitor the status of the device, or can be used to draw statistics graphs.

There are various open-source SNMP suites available that can be used in FreeBSD. This chapter discusses two important SNMP implementations in FreeBSD as shown here:

- Net-SNMP, that is available via ports system, is a very popular open-source SNMP toolkit.
- bsnmpd is a light-weight SNMP agent that is available in FreeBSD's base system.

bsnmpd

The `bsnmpd(1)` daemon is a very light-weight SNMP daemon that is supposed to serve only the basic SNMP MIBS, and the other MIBS through loadable modules. The `bsnmpd(1)` is available in FreeBSD base system, out of the box.

Setting up a basic SNMP server using bsnmpd is pretty straightforward:

```
bsnmpd_enable="YES"
```

Adding this line to `/etc/rc.conf` file will enable the daemon so that it is started automatically, upon system start up. You should then start the daemon, manually, for the first time:

```
# /etc/rc.d/bsnmpd start
```

And you are set.

Now `bsnmpd(1)` is running with the default configuration (which is not always secure) and it is highly recommended that you customize the configuration for your needs.

The configuration file is located at `/etc/snmpd.config`. You need to change a few basic things, such as `location` and contact fields, and most importantly, the read and write to `community` strings.

In SNMP, the community strings are almost equal to passwords. Anyone who knows your community string can poll status information from your SNMP server, or even change the variables over the network.

Following is a sample of secured `snmpd.config` file:

```
location := "Datacenter"
contact := "sysadmin@example.com"
system := 1       # FreeBSD
traphost := localhost
trapport := 162
read := "p^49Gb*z0n$0"
write := "wMt54%z@0Rcj3"
```

The sample configuration file also contains a modules section in which it loads appropriate modules, if necessary. One module that is loaded by default is SNMP MIB II module that contains basic information about the host. There are also a few other modules available such as Netgraph Module, PF Module, and Bridge Module.

For more information about the other modules, please see documents and MIBs under the `/usr/share/snmp` directory.

NET-SNMP

NET-SNMP is a complete suite of open-source SNMP tools, including client and server components, and supports the SNMP v1, v2c, and v3 protocols. NET-SNMP is very popular, and has many modules that can be used to extend its functionality.

Unlike `bsnmpd(1)`, the NET-SNMP is a fully loaded SNMP toolkit that contains many MIBs and supports many protocol extensions, and also includes a handful of client and test tools. NET-SNMP is the right choice for a complex SNMP scenario.

NET-SNMP is available in ports tree under the `/usr/ports/net-mgmt/net-snmp` directory. After installing the port, you can enable the NET-SNMP in the `/etc/rc.conf` file using appropriate configuration variable:

```
snmpd_enable="YES"
```

You can then manually start the daemon by issuing the following command:

```
# /usr/local/etc/rc.d/snmpd start
```

The NET-SNMP configuration is somehow complicated, as compared to bsnmpd. The configuration consists of a set of configuration files that can be found under the /usr/local/share/snmp subdirectory. The most important configuration file is snmpd.conf, which contains configuration information for the SNMP server component.

You do not have to edit the configuration files manually. The snmpconf(1) utility can be used to edit the configuration in a step-by-step manner.

You need to perform some basic initial setup for your NET-SNMP daemon, before you can actually use it. These configuration parameters consist of the basic contact and location information, as well as community names and network access policies. All these steps can be done using the following command:

```
# snmpconf -i
```

The snmpconf(1) utility then asks you, which component you want to configure and starts asking you questions about your preferred setup parameters. Once finished, it will automatically install the configuration file in the correct location, and all you need to do is to start or restart the SNMP daemon.

Client Tools

The NET-SNMP is bundled with a Swiss army knife of SNMP client and test tools. Using these utilities, you can perform various SNMP operations from the command line. The client set consists of the following tools:

Utility Name	Description of functionality
snmpget	Queries SNMP server for a specific variable using GET request.
snmpgetnext	Queries SNMP server for a specific variable using GETNEXT request.
snmpset	Sends a SET request to SNMP server to update a specific variable.
snmpwalk	Retrieves a subtree of variables from SNMP server.
snmpbulkget	Queries SNMP server for a set of variables using GETBULK request.
snmpbulkwalk	Retrieves a subtree of variable from SNMP server using GETBULK request.
snmpdelta	Monitors delta differences in SNMP counter values.
snmpinform	Sends an INFORM-PDU to the trap receiver.
snmpnetstat	Displays network status and configuration information of a SNMP server.

Utility Name	Description of functionality
snmptest	Communicates with SNMP servers using user specified SNMP requests.
snmpstatus	Retrieves a fixed set of management information from SNMP server.
snmptable	Retrieves an SNMP table and displays it in tabular format.
snmptranslate	Translates OID names from numeric to text and vice versa.
snmpusm	Manages SNMPv3 users on SNMP servers.
snmpvacm	Manages SNMPv3 View-based Access Control on SNMP servers.
snmpdf	Retrieves disk usage information from SNMP server.
snmptrap	Sends TRAP-PDU or TRAP2-PDU to trap receiver.

The snmpget(1) utility is a handy tool to retrieve SNMP variables from an SNMP agent.

```
# snmpget -v 1 -c public 10.10.1.3 sysName.0

    SNMPv2-MIB::sysName.0 = STRING: server01.example.org
```

This example shows retrieveing sysName variable from host 10.10.1.3. This query is initiaited using SNMP version 1 (hence the -v parameter) and a read-only community named public is configured on the SNMP server.

On the other hand, snmpwalk(1) actually retrieves a complete sub-tree from the SNMP server. It can be used to populate a complete set of data from an SNMP-enabled host.

```
# snmpwalk -v 1 -c public 10.10.1.3 IF-MIB::ifDescr

    IF-MIB::ifDescr.1 = STRING: sis0
    IF-MIB::ifDescr.2 = STRING: xl0
    IF-MIB::ifDescr.3 = STRING: lo0
```

This example shows how to retrieve the ifDescr sub-tree from IF-MIB. Note that you can retrieve the complete SNMP MIB tree from the host, if you do not specify any SNMP OID in parameters. This will most likely give a huge amount of output, but it is useful to see what kind of information you can get from the host.

Printing

Obviously FreeBSD can be used to connect to printers and communicate with them. This is not a big deal, since pretty much every other operating system has a printing interface that can be hooked up to standard printers, and print documents. Besides that, FreeBSD can be used as a full-featured print server. As a print server, your FreeBSD host can receive print jobs from multiple hosts over the network, and spool the jobs and then print them respectively.

FreeBSD has its own built-in generic print spooler called lpd(8) based on RFC 1179 definitions. There are also various alternatives to the built-in print spooler such as LPRng (available in ports tree as sysutils/LPRng) that is a more advanced print spooler as compared to FreeBSD's built-in spooler.

Another very popular and more complex print spooler is CUPS (for Common UNIX Printing System) that supports more protocols and is easier to configure.

lpd—Print Spooler Daemon

The lpd(8) utility is the legacy print spooler daemon that is built-in to the FreeBSD distribution. It can handle incoming print requests from the network (or locally) and store them in the spool directory, and then take care of printing documents correctly.

LPD relies on the /etc/printcap file in order to communicate with your printer. This file contains printer definitions. LPD reads this file anytime it needs to communicate with a printer. Therefore, you should setup your printer and add appropriate configuration to this file before anything else. Setting up the printcap entries manually is somewhat complex. Luckily there are tools that would make your life easier by taking care of configuring printcap for you, based on an interactive interface. One such tool is apsfilter program that is available in ports collection as print/apsfilter. The apsfilter program helps you in choosing the correct printer drivers and configuration, and finally creating relevant entries in the /etc/printcap file.

Once you have configured your printer driver, you should enable lpd, so that your host can receive print jobs and send them to its attached printer.

LPD can be enabled from the rc.conf file by adding the following line:

```
lpd_enable="YES"
```

You can then start the LPD service manually, by running the following command:

```
# /etc/rc.d/lpd start
```

Now LPD is ready to accept print jobs. You can test your setup by sending a sample text file to the printer. The following command is run to test your print setup:

```
# lpr /etc/motd
```

This should print the /etc/motd file to your recently configured printer.

Common UNIX Printing System (CUPS)

CUPS provides you with a friendly interface for printing. Unlike legacy LPD, CUPS automatically takes care of your printer configuration, and deals with the `printcap` file in the background. In addition to LPD protocol, CUPS supports Internet Printing Protocol (IPP) as the default protocol, as well as SMB and HP JetDirect protocols. IPP is an advanced remote printing protocol that covers many shortcomings of older protocols by adding many advanced features such as Access Control, Encryption, and Authentication.

CUPS can be found in ports collection under the `print/cups` directory.

 If you have already configured your `/etc/printcap` file, make sure you take a backup prior to installing CUPS as it will overwrite the existing `printcap` file.

Just like any other daemon in FreeBSD, CUPS should be enabled by adding this line to your `/etc/rc.conf` file:

```
cupsd_enable="YES"
```

While running, CUPS listens on TCP 631 (bound to 127.0.0.1) and UDP 631, on all interfaces. You can manage CUPS configuration using the Web GUI by pointing your browser to `http://127.0.0.1:631/` on the same host you are running CUPS. If you want to manage CUPS configuration remotely, you should change the default configuration file that is located at `/usr/local/etc/cups/cupsd.conf`.

Using the Web GUI, you can manage printers, classes (group of printers), and print jobs. CUPS updates the `/etc/printcap` file, when you add or modify printer settings. So when you configure a printer using CUPS, any other print spooler (for example LPD or LPRng) can use the `printcap` file to communicate with the printers.

CUPS Management Interface shows a sample print job in the following screenshot:

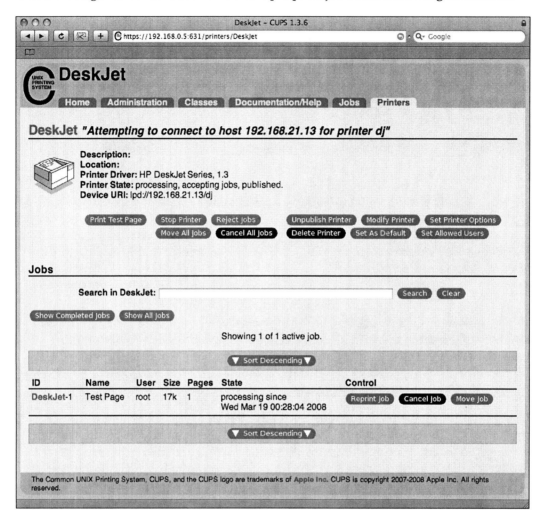

Network Information System (NIS)

NIS (formerly YP) is to UNIX, what a Domain Controller is to Windows. Basically, NIS allows a group of workstations to share a common set of configuration files such as passwords database, group database, hosts files, and so on.

NIS in conjunction with NFS can offer roaming users profile that will allow users to log into any of the NIS member workstations and feel like they're at home (same home directory and configuration).

Obviously, NIS follows Client/Server model in which there is at least one server (master server), and optionally one or more slave servers.

There are also one or more clients that are members of the "NIS Domain". This is called **binding**. The ypbind(8) daemon takes care of binding on the client machines.

NIS Server

To set up a NIS server, you should take a few steps. The first step is choosing your NIS domain name. The NIS domain name is a name that your NIS domain is identified with. The benefit of identifying a domain by name is that you may have multiple domains, each with its own set of workstations running on the same network without any interference.

 As the NIS domain name is not necessarily your DNS domain name, it does not follow DNS naming rules. You may choose your own NIS domain name in order to avoid confusion. However, you are also free to use your DNS domain name as NIS domain name.

Either on a server or a client, you should specify the domain name in the /etc/rc.conf configuration file:

```
nisdomainname="example-domain"
```

You should also enable NIS server daemon to run during system startup, as shown here:

```
nis_server_enable="YES"
```

These are the two parameters which you need to set up a NIS domain server. However, there are a few other variables that we will discuss later in this chapter.

Initializing NIS Server

It is necessary to initialize the NIS server. By initializing you will create a default set of centralized database files and make your server ready to serve the configuration databases to the clients.

NIS database files are kept under the /var/yp subdirectory. On a brand-new installation, you will have a Makefile under this directory, that will be used later to initialize the NIS server.

First, you need to make a copy of the password file in the /var/yp directory
as follows:

```
# cp /etc/master.passwd /var/yp/
```

Then you should edit the password file and remove unnecessary accounts. This
includes the system accounts such as daemon, operator, bin, etc. Please note that
the system accounts use UID lesser than 1000. You may also want to keep the root
account, and add a few accounts to the file, before initializing the server.

When you are finished with the password file, you are ready to initialize the NIS
server for the first time. To do so, the ypinit(8) command will be used. The
ypinit(8) command initializes a master or slave NIS domain server for the first
time. It creates initial databases and appropriate directory structure that is needed by
the NIS server. The ypinit command uses the Makefile from the /var/yp directory
to set up the server, so that you do not have to run the Makefile manually.

```
# ypinit -m example-domain

    Server Type: MASTER Domain: example-domain

    Creating an YP server will require that you answer a few questions.
    Questions will all be asked at the beginning of the procedure.

    Do you want this procedure to quit on non-fatal errors? [y/n: n]

    Ok, please remember to go back and redo manually whatever fails.
    If you don't, something might not work.

    At this point, we have to construct a list of this domains YP servers.
    server.example.org is already known as master server.
    Please continue to add any slave servers, one per line. When you are
    done with the list, type a <control D>.
            master server   :   server.example.org
            next host to add:   ^D
    The current list of NIS servers looks like this:
    server.example.org

    Is this correct?   [y/n: y]
    Building /var/yp/example-domain/ypservers...
    Running /var/yp/Makefile...
    NIS Map update started on Sun Dec 16 00:32:45 IRST 2007 for domain
    example-domain
    Updating hosts.byname...
    Updating hosts.byaddr...
    yp_mkdb: duplicate key '192.168.0.5' - skipping
    Updating networks.byaddr...
    yp_mkdb: no key -- check source file for blank lines
```

```
yp_mkdb: no key -- check source file for blank lines
Updating networks.byname...
yp_mkdb: no key -- check source file for blank lines
yp_mkdb: no key -- check source file for blank lines
Updating protocols.bynumber...
Updating protocols.byname...
Updating rpc.byname...
yp_mkdb: duplicate key 'rpcbind' - skipping
Updating rpc.bynumber...
Updating services.byname...
yp_mkdb: duplicate key 'compressnet/tcp' - skipping
yp_mkdb: duplicate key 'compressnet/udp' - skipping
yp_mkdb: duplicate key 'mit-ml-dev/tcp' - skipping
yp_mkdb: duplicate key 'mit-ml-dev/udp' - skipping
Updating shells...
Updating group.byname...
Updating group.bygid...
Updating passwd.byname...
Updating passwd.byuid...
Updating master.passwd.byname...
Updating master.passwd.byuid...
Updating netid.byname...
Updating amd.map...
NIS Map update completed.

server.example.org has been setup as an YP master server without any
errors.
```

Now your server is initialized. The /var/yp directory should now contain two new files and a folder. The passwd file is just like a typical password file created using the custom master.passwd that we created for our NIS server. The ypservers file also contains the names of all master and slave servers for the domain.

A directory named example-domain (which is the same as the domain name on your system) containing NIS server's database files is also created with the default values.

Now you can start your NIS server by running appropriate rc script manually, or by rebooting the server:

```
# /etc/rc.d/ypserve start
```

Summary

FreeBSD offers a sound platform for local network services. In this chapter we learned to deal with a few of the local network services and protocols – DHCP, TFTP, NFS, SMB, SNMP, Printing, and NIS/YP. FreeBSD provides some of these services as built-in, while the others require the network administrators to configure them separately using the built-in utilities (such as NFS).

DHCP describes a means by which network devices access network configuration details from the server for communication. This section covers dhclient(8), and ISC DHCPD daemon and its configuration. TFTP is a simpler version of FTP and requires the inetd server to run. NFS is a client/server protocol used for file sharing for *nix operating systems. Samba implements SMB protocol, and is used for interface in Microsoft environments. SNMP monitors and controls the network devices. This chapter discusses the two open source SNMP utilities – Net-SNMP and bsnmpd. FreeBSD has its own print spooler daemons – lpd and CUPs. The final services that this chapter discusses are NIS, where a group of workstations share a set of configuration files.

Index

Symbols

/boot/loader.conf file 98
/etc/make.conf file
  about 97
  CFLAGS, variables 98
  COPTFLAGS, variables 98
  CPUTYPE, variables 97
  variables 97

A

AH protocol 137
Autonomous System 166

B

bridging
  about 169, 171
  bridge, creating 170, 171
  bridge interface configuration, verifying
    170, 171
  filtering bridges 171
  filtering bridges, configuring 172
  flags 171
  interface, removing from bridge group 170,
    171
  network bridge 169, 171

C

CIDR method 175
CIFS. *See* SMB
CVSup
  -CURRENT, tracking 33, 34
  -STABLE, tracking 31-33
  -STABLE, tracking supfile used 31

about 31
branch tag 30
HEAD tag 30
release tag 30
RELENG_7 tag 30
revision tag 30

D

DHCP, network services
  about 236
  Dhclient 236
  DHCPD configuration 237, 238
  ISC DHCPD 236
disk
  file limits 92
  i/o performance 92, 93
  partition layout 7
  RAID 93
  RAID, levels 93
  sizes 7
  swap partitions 9
DNS, internet services
  about 215
  authoritative, operating modes 217, 218
  BIND software 215
  BIND software, authoritative mode 215
  BIND software, caching forwarder mode
    216
  BIND software, modes 215
  caching, operating modes 216
  forwarding, operating modes 216
  monitoring, operating modes 219
  operating modes 215
  optimizations, operating modes 219, 220

Domain Name System. *See* DNS
Dynamic Host Configuration Protocol. *See*
    DHCP

E

Encapsulated Security Payload protocol. *See*
    ESP protocol
ESP protocol 137

F

file system backup, system configuration
  about 18
  cpio utility 23
  dump utility 18-21
  pax utility 23
  restore utility 18-21
  snapshots 23
  tarball 22
  tar utility 22
FreeBSD
  /, disk partitions 8
  /tmp, disk partitions 8
  /usr, disk partitions 8
  /var, disk partitions 8
  bridging 169, 171
  chroot environment 75, 76
  disklabel editor, with partitions 8, 9
  disk partitions 8
  internet services 203
  IP forwarding 158
  IPFW 183
  IPv6 176
  jail 75, 76
  Multicast routing 181
  network, variables 94
  network address translation, PF and IPFW
    used 199, 200
  network configuration 101
  network services 235
  OpenBGPD 166
  OpenOSPFD 163
  package management tools 55
  Perforce version control system, used 30
  PF 183, 193
  PF and IPFW combinations, for NAT
    implementing 199

  ports and packages 48
  process accounting 72, 73
  process management 63
  proxy ARP 172
  RAID-GEOM framework 24
  resource management 69
  RIP6 180
  route6d(8) 162
  routed(8) 162
  routing daemons 162, 163
  softwares 157
  static routing 160
  swap, disk partitions 8
  swap encryption 12
  swap partitions, creating 9
  system configuration 7
  upgrading 29
FreeBSD, performance
  /boot/loader.conf file 98
  /etc/make.conf file 97
  disk, tweaking 92
  kernel, tweaking 89, 90
  kernel variables, tweaking using sysctl 88,
    89
  network, tweaking 94
  SMP, tweaking 91
FreeBSD, softwares
  OpenBGPD 157
  OpenOSPFD 157
  Quagga 157
  XORP 157
  Zebra 157
FreeBSD, upgrading
  binary update 42
  binary update, installing 43
  binary update, methods 42
  customized kernel, loading 44
  custom kernel, advantages 38
  custom kernel, building 39
  custom kernel, considerations 40
  custom kernel file, creating 39
  CVSup 30
  kernel, customizing 38
  kernel, subdirectory and platform 38
  new kernel, installing 43
  ports collection 34
  security 36

world, rebuilding 40, 41
world rebuilding, precautions 41
world rebuilding, tricks 42
FTP, internet services
about 221
anonymous FTP server 221, 222

G

Generic Routing Encapsulation. *See* **GRE**
GRE
about 134
gre(4) interface, creating 134
gre(4) interface, removing 134
GRE tunnel, establishing between Host A
  and Host B 135, 136

I

ifconfig utility
about 101
address families 106
advanced options 113
Apple Talk, configuring 108
FEC (Fast EtherChannel), configuring 118
inet keyword 106
interface flags 102, 103
IP address, configuring 106
IPv6 address, assigning to interface 106
IPX, configuring 107, 108
layer2 address, configuring 107
media options, configuring 110, 111
NIC options 103, 104
secondary(alias) IP address, configuring
  109, 110
uses 102
VLANs, configuring 112, 113
ifconfig utility, advanced options
ARP (Address Resolution Protocol) 116
hardware, offloading 114
monitor mode 118
MTU (Maximum Transmission Unit) 116
promiscuous mode 115
static ARP 117
TCP/IP checksum calculations, offloading
  114
TCP Large Receive, offloading 114
TCP segmentation, offloading 114

VLAN tagging, offloading 114
inetd daemon, internet services
about 204, 205
tcdp 206
internet services
DNS 215
FTP 221
inetd daemon 204
mail 223
NTP 213
proxy 230
SSH 207
web 227
IPFIREWALL. *See* **IPFW**
IP forwarding
about 158
flags 159, 160
IPv6 routing table, displaying current
  status 159
IPv6 routing table, displaying status and
  content 158
routing entry, fields 159
routing table, modifying methods 158
IPFW
about 184
basic configuration 185, 186
configuration parameters, for pipes 193
customized rulesets 188
enabling 184
logging 190
NAT (Network Address Translation) 191
NAT configuration 191
NAT configuration, keywords 191
pipe, traffic shaping 192
queue, traffic shaping 192
ruleset templates 187
traffic shaping 192
IPSec
about 136
IPSec Tunneling 137
IPSec VPN 137
operating modes 137
transport mode, operating modes 137
tunnel mode 138
tunnel mode, operating modes 137
IPSec, tunnel mode
components, encryption setup 139

encryption, applying on packets 139
routing table updates, verifying 139
site to site IPSec tunnel, creating 138-143
static routes, adding 139
IPv4
about 175
issues 175
IPv6
about 176
GIF tunneling 181
interfaces, configuring 177, 178
multicast routing 181
reserved addresses 179
RIP6 180
routing 179, 180
tunnelling 181
using 177
IPv6, facts
addressing 176
address types 176
ARP 176
interface confiugration 177

J

jail
about 75, 76
automatic startup 81
devfs(5) mount 84
devfs(5) ruleset 84
host system, configuring 78-80
initial configuration 80
limitations 85
managing 82, 83
running 81
security 84
service jail 76
setting up 77, 78
shutting down 82
steps 80

M

mail, internet services
about 223
postfix 226
sendmail 224, 225
sendmail, catchall method 226

Mail Transfer Agent. *See* **MTA**
MTA 223

N

NAT method 175
network, variables
network interface polling 96
RFC 1323 extensions 95
TCP buffer space 95
TCP delayed ACK 94
TCP listen queue size 95
network configuration
about 101
default routing 119
GIF, tunneling protocols 133
GRE, tunneling protocols 133, 134
host name, translating to IP address 120
ifconfig utility 101
IPSEC, tunneling protocols 133
IPSec protocol 136
name resolution 120, 121
network interfaces 101
network testing tools 121
NOS, tunneling protocols 133
tunneling 133
tunneling protocols 133
Network File System. *See* **NFS**
Network Information System. *See* **NIS**
network interfaces
logical network interfaces 102
physical network interfaces 101
network services
DHCP 236
NFS 240
NIS 254
printing 251
SMB 243
SNMP 248
TFTP 239
network testing tools, network
configuration
ARP 125, 126
netstat 124, 125
netstat parameters 124
ping 121, 122
sockstat 123, 124

tcpdump 126-130
traceroute 122
NFS, network services
about 240
client 241, 242
locking 243
server 240, 241
NIS, network services
about 254
NIS server, initializing 255, 257
server 255
NTP, internet services
about 213
NTP server 214, 215
syncing 213, 214

O

OpenBGPD
about 166
bgpd.conf example 166, 168
BGP protocol 166
OpenOSPFD
about 163, 165
OSPF network 164

P

package management tools
about 55
pkg_deinstall, portupgrade 57
pkg_which, portupgrade 59
portinstall, portupgrade 56
portmaster 60
portsclean, portupgrade 59
portupgrade 56, 58
portversion, portupgrade 58
utilities, portupgrade 56
PF
about 193
controlling 197
keywords, used with -s flag 198
PF configuration syntax 194, 195
PF configuration syntax
filter rules 197
macros 195
options 196
queuing 196

Scrub 196
tables 196
translation 197
ports and packages, FreeBSD
about 48
FreeBSD website, software directories 49
freshports, software directories 49
legacy method 48, 49
local ports repository, software
directories 49
make arguments, ports 52, 53
packages 49, 50
ports 51
resources, for searching application 49
search facility, ports 52
software directories 49
ports collection
ports, tracking 34, 35
portsnap 35
portsnap, advantages 35
ports tree, downloading 36
ports tree, updating ways 34
printing, network services
CUPS(Common UNIX Printing System)
253
lpd, print spooler daemon 252
process accounting 72
process management
daemon 64
process 64
running processes, information 65
signal 64
signals 64
proxy, internet services
HTTP proxy server 230
web proxy server 230

Q

quotas, system configuration
about 15, 16
assigning 16, 17
high limit, quota limits 16
important notes 18
quota limits 16
soft limit, quota limits 17

R

RAID-GEOM framework, system configuration
about 24
disk concatenation 27
gconcat(8) utility 27
GEOM stripe sets, devices 25
gmirror(8) utility 26
gmirror(8) utility, commands 26
gstripe(8) utility 24
RAID0, striping 24
RAID1, mirroring 26
RAID1, mirroring, balance algorithms 26
resource management
about 69
iostat, system resource monitoring tools 70
pstat, system resource monitoring tools 70
systat, system resource monitoring tools 71
system resource monitoring tools 69
vmstat, system resource monitoring tools 69
running processes, process management
information 65
killall command, sending signals 68
kill command, sending signals 67
pgrep command, getting information 67
pkill command, sending signals 68
prioritizing, nice command 68
prioritizing, renice command 68, 69
ps command, getting information 65
top command, getting information 65

S

Samba Web Administration Tool. *See* SWAT
security, FreeBSD
about 36
CVS branch tag 37
VuXML(Vulnerability and eXposure Markup Language) 37
Server Message Block. *See* SMB
Simple Network Management Protocol. *See* SNMP
SMB, network services
about 243

client 243
SAMBA 244
server 244
server, authentication 246
SWAT 246
snapshots, system configuration 13-15
SNMP, network services
about 248
bsnmpd 248
MIBs (Management Information Bases) 248
NET-SNMP 249
NET-SNMP, client tools 250
softupdates, system configuration 12
Squid
about 230
configuring 231, 232
installing 231
SSH, internet services
about 207
command, running remotely 208
SSH authentication agent, SSH keys 210
SSH keys 208
SSH keys, advantages 208
SSH keys, protecting 209
SSH port forwarding, SSH keys 212
SSH tunnel, dynamic forwarding mode 212
SSH tunnel, establishing modes 212
SSH tunnel, static forwarding mode 212
SSH tunneling, SSH keys 212
static routing
about 160
add command, routing table 161
adding, to routing table 160
change command, routing table 161
default gateway, adding to routing table 160
delete command, routing table 161
example 162
existing route, removing from routing table 161
routing table, cleaning up 161
routing table, manipulating 160
routing table, updating 161
routing table entries, viewing 161
supfile 31

swap, system configuration
  about 9
  partitions, creating 9
SWAT 246
system configuration
  disks 7
  file system backup 18
  quotas 15
  RAID-GEOM framework 24
  snapshots 13
  softupdates 12
  swap 9
  swap space, adding 10, 11

T

TFTP, network services 239
Trivial File Transfer Protocol. *See* **TFTP**
tunneling, network configuration 133

U

UFS2 file system
  about 92
  mounting modes 92

V

virtual server 76

W

web, internet services
  about 227
  alternative HTTP servers 230
  Apache 228
  Apache, virtual hosts 229

Y

yellow pages. *See* **NIS**

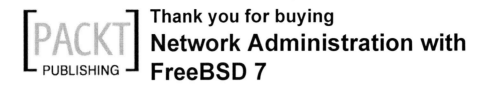

Thank you for buying
Network Administration with
FreeBSD 7

Packt Open Source Project Royalties

When we sell a book written on an Open Source project, we pay a royalty directly to that project. Therefore by purchasing Network Administration with FreeBSD 7, Packt will have given some of the money received to the FreeBSD Project.

In the long term, we see ourselves and you—customers and readers of our books—as part of the Open Source ecosystem, providing sustainable revenue for the projects we publish on. Our aim at Packt is to establish publishing royalties as an essential part of the service and support a business model that sustains Open Source.

If you're working with an Open Source project that you would like us to publish on, and subsequently pay royalties to, please get in touch with us.

Writing for Packt

We welcome all inquiries from people who are interested in authoring. Book proposals should be sent to authors@packtpub.com. If your book idea is still at an early stage and you would like to discuss it first before writing a formal book proposal, contact us; one of our commissioning editors will get in touch with you.

We're not just looking for published authors; if you have strong technical skills but no writing experience, our experienced editors can help you develop a writing career, or simply get some additional reward for your expertise.

About Packt Publishing

Packt, pronounced 'packed', published its first book "Mastering phpMyAdmin for Effective MySQL Management" in April 2004 and subsequently continued to specialize in publishing highly focused books on specific technologies and solutions.

Our books and publications share the experiences of your fellow IT professionals in adapting and customizing today's systems, applications, and frameworks. Our solution-based books give you the knowledge and power to customize the software and technologies you're using to get the job done. Packt books are more specific and less general than the IT books you have seen in the past. Our unique business model allows us to bring you more focused information, giving you more of what you need to know, and less of what you don't.

Packt is a modern, yet unique publishing company, which focuses on producing quality, cutting-edge books for communities of developers, administrators, and newbies alike. For more information, please visit our website: www.PacktPub.com.

Printed in the United States
PP4060500001B/1/P

9 781847 192646